GW00707822

UNIX® System V/386
Release 3.2
User's Guide

Prentice Hall, Englewood Cliffs, New Jersey 07632

Library of Congress Catalog Card Number: 88-62533

Editorial/production supervision: Karen Skrable Fortgang
Manufacturing buyer: Mary Ann Gloriande

NOTICE
The information in this document is subject to change without notice.
AT&T assumes no responsibility for any errors that may appear in
this document.

Intel is a registered trademark of Intel Corporation.
MS-DOS and XENIX are registered trademarks of Microsoft Corporation.
UNIX is a registered trademark of AT&T.

The publisher offers discounts on this book when ordered
in bulk quantities. For more information, write or call:

> Special Sales
> Prentice-Hall, Inc.
> College Technical and Reference Division
> Englewood Cliffs, NJ 07632
> (201) 592-2498

Printed in the United States of America

10 9 8 7 6 5 4 3

ISBN 0-13-944869-1

Prentice-Hall International (UK) Limited, *London*
Prentice-Hall of Australia Pty. Limited, *Sydney*
Prentice-Hall Canada Inc., *Toronto*
Prentice-Hall Hispanoamericana, S.A., *Mexico*
Prentice-Hall of India Private Limited, *New Delhi*
Prentice-Hall of Japan, Inc., *Tokyo*
Simon & Schuster Asia Pte. Ltd., *Singapore*
Editora Prentice-Hall do Brasil, Ltda., *Rio de Janeiro*

Table of Contents

Table of Contents ―――――――――――――――――――――――

4   Overview of the Tutorials

5   Line Editor Tutorial (ed)

6   Screen Editor Tutorial (vi)

7   Shell Tutorial

List of Figures

List of Figures ───────────────────────────────────

Preface

The material in this guide is organized into two major parts: an overview of the UNIX operating system and a set of tutorials on the main tools available on the UNIX system. A brief description of each part follows. The last section of this Preface, "Notation Conventions," describes the typographical notation with which all the chapters of this *Guide* conform. You may want to refer back to this section from time to time as you read the *Guide*.

System Overview

This part consists of Chapters 1–3, which introduce you to the basic principles of the UNIX operating system. Each chapter builds on information presented in preceding chapters, so it is important to read them in sequence.

- Chapter 1, "What is the UNIX System?", provides an overview of the operating system.

- Chapter 2, "Basics for UNIX System Users," discusses the general rules and guidelines for using the UNIX system. It covers topics related to using your terminal, obtaining a system account, and establishing contact with the UNIX system.

- Chapter 3, "Using the File System," offers a working perspective of the file system. It introduces commands for building your own directory structure, accessing and manipulating the subdirectories and files you organize within it, and examining the contents of other directories in the system for which you have access permission.

UNIX System Tutorials

The second part of the *Guide* consists of tutorials on the following topics: the **ed** text editor, the **vi** text editor, the shell command language and programming language, and electronic communication tools. For a thorough understanding of the material, we recommend that you work through the examples and exercises as you read each tutorial. The tutorials assume you understand the concepts introduced in Chapters 1–3.

■ Chapter 4, "UNIX System Capabilities," introduces the four chapters of tutorials in the second half of the *Guide*. It highlights UNIX system capabilities such as command execution, text editing, electronic communication, programming, and aids to software development.

■ Chapter 5, "Line Editor Tutorial (**ed**)," teaches you to how to use the **ed** text editor to create and modify text on a video display terminal or paper printing terminal.

■ Chapter 6, "Screen Editor Tutorial (**vi**)," teaches you how to use the visual text editor, **vi**, to create and modify text on a video display terminal.

vi, the visual editor, is based on software developed by The University of California, Berkeley, California; Computer Science Division, Department of Electrical Engineering and Computer Science, and such software is owned and licensed by the Regents of the University of California.

■ Chapter 7, "Shell Tutorial," teaches you to how to use the shell, both as a command interpreter and as a programming language used to create shell programs.

■ Chapter 8, "Communication Tutorial," teaches you how to send messages and files to users of both your UNIX system and other UNIX systems.

Reference Information

Six appendices and a glossary of UNIX system terms are also provided for reference.

■ Appendix A, "Summary of the File System," illustrates how information is stored in the UNIX operating system.

■ Appendix B, "Summary of UNIX System Commands," describes, in alphabetical order, each UNIX system command discussed in the *Guide*.

■ Appendix C, "Quick Reference to **ed** Commands," is a quick reference for the line editor, **ed**. (For details, see Chapter 5, "Line Editor
Tutorial.") The commands are organized by topic, as they are covered
in Chapter 5.

■ Appendix D, "Quick Reference to **vi** Commands," is a reference for
the full screen editor, **vi**, discussed in Chapter 6, "Screen Editor
Tutorial (**vi**)." Commands are organized by topic, as covered in
Chapter 6.

■ Appendix E, "Summary of Shell Command Language," is a summary
of the shell command language, notation, and programming constructs,
as discussed in Chapter 7, "Shell Tutorial."

■ Appendix F, "Setting Up the Terminal," explains how to configure
your terminal for use with the UNIX system, and create multiple windows on the screens of terminals with windowing capability.

■ The Glossary defines terms pertaining to the UNIX system used in this
book.

Notation Conventions

The following notation conventions are used throughout this *Guide*.

bold
User input, such as commands, options and arguments to commands, variables, and the names of directories and files, appear in **bold**.

italic
Names of variables to which values must be assigned (such as *password*) appear in *italic*.

constant width
UNIX system output, such as prompt signs and responses to commands, appear in constant width.

<>
Input that does not appear on the screen when typed, such as passwords, tabs, or RETURN, appear between angle brackets.

<^char>
Control characters are shown between angle brackets because they do not appear on the screen when typed. The circumflex (^) represents the control key (usually labeled CTRL). To type a control character, hold down the control key while you type the character specified by *char*. For example, the notation <^**d**> means to hold down the control key while pressing the D key; the letter D will not appear on the screen.

[ ]
Command options and arguments that are optional, such as **[-msCj]**, are enclosed in square brackets.

¦
The vertical bar separates optional arguments from which you may choose one. For example, when a command line has the following format:

command [arg1 ¦ arg2]

You may use either *arg1* or *arg2* when you issue the *command*.

...

Ellipses after an argument mean that more than one argument may be used on a single command line.

Arrows on the screen (shown in examples in Chapter 6) represent the cursor.

command(number)

A command name followed by a number in parentheses refers to the part of a UNIX system reference manual that documents that command. (There are three reference manuals: the *User's Reference Manual, Programmer's Reference Manual,* and *System Administrator's Reference Manual*.) For example, the notation **cat**(1) refers to the page in section 1 (of the *User's Reference Manual*) that documents the **cat** command.

In sample commands the $ sign is used as the shell command prompt. This is not true for all systems. Whichever symbol your system uses, keep in mind that prompts are produced by the system; although a prompt is some-times shown at the beginning of a command line as it would appear on your screen, you are not meant to type it. (The $ sign is also used to reference the value of positional parameters and named variables; see Chapter 7 for details.)

In all chapters, full and partial screens are used to display examples of how your terminal screen will look when you interact with the UNIX system. These examples show how to use the UNIX system editors, write short pro-grams, and execute commands. The input (characters typed by you) and out-put (characters printed by the UNIX system) are shown in these screens in accordance with the conventions listed above. All examples apply regardless of the type of terminal you use.

The commands discussed in each section of a chapter are reviewed at the end of that section. A summary of **vi** commands is found in Appendix D, where they are listed by topic. At the end of some sections, exercises are also provided so you can experiment with the commands. The answers to all the exercises in a chapter are at the end of that chapter.

The text in the *User's Guide* was prepared with the UNIX system text editors described in the *Guide* and formatted with the DOCUMENTER'S WORK-BENCH Software: **troff**, **tbl**, **pic**, and **mm** macros.

1 What Is the UNIX System?

What the UNIX System Does

The UNIX Operating System is a set of programs (or software) that controls the computer, acts as the link between you and the computer, and provides tools to help you do your work. It is designed to provide an uncomplicated, efficient, and flexible computing environment. Specifically, the UNIX System offers the following advantages:

- a general purpose system for performing a wide variety of jobs or applications

- an interactive environment that allows you to communicate directly with the computer and receive immediate responses to your requests and messages

- a multi-user environment that allows you to share the computer's resources with other users without sacrificing productivity

   This technique is called timesharing. The UNIX System interacts between users on a rotating basis so quickly that it appears to be interacting with all users simultaneously.

- a multi-tasking environment that enables you to execute more than one program simultaneously.

The organization of the UNIX System is based on four major components:

the kernel	The kernel is a program that constitutes the nucleus of the operating system; it coordinates the functioning of the computer's internals (such as allocating system resources). The kernel works invisibly; you need never be aware of it while doing your work.
the file system	The file system provides a method of handling data that makes it easy to store and access information.
the shell	The shell is a program that serves as the command interpreter. It acts as a liaison between you and the kernel, interpreting and executing your commands. Because it reads input from you and sends you messages, it is described as interactive.

commands   Commands are the names of programs that you request the computer to execute. Packages of programs are called tools. The UNIX System provides tools for jobs such as creating and changing text, writing programs and developing software tools, and exchanging information with others via the computer.

How the UNIX System Works

Figure 1-1 is a model of the UNIX System. Each circle represents one of the major components of the UNIX System: the kernel, the shell, and user programs or commands. The arrows suggest the shell's role as the medium through which you and the kernel communicate. The remainder of this chapter describes each of these components, along with another component of the UNIX System, the file system.

User Programs

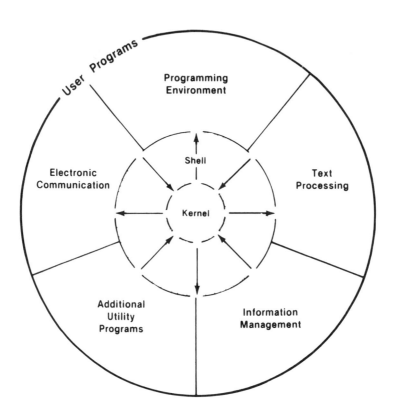

Figure 1-1: Model of the UNIX System

The Kernel

The nucleus of the UNIX System is called the kernel. The kernel controls access to the computer, manages the computer's memory, maintains the file system, and allocates the computer's resources among users. Figure 1-2 is a functional view of the kernel.

Kernel

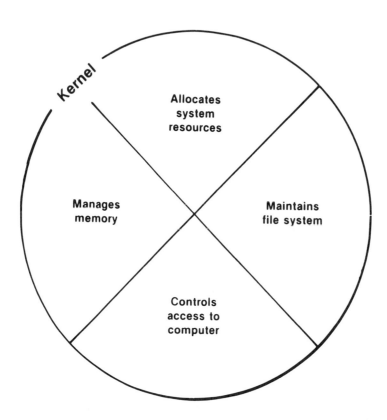

Figure 1-2: Functional View of the Kernel

The File System

The file system is the cornerstone of the UNIX Operating System. It provides a logical method of organizing, retrieving, and managing information. The structure of the file system is hierarchical; if you could see it, it might look like an organization chart or an inverted tree (Figure 1-3).

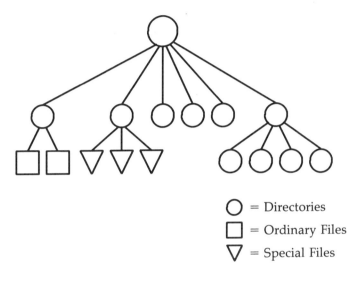

O = Directories
□ = Ordinary Files
▽ = Special Files

Figure 1-3: The Hierarchical Structure of the File System

The file is the basic unit of the UNIX System, and it can be any one of three types: an ordinary file, a directory, or a special file. (See Chapter 3, "Using the File System.")

Ordinary Files

An ordinary file is a collection of characters that is treated as a unit by the system. Ordinary files are used to store any information you want to save. They may contain text for letters or reports, code for the programs you write, or commands to run your programs. Once you have created a file, you can add material to it, delete material from it, or remove it entirely when it is no longer needed.

Directories

A directory is a super-file that contains a group of related files. For example, a directory called **sales** may hold files containing monthly sales figures called **jan, feb, mar**, and so on. You can create directories, add or remove files from them, or remove directories themselves at any time.

Your home directory is a directory assigned to you by the system when you receive a recognized login. You have control over this directory; no one else can read or write files in it without your explicit permission, and you determine its structure.

The UNIX System also maintains several directories for its own use. The structure of these directories is much the same on all UNIX Systems. These directories, which include **/unix** (the kernel) and several important system directories, are located directly under the root directory in the file hierarchy. The root directory (designated by **/**) is the source of the UNIX file structure; all directories and files are arranged hierarchically under it.

Special Files

Special files constitute the most unusual feature of the file system. A special file represents a physical device such as a terminal, disk drive, magnetic tape drive, or communication link. The system reads and writes to special files in the same way it does to ordinary files. However, the system's read and write requests do not activate the normal file access mechanism; instead, they activate the device handler associated with the file.

Some operating systems require you to define the type of file you have and to use it in a specified way. In those cases, you must consider how the files are stored since they might be sequential, random-access, or binary files. To the UNIX System, however, all files are alike. This makes the UNIX System file structure easy to use. For example, you need not specify memory requirements for your files since the system automatically does this for you. Or if you or a program you write needs to access a certain device, such as a printer, you specify the device just as you would another one of your files. In the UNIX System, there is only one interface for all input from you and output to you; this simplifies your interaction with the system.

Figure 1-4 shows an example of a typical file system. Notice that the root directory contains the kernel (**/unix**) and several important system directories.

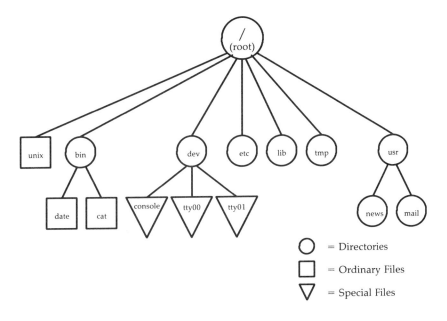

Figure 1-4: Example of a File System

/bin	contains many executable programs and utilities
/dev	contains special files that represent peripheral devices such as the console, the line printer, user terminals, and disks
/etc	contains programs and data files for system administration
/lib	contains libraries for programs and languages
/tmp	contains temporary files that can be created by any user
/usr	contains other directories, including **mail**, which contain files for storing electronic mail, and **news**, which contains files for storing newsworthy items.

In summary, the directories and files you create comprise the portion of the file system that you control. Other parts of the file system are provided and maintained by the operating system, such as **/bin, /dev, /etc, /lib, /tmp** and **/usr**, and have much the same structure on all UNIX Systems.

You will learn more about the file system in other chapters. Chapter 3 shows how to organize a file system directory structure, and access and manipulate files. Chapter 4 gives an overview of UNIX System capabilities. The effective use of these capabilities depends on your familiarity with the file system and your ability to access information stored within it. Chapters 5 and 6 are tutorials designed to teach you how to create and edit files.

The Shell

The shell is a unique command interpreter that allows you to communicate with the operating system. The shell reads the commands you enter and interprets them as requests to execute other programs, access files, or provide output. The shell is also a powerful programming language, not unlike the C programming language, that provides conditional execution and control flow features. The model of a UNIX System in Figure 1-1 shows the two-way flow of communication between you and the computer via the shell.

In addition, this version of UNIX supports the C-shell, a command interpreter with a C-like syntax. Like the standard shell, the C-shell is an interface between you and the UNIX commands and programs.

Chapter 4 describes the shell's capabilities. Chapter 7 is a tutorial that teaches you to write simple shell programs called shell scripts and custom tailor your environment. Chapter 8 describes the C-shell and provides examples for customizing your C-shell environment, as well as writing C-shell scripts.

Commands

A program is a set of instructions to the computer. Programs that can be executed by the computer without need for translation are called executable programs or commands. As a typical user of the UNIX System, you have many standard programs and tools available to you. If you use the UNIX System to write programs and develop software, you can also draw on system calls, subroutines, and other tools. Of course, any programs you write yourself will be at your disposal, too.

This book introduces you to many of the UNIX System programs and tools that you will use on a regular basis. If you need additional information on these or other standard programs, refer to the *User's/System Administrator's Reference Manual*. For information on tools and routines related to programming and software development, consult the *Programmer's Reference Manual*. The *Documentation Roadmap* describes and explains how to order all UNIX System documents from AT&T.

What Commands Do

The outer circle of the UNIX System model in Figure 1-1 organizes the system programs and tools into functional categories. These functions include

text processing	The system provides programs such as line and screen editors for creating and changing text, a spelling checker for locating spelling errors, and optional text formatters for producing high-quality paper copies that are suitable for publication.
information management	The system provides many programs that allow you to create, organize, and remove files and directories.
electronic communication	Several programs, such as **mail**, enable you to transmit information to other users and to other UNIX Systems.
software development	Several UNIX System programs establish a friendly programming environment by

providing UNIX-to-programming-language interfaces and by supplying numerous utility programs.

additional utilities

The system also offers capabilities for generating graphics and performing calculations.

How to Execute Commands

To make your requests comprehensible to the UNIX System, you must present each command in the correct format, or command line syntax. This syntax defines the order in which you enter the components of a command line. Just as you must put the subject of a sentence before the verb in an English sentence, so must you put the parts of a command line in the order required by the command line syntax. Otherwise, the UNIX System shell will not be able to interpret your request. Here is an example of the syntax of a UNIX System command line:

> *command*   *option(s)*   *argument(s)*<**CR**>

On every UNIX System command line, you must type at least two components: a command name and the <RETURN> key. (The notation <**CR**> is used as an instruction to press the <RETURN> key throughout this *Guide*.) A command line may also contain either options or arguments, or both. What are commands, options, and arguments?

- A *command* is the name of the program you want to run.

- An *option* modifies how the command runs.

- An *argument* specifies data on which the command is to operate (usually the name of a directory or file).

In command lines that include options and/or arguments, the component words are separated by at least one blank space. (You can insert a blank by pressing the space bar.) If an argument name contains a blank, enclose that name in double quotation marks. For example, if you want the argument to your command to be **sample 1**, you must type it as **"sample 1"**. If you forget the double quotation marks, the shell will interpret **sample** and **1** as two separate arguments.

Some commands allow you to specify multiple options and/or arguments on a command line. Consider the following command line:

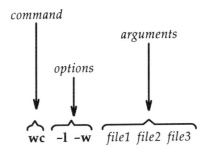

In this example, **wc** is the name of the command and **–l** and **–w** are two options that have been specified. (The UNIX System usually allows you to group options such as these to read **–lw** if you prefer.) In addition, three files (*file1*, *file2*, and *file3*) are specified as arguments. Although most options can be grouped together, arguments cannot.

The following examples show the proper sequence and spacing in command line syntax:

Incorrect	Correct
wc*file*	**wc** *file*
wc–l*file*	**wc –l** *file*
wc –l w *file*	**wc –lw** *file*
	or
	wc –l –w *file*
wc *file1file2*	**wc** *file1 file2*

Remember, regardless of the number of components, you must end every command line by pressing the <RETURN> key.

How Commands Are Executed

Figure 1-5 shows the flow of control when the UNIX System executes a command.

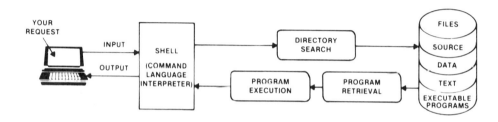

Figure 1-5: Execution of a UNIX System Command

To execute a command, enter a command line when a prompt (such as a $ sign) appears on your screen. The shell considers your command as input, searches through one or more directories to retrieve the program you specified, and conveys your request, along with the program requested, to the kernel. The kernel then follows the instructions in the program and executes the command you requested. After the program has finished running, the shell signals that it is ready for your next command by printing another prompt.

This chapter has described some basic principles of the UNIX Operating System. The following chapters will help you apply these principles according to your computing needs.

2 Basics for UNIX System Users

Getting Started

This chapter acquaints you with the general rules and guidelines for working on the UNIX System. Specifically, it lists the required terminal settings and explains how to use the keyboard, obtain a login, log on to and off of the system, and enter simple commands.

To establish contact with the UNIX System, you need

■ a terminal

■ a login name (a name by which the UNIX System identifies you as one of its authorized users)

■ a password that verifies your identity

■ instructions for dialing in and accessing the UNIX System if your terminal is not directly connected or hard-wired to the computer

The Terminal

A terminal is an input/output device: you use it to enter requests to the UNIX System, and the system uses it to send its responses to you. There are two basic types of terminals: video display terminals and printing terminals (see Figure 2-1).

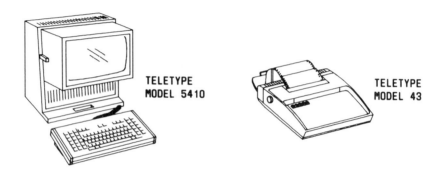

TELETYPE
MODEL 5410

TELETYPE
MODEL 43

Figure 2-1: A Video Display Terminal and a Printing Terminal

The video display terminal shows input and output on a display screen; the printing terminal, on continuously fed paper. In most respects, this difference has no effect on the user's actions or the system's responses. Instructions throughout this book that refer to the terminal screen apply in the same way to the paper in a printing terminal, unless otherwise noted.

Required Terminal Settings

Regardless of the type of terminal you use, you must configure it properly to communicate with the UNIX System. If you have not set terminal options before, you might feel more comfortable seeking help from someone who has.

How you configure a terminal depends on the type of terminal you are using. Some terminals are configured with switches; others are configured directly from the keyboard by using a set of function keys. To determine how to configure your terminal, consult the owner's manual provided by the manufacturer.

The following is a list of configuration checks you should perform on any terminal before trying to log in on the UNIX System:

1. Turn on the power.

2. Set the terminal to ON-LINE or REMOTE operation. This setting ensures the terminal is under the direct control of the computer.

3. Set the terminal to FULL DUPLEX mode. This mode ensures two-way communication (input/output) between you and the UNIX System.

4. If your terminal is not directly connected or hard-wired to the computer, make sure the acoustic coupler or data phone set you are using is set to the FULL DUPLEX mode.

5. Set character generation to LOWERCASE. If your terminal generates only uppercase letters, the UNIX System will accommodate it by printing everything in uppercase letters.

6. Set the terminal to NO PARITY.

7. Set the baud rate. This is the speed at which the computer communicates with the terminal, measured in characters per second. (For example, a terminal set at a baud rate of 4800 sends and receives 480 characters per second.) Depending on the computer and the terminal, baud rates between 300 and 19200 are available. Some computers may be capable of processing characters at higher speeds.

Keyboard Characteristics

There is no standard layout for terminal keyboards. However, all terminal keyboards share a standard set of 128 characters called the ASCII character set. (ASCII is an acronym for American Standard Code for Information Interchange.) While the keys are labeled with characters that are meaningful to you (such as the letters of the alphabet), each one is also associated with an ASCII code that is meaningful to the computer.

The keyboard layout on a typical ASCII terminal is basically the same as a typewriter's, with a few additional keys for functions such as interrupting tasks. Figure 2-2 shows an example of a keyboard on an ASCII terminal.

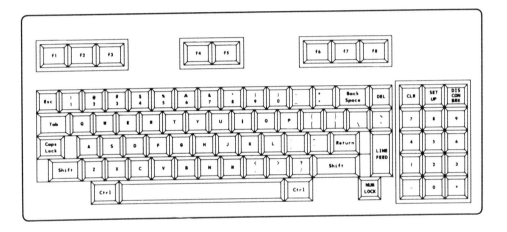

Figure 2-2: Keyboard Layout of a Teletype 5410 Terminal

The keys correspond to the following:

- the letters of the English alphabet (both uppercase and lowercase)

- the numerals (0 through 9)

- a variety of symbols (including ! @ # $ % ˆ & ( ) _ – + = ~ ' { } [ ]
  \ : ; " ' < > , ? /)

- specially defined words (such as <RETURN> and <BREAK>) and
  abbreviations (such as <DEL> for delete, <CTRL> for control, and
  <ESC> for escape)

While terminal and typewriter keyboards both have alphanumeric keys,
terminal keyboards also have keys designed for use with a computer. These
keys are labeled with characters or symbols that remind the user of their functions. However, their placement may vary from terminal to terminal because
there is no standard keyboard layout.

Typing Conventions

To interact effectively with the UNIX System, you should be familiar with
its typing conventions. The UNIX System requires that you enter commands
in lowercase letters (unless the command includes an uppercase letter). Other
conventions enable you to perform tasks, such as erasing letters or deleting
lines, simply by pressing one key or entering a specific combination of characters. Characters associated with tasks in this way are known as special characters. Figure 2-3 lists the conventions based on special characters. Detailed
explanations of them are provided on the next few pages.

Key(s)	Meaning
$	System's command prompt (your cue to issue a command).
#*	Erases a character.
@	Erases or kills an entire line.
\<BREAK\>	Stops execution of a program or command.
\<DEL\>	Deletes or kills the current command line.
\<ESC\>	When used with another character, performs a specific function (called an escape sequence).
	When used in an editing session with the **vi** editor, ends the text input mode and returns you to the command mode.
\<CR\>	Press the \<RETURN\> key. This ends a line of typing and puts the cursor on a new line.
\<^d\>†	Stops input to the system or logs off.
\<^h\>	Backspaces for terminals without a backspace key.
\<^i\>	Tabs horizontally for terminals without a tab key.
\<^s\>	Temporarily stops output from printing on the screen.
\<^q\>	Makes the output resume printing on the screen after it has been stopped by the \<^s\> command.

*   Nonprinting characters are shown in angle brackets (\< \>).

†   Characters preceded by a circumflex (^) are called control characters and are pronounced control-*letter*. To type a control character, hold down the \<CTRL\> key and press the specified letter.

Figure 2-3: UNIX System Typing Conventions

The Command Prompt

The standard UNIX System command prompt is the dollar sign ($). When the prompt appears on your terminal screen, the UNIX System is waiting for instructions from you. The appropriate response to the prompt is to issue a command and press the RETURN key.

The $ sign is the default value for the command prompt. Chapter 7 explains how to change it if you would prefer another character or character string as your command prompt.

Correcting Typing Errors

There are two keys you can use to delete text so that you can correct typing errors. The @ (at) sign key kills the current line and the # (pound) sign key erases the last character typed. These keys are available by default to perform these functions. However, if you want to use other keys, you can reassign the erase and kill functions. (For instructions, see "Reassigning the Delete Functions" later in this section and "Setting Terminal Options" in Chapter 7.)

Deleting the Current Line: the @ Sign

The @ sign key kills the current line. When you press it, an @ sign is added to the end of the line, and the cursor moves to the next line. The line containing the error is not erased from the screen but is ignored.

The @ sign key works only on the current line; be sure to press it before you press the RETURN key if you want to kill a line. In the following example, a misspelled command is typed on a command line, and the command is cancelled with the @ sign:

       whooo@
       who<CR>

Deleting the Last Characters Typed: the # Sign Key

The # sign key deletes the character(s) last typed on the current line. When you type a # sign, the cursor backs up over the last character and lets you retype it, thus effectively erasing it. This is an easy way to correct a typing error.

You can delete as many characters as you like as long as you type a corresponding number of # signs. For example, in the following command line, two characters are deleted by typing two # signs:

       dattw##e<CR>

The UNIX System interprets this as the **date** command, typed correctly.

The BACKSPACE Key

Many people prefer to use the BACKSPACE key for the erase function instead of the # sign key. When you press the BACKSPACE key, the cursor backs up over your errors, erasing them as it goes. It does not print anything, unlike the # sign key, which prints a # sign on your screen between an error and a correction. When you have finished correcting an error with the BACK-SPACE key, the line of text on the screen looks as though it was typed perfectly.

The # sign and BACKSPACE keys are equally effective at deleting characters, but using the BACKSPACE key gives you better visual information about what you are doing.

 Some terminals may not recognize the # sign key as a delete character.

Reassigning the Delete Functions

As stated earlier, you can change the keys that kill lines and erase characters. If you want to change these keys for a single working session, you can issue a command to the shell to reassign them; the delete functions will revert to the default keys (# and @) as soon as you log off. If you want to use other keys regularly, you must specify the reassignment in a file called **.profile**. Instructions for making both temporary and permanent key reassignments, along with a description of the **.profile**, are given in Chapter 7.

There are three points to keep in mind if you reassign the delete functions to non-default keys. First, the UNIX System allows only one key at a time to perform a delete function. When you reassign a function to a non-default key, you also take that function away from the default key. For example, if you reassign the erase function from the # sign key to the BACKSPACE key, you will no longer be able to use the # sign key to erase characters.

Secondly, such reassignments are inherited by any other UNIX System program that allows you to perform the function you have reassigned. For example, the interactive text editor called **ed** (described in Chapter 5) allows you to delete text with the same key you use to correct errors on a shell command line (as described in this section). Therefore, if you reassign the erase function to the BACKSPACE key, you will have to use the BACKSPACE key to erase characters while working in the **ed** editor, as well. The # sign key will no longer work.

Finally, keep in mind that any reassignments you have specified in your **.profile** do not become effective until after you log in. Therefore, if you make an error while typing your login name or password, you must use the # sign key to correct it.

Whichever keys you use, remember that they work only on the current line. Be sure to correct your errors before pressing the RETURN key at the end of a line.

Using Special Characters as Literal Characters

What happens if you want to use a special character with literal meaning as a unit of text? Since the UNIX System's default behavior is to interpret special characters as commands, you must tell the system to ignore or escape from a character's special meaning whenever you want to use it as a literal character. The backslash (\) enables you to do this. Type a \ before any special character that you want to have treated as it appears. By doing this you essentially tell the system to ignore this character's special meaning and treat it as a literal unit of text.

For example, suppose you want to add the following sentence to a file:

Only one # appears on this sheet of music.

To prevent the UNIX System from interpreting the **#** sign as a request to delete a character, enter a \ in front of the **#** sign. If you do not, the system will erase the space after the word one and print your sentence as follows:

`Only one appears on this sheet of music.`

To avoid this, type your sentence as follows:

Only one \# appears on this sheet of music.

Typing Speed

After the prompt appears on your terminal screen, you can type as fast as you want, even when the UNIX System is executing a command or responding to one. Since your input and the system's output appear on the screen simultaneously, the printout on your screen will appear garbled. However, while this may be inconvenient for you, it does not interfere with the UNIX System's work because the UNIX System has read-ahead capability. This capability allows the system to handle input and output separately. The system takes and stores input (your next request) while it sends output (its response to your last request) to the screen.

Stopping a Command

If you want to stop the execution of a command, simply press the BREAK or DELETE key. The UNIX System will stop the program and print a prompt on the screen. This is its signal that it has stopped the last command from running and is ready for your next command.

Using Control Characters

Locate the control key on your terminal keyboard. It may be labeled CONTROL or CTRL and is probably to the left of the A key or below the Z key. The control key is used in combination with other characters to perform physical controlling actions on lines of typing. Commands entered in this way are called control characters. Some control characters perform mundane tasks such as backspacing and tabbing. Others define commands that are specific to the UNIX System. For example, CONTROL-s temporarily halts output that is being printed on a terminal screen.

To type a control character, hold down the control key and press the appropriate alphabetic key. Most control characters do not appear on the screen when typed and therefore are shown between angle brackets (see "Notational Conventions" in the Preface). The control key is represented by a circumflex (ˆ) before the letter. Thus, for example, < ˆs> designates the CONTROL-s character.

The two functions for which control characters are most often used are to control the printing of output on the screen and to log off the system. To prevent information from rolling off the screen on a video display terminal, type < ˆs>; the printing will stop. When you are ready to read more output, type < ˆq> and the printing will resume.

To log off the UNIX System, type < ˆd>.

In addition, the UNIX System uses control characters to provide capabilities that some terminals fail to make available through function-specific keys. If your keyboard does not have a BACKSPACE key, you can use the < ^h> key instead. You can also set tabs without a TAB key by typing < ^i> if your terminal is set properly. (Refer to the section entitled "Possible Problems When Logging In" for information on how to set the TAB key.)

Now that you have configured the terminal and inspected the keyboard, one step remains before you can establish communication with the UNIX System: you must obtain a login name.

Obtaining a Login Name

A login name is the name by which the UNIX System verifies that you are an authorized user of the system when you request access to it. It is so called because you must enter it every time you want to log in. (The expression logging in is derived from the fact that the system maintains a log for each user, in which it records the type and amount of system resources being used.)

To obtain a login name, set up a UNIX System account through your system administrator. There are few rules governing your choice of a login name. Typically, it is three to eight characters long. It can contain any combination of lowercase alphanumeric characters, as long as it starts with a letter. It cannot contain any symbols.

However, your login name will probably be determined by local practices. The users of your system may all use their initials, last names, or nicknames as their login names. Here are a few examples of legal login names: **starship**, **mary2**, and **jmrs**.

Establishing Contact with the UNIX System

Typically, you will be using either a terminal that is wired directly to a computer or a terminal that communicates with a computer over a telephone line.

 This section describes a typical procedure for logging in, but it may not apply to your system. There are many ways to log in on a UNIX System over a telephone line. Security precautions on your system may require that you use a special telephone number or other security code. For instructions on logging in on your UNIX System from outside your computer installation site, see your system administrator.

Turn on your terminal. If it is directly connected, the login: prompt will immediately appear in the upper left-hand corner of the screen.

If you are going to communicate with the computer over a telephone line, you must now establish a connection. The following procedure is an example of a method you might use to do this. (For the procedure required by your system, see your system administrator.)

1. Dial the telephone number that connects you to the UNIX System. You will hear one of the following:

   □ A busy signal. This means that either the circuits are busy or the line is in use. Hang up and dial again.

   □ Continuous ringing and no answer. This usually means that there is trouble with the telephone line or that the system is inoperable because of mechanical failure or electronic problems. Hang up and dial again later.

   □ A high-pitched tone. This means that the system is accessible.

2. When you hear the high-pitched tone, place the handset of the phone in the acoustic coupler or momentarily press the appropriate button on the data phone set (see the owner's manual for the appropriate equipment). Then replace the handset in the cradle (see Figure 2-4).

3. After a few seconds, the login: prompt will appear in the upper left hand corner of the screen.

4. A series of meaningless characters may appear on your screen. This means that the telephone number you called serves more than one baud rate; the UNIX System is trying to communicate with your terminal, but is using the wrong speed. Press the BREAK or RETURN key; this signals the system to try another speed. If the UNIX System does not display the login: prompt within a few seconds, press the BREAK or RETURN key again.

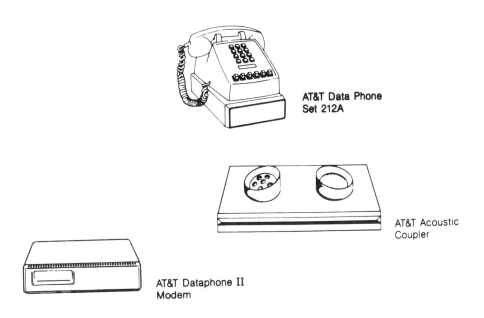

AT&T Data Phone
Set 212A

AT&T Acoustic
Coupler

AT&T Dataphone II
Modem

Figure 2-4: Data Phone Set, Modem, and Acoustic Coupler

Login Procedure

When the login: prompt appears, type your login name and press the RETURN key. For example, if your login name is **starship**, your login line will look like the following:

login: **starship**<CR>

Remember to type in lowercase letters. If you use uppercase from the time you log in, the UNIX System will expect and respond in uppercase exclusively until the next time you log in. It will accept and run many commands typed in uppercase but will not allow you to edit files.

Password

Next, the system prompts you for your password. Type your password and press the RETURN key. For security reasons, the UNIX System does not print (or echo) your password on the screen.

If both your login name and password are acceptable to the UNIX System, the system may print the message of the day and/or current news items and then the default command prompt ($). (The message of the day might include a schedule for system maintenance, and news items might include an announcement of a new system tool.) When you have logged in, your screen will look similar to the following:

```
login: starship<CR>
password:
UNIX System news
$
```

If you make a typing mistake when logging in, the UNIX System prints the message login incorrect on your screen. Then, it gives you a second chance to log in by printing another login: prompt.

```
login: ttarship<CR>
password:
login incorrect
login:
```

The login procedure may also fail if the communication link between your terminal and the UNIX System has been dropped. If this happens, you must reestablish contact with the computer (specifically, with the data switch that links your terminal to the computer) before trying to log in again. Since procedures for doing this vary from site to site, ask your system administrator to give you exact instructions for getting a connection on the data switch.

If you have never logged in on the UNIX System, your login procedure may differ from the one just described. This is because some system administrators follow the optional security procedure of assigning temporary passwords to new users when they set up their accounts. If you have a temporary password, the system will force you to choose a new password before it allows you to log in.

By forcing you to choose a password for your exclusive use, this extra step helps to ensure a system's security. Protection of system resources and your personal files depends on your keeping your password private.

The actual procedure you follow will be determined by the administrative procedures at your computer installation site. However, it will probably be similar to the following example of a first-time login procedure:

1. You establish contact; the UNIX System displays the login: prompt. Type your login name and press the RETURN key.

2. The UNIX System prints the password prompt. Type your temporary password and press the RETURN key.

3. The system tells you your temporary password has expired and you must select a new one.

4. The system asks you to type your old password again. Type your temporary password.

5. The system prompts you to type your new password. Type the password you have chosen.

    Passwords must meet the following requirements:

    ☐ Each password must have at least six characters. Only the first eight characters are significant.

    ☐ Each password must contain at least two alphabetic characters and at least one numeric or special character. Alphabetic characters can be uppercase or lowercase letters.

☐ Each password must differ from your login name and any reverse or circular shift of that login name. For comparison purposes, an uppercase letter and its corresponding lowercase letter are equivalent.

☐ A new password must differ from the old by at least three characters. For comparison purposes, an uppercase letter and its corresponding lowercase letter are equivalent.

Examples of valid passwords are: **mar84ch**, **Jonath0n**, and **BRAV3S**.

 NOTE The UNIX System you are using may have different requirements to consider when choosing a password. Ask your system administrator for details.

6. For verification, the system asks you to re-enter your new password. Type your new password again.

7. If you do not re-enter the new password exactly as typed the first time, the system tells you the passwords do not match and asks you to try the procedure again. On some systems, however, the communication link may be dropped if you do not re-enter the password exactly as typed the first time. If this happens, you must return to step 1 and begin the login procedure again. When the passwords match, the system displays the prompt.

The following screen summarizes this procedure (steps 1 through 6) for first-time UNIX System users.

```
login: starship    <CR>
password: <CR>
Your password has expired.
Choose a new one.
Old password: <CR>
New password: <CR>
Re-enter new password: <CR>
$
```

Possible Problems when Logging In

A terminal usually behaves predictably when you have configured it properly. Sometimes, however, it may act peculiarly. For example, the carriage return may not work properly.

Some problems can be corrected simply by logging off the system and logging in again. If logging in a second time does not remedy the problem, you should first check the following and try logging in once again:

the keyboard	Keys labeled CAPS, NUM, SCROLL, and so on should not be enabled (put into the locked position). You can usually disable these keys simply by pressing them.
the data phone set or modem	If your terminal is connected to the computer via telephone lines, verify that the baud rate and duplex settings are correctly specified.
the switches	Some terminals have several switches that must be set to be compatible with the UNIX System. If this is the case with the terminal you are using, make sure they are set properly.

Refer to the section "Required Terminal Settings" in this chapter if you need information to verify the terminal configuration. If you need additional information about the keyboard, terminal, data phone, or modem, check the owner's manuals for the appropriate equipment.

Figure 2-5 presents a list of procedures you can follow to detect, diagnose, and correct some problems you may experience when logging in. If you need further help, contact your system administrator.

Problem†	Possible Cause	Action/Remedy
Meaningless characters	UNIX System at wrong speed	Press RETURN or BREAK key
Input/output appears in UPPER CASE letters	Terminal configuration includes UPPER CASE setting	Log off and set character generation to lower case
Input appears in UPPER CASE, output in lower case	Key labeled CAPS (or CAPS LOCK) is enabled	Press CAPS or CAPS LOCK key to disable setting
Input is printed twice	Terminal is set to HALF DUPLEX mode	Change setting to FULL DUPLEX mode
Tab key does not work properly	Tabs are not set correctly	Type **stty –tabs**‡
Communication link cannot be established although high pitched tone is heard when dialing in	Terminal is set to LOCAL or OFF-LINE mode	Set terminal to ON-LINE mode try logging in again
Communication link (terminal to UNIX System) is repeatedly dropped	Bad telephone line or bad communications port	Call system administrator

*   Numerous problems can occur if your terminal is not configured properly. To eliminate these possibilities before attempting to log in, perform the configuration checks listed under "Required Terminal Settings."

†   Some problems may be specific to your terminal, data phone set, or modem. Check the owner's manual for the appropriate equipment if suggested actions do not remedy the problem.

‡   Typing **stty –tabs** corrects the tab setting only for your current computing session. To ensure a correct tab setting for all sessions, add the line **stty –tabs** to your **.profile** (see Chapter 7).

Figure 2-5: Troubleshooting Problems When Logging In*

Simple Commands

When the prompt appears on your screen, the UNIX System has recognized you as an authorized user and is waiting for you to request a program by entering a command.

For example, try running the **date** command. After the prompt, type the command and press the RETURN key. The UNIX System accesses a program called **date**, executes it, and prints its results on the screen, as shown below.

```
$ date<CR>
Wed Oct 15 09:49:44 EDT 1986
$
```

As you can see, the **date** command prints the date and time, using the 24-hour clock.

Now type the **who** command and press the RETURN key. Your screen will look something like this:

```
$ who<CR>
starship        tty00       Oct 12      8:53
mary2           tty02       Oct 12      8:56
acct123         tty05       Oct 12      8:54
jmrs            tty06       Oct 12      8:56
$
```

The **who** command lists the login names of everyone currently working on your system. The tty designations refer to the special files that correspond to each user's terminal. The date and time at which each user logged in are also shown.

Logging Off

When you have completed a session with the UNIX System, type <^d> after the prompt. (Remember that control characters such as <^d> are typed by holding down the control key and pressing the appropriate alphabetic key. Because they are nonprinting characters, they do not appear on your screen.) After several seconds, the UNIX System will display the login: prompt again.

```
$ <^d>
login:
```

This shows that you have logged off successfully and the system is ready for someone else to log in.

 Always log off the UNIX System by typing <^d> before you turn off the terminal or hang up the telephone. If you do not, you may not be actually logged off the system.

The **exit** command also allows you to log off but is not used by most users. It may be convenient if you want to include a command to log off within a shell program. (For details, see the "Special Commands" section of the **sh**(1) page in the *User's/System Administrator's Reference Manual.*)

3 Using the File System

Printing Files   3-72

Introduction

To use the UNIX file system effectively you must be familiar with its structure, know something about your relationship to this structure, and understand how the relationship changes as you move around within it. This chapter prepares you to use this file system.

The first two sections ("How the File System is Structured" and "Your Place in the File System") offer a working perspective of the file system. The rest of the chapter introduces UNIX System commands that allow you to build your own directory structure, access and manipulate the subdirectories and files you organize within it, and examine the contents of other directories in the system for which you have access permission.

Each command is discussed in a separate subsection. Tables at the end of these subsections summarize the features of each command so that you can later review a command's syntax and capabilities quickly. Many of the commands presented in this section have additional, sophisticated uses. These, however, are left for more experienced users and are described in other UNIX System documentation. All the commands presented here are basic to using the file system efficiently and easily. Try using each command as you read about it.

How the File System is Structured

The file system is made up of a set of ordinary files, special files, and directories. These components provide a way to organize, retrieve, and manage information electronically. Chapter 1 introduced the properties of directories and files; this section will review them briefly before discussing how to use them.

- An ordinary file is a collection of characters stored on a disk. It may contain text for a report or code for a program.

- A special file represents a physical device, such as a terminal or disk.

- A directory is a collection of files and other directories (sometimes called subdirectories). Use directories to group files together on the basis of any criteria you choose. For example, you might create a directory for each product that your company sells or for each of your student's records.

The set of all the directories and files is organized into a tree shaped structure. Figure 3-1 shows a sample file structure with a directory called root (/) as its source. By moving down the branches extending from root, you can reach several other major system directories. By branching down from these, you can, in turn, reach all the directories and files in the file system.

In this hierarchy, files and directories that are subordinate to a directory have what is called a parent/child relationship. This type of relationship is possible for many layers of files and directories. In fact, there is no limit to the number of files and directories you may create in any directory that you own. Neither is there a limit to the number of layers of directories that you may create. Thus, you have the capability to organize your files in a variety of ways, as shown in Figure 3-1.

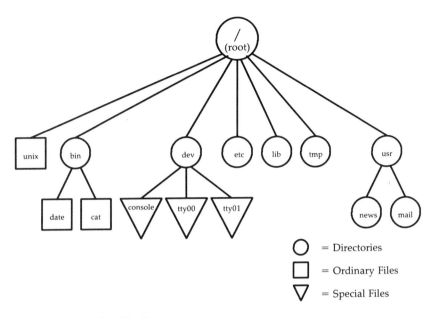

Figure 3-1: A Sample File System

Your Place in the File System

Whenever you interact with the UNIX System, you do so from a location in its file system structure. The UNIX System automatically places you at a specific point in its file system every time you log in. From that point, you can move through the hierarchy to work in any of your directories and files and to access those belonging to others that you have permission to use.

The following sections describe your position in the file system structure and how this position changes as you move through the file system.

Your Home Directory

When you successfully complete the login procedure, the UNIX System places you at a specific point in its file system structure called your login or home directory. The login name assigned to you when your UNIX System account was set up is usually the name of this home directory. Every user with an authorized login name has a unique home directory in the file system.

The UNIX System is able to keep track of all these home directories by maintaining one or more system directories that organize them. For example, the home directories of the login names **starship**, **mary2**, and **jmrs** are contained in a system directory called **user1**. Figure 3-2 shows the position of a system directory such as **user1** in relation to the other important UNIX System directories discussed in Chapter 1.

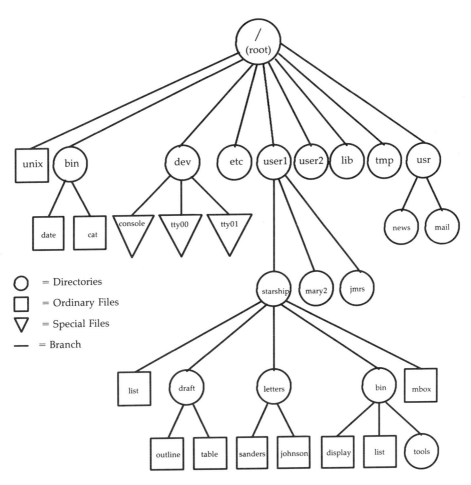

Figure 3-2: Directory of Home Directories

Within your home directory, you can create files and additional directories (called subdirectories) in which to group them. You can move and delete your files and directories, and you can control access to them. You have full responsibility for everything you create in your home directory because you own it. Your home directory is a vantage point from which to view all the files and directories it holds, and the rest of the file system, all the way up to root.

Your Current Directory

As long as you continue to work in your home directory, it is considered your current working directory. If you move to another directory, that directory becomes your new current directory.

The **pwd** command (short for print working directory) prints the name of the directory in which you are now working. For example, if your login name is **starship** and you execute the **pwd** command in response to the first prompt after logging in, the UNIX System responds as follows:

```
$ pwd<CR>
/user1/starship
$
```

The system response gives you both the name of the directory in which you are working (**starship**) and the location of that directory in the file system. The path name /user1/starship tells you that the root directory (shown by the leading / in the line) contains the directory **user1** which, in turn, contains the directory **starship**. (All other slashes in the path name other than root are used to separate the names of directories and files, and to show the position of each directory relative to root.) A directory name that shows the directory's location in this way is called a full or complete directory name or path name. In the next few pages we will analyze and trace this path name so you can start to move around in the file system.

Remember, you can determine your position in the file system at any time simply by issuing the **pwd** command. This is especially helpful if you want to read or copy a file and the UNIX System tells you the file you are trying to access does not exist. You may be surprised to find you are in a different directory than you thought.

Figure 3-3 provides a summary of the syntax and capabilities of the **pwd** command.

Command Recap		
pwd – prints full name of working directory		
command	*options*	*arguments*
pwd	none	none
Description:	**pwd** prints the full path name of the directory in which you are currently working.	

Figure 3-3: Summary of the **pwd** Command

Path Names

Every file and directory in the UNIX System is identified by a unique path name. The path name shows the location of the file or directory and provides directions for reaching it. Knowing how to follow the directions given by a path name is your key to moving around the file system successfully. The first step in learning about these directions is to learn about the two types of path names: full and relative.

Full Path Names

A full path name (sometimes called an absolute path name) gives directions that start in the root directory and lead you down through a unique sequence of directories to a particular directory or file. You can use a full path name to reach any file or directory in the UNIX System in which you are working.

Because a full path name always starts at the root of the file system, its leading character is always a **/** (slash). The final name in a full path name can be either a file name or a directory name. All other names in the path must be directories.

To understand how a full path name is constructed and how it directs you, consider the following example. Suppose you are working in the **star-ship** directory, located in **/user1**. You issue the **pwd** command and the system responds by printing the full path name of your working directory: /user1/starship. Analyze the elements of this path name using the following diagram and key.

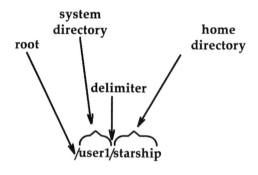

/ (leading)	= the slash that appears as the first character in the path name is the root of the file system
user1	= system directory one level below root in the hierarchy to which root points or branches
/ (subsequent)	= the next slash separates or delimits the directory names **user1** and **starship**
starship	= current working directory

Now follow the bold lines in Figure 3-4 to trace the full path to
/user1/starship.

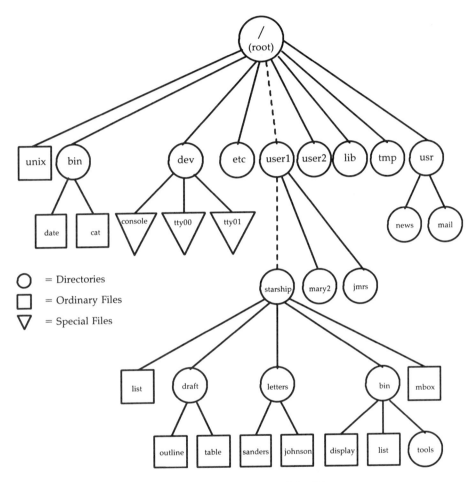

Figure 3-4: Full Path Name of the **/user1/starship** Directory

Relative Path Names

A relative path name gives directions that start in your current working directory and lead you up or down through a series of directories to a particular file or directory. By moving down from your current directory, you can access files and directories you own. By moving up from your current directory, you pass through layers of parent directories to the grandparent of all system directories, root. From there you can move anywhere in the file system.

A relative path name begins with one of the following: a directory or file name; a . (pronounced dot), which is a shorthand notation for your current directory; or a .. (pronounced dot dot), which is a shorthand notation for the directory immediately above your current directory in the file system hierarchy. The directory represented by .. (dot dot) is called the parent directory of . (your current directory).

For example, say you are in the directory **starship** in the sample system and **starship** contains directories named **draft**, **letters**, and **bin** and a file named **mbox**. The relative path name to any of these is simply its name, such as **draft** or **mbox**. Figure 3-5 traces the relative path from **starship** to **draft**.

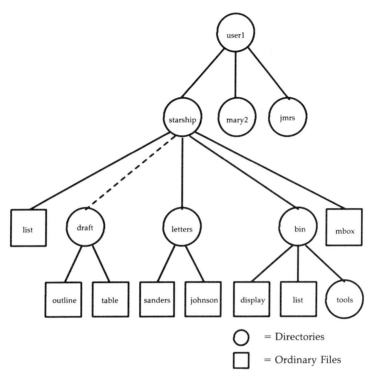

Figure 3-5: Relative Path Name of the **draft** Directory

The **draft** directory belonging to **starship** contains the files **outline** and **table**. The relative path name from **starship** to the file **outline** is **draft/outline**.

Figure 3-6 traces this relative path. Notice that the slash in this path name separates the directory named **draft** from the file named **outline**. Here, the slash is a delimiter showing that **outline** is subordinate to **draft**; that is, **outline** is a child of its parent, **draft**.

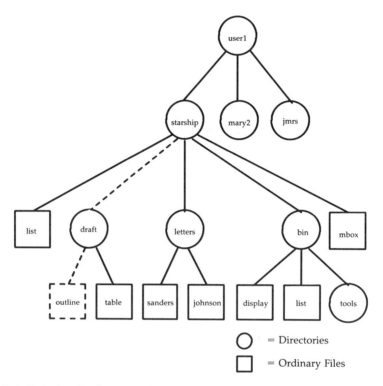

⃝ = Directories

☐ = Ordinary Files

Figure 3-6: Relative Path Name from **starship** to **outline**

So far, the discussion of relative path names has covered how to specify names of files and directories that belong to, or are children of, your current directory. You now know how to move down the system hierarchy level by level until you reach your destination. However, you can also ascend the levels in the system structure or ascend and subsequently descend into other files and directories.

To ascend to the parent of your current directory, you can use the .. notation. This means that if you are in the directory named **draft** in the sample file system, **..** is the path name to **starship**, and **../..** is the path name to **starship**'s parent directory, **user1**.

From **draft**, you can also trace a path to the directory **sanders** by using the path name **../letters/sanders**. The **..** brings you up to **starship**. Then the names **letters** and **sanders** take you down through the **letters** directory to the **sanders** directory.

Keep in mind that you can always use a full path name in place of a relative one.

Figure 3-7 shows some examples of full and relative path names.

Path Name	Meaning
/	full path name of the root directory
/bin	full path name of the **bin** directory (contains most executable programs and utilities)
/user1/starship/bin/tools	full path name of the **tools** directory belonging to the **bin** directory that belongs to the **starship** directory belonging to **user1** that belongs to root
bin/tools	relative path name to the directory **tools** in the directory **bin**
	If the current directory is **/**, then the UNIX System searches for **/bin/tools**. However, if the current directory is **starship**, then the system searches the full path **/user1/starship/bin/tools**.
tools	relative path name of the directory **tools** in the current directory.

Figure 3-7: Example Path Names

You may need some practice before you can use path names such as these to move around the file system with confidence. However, this is to be expected when learning a new concept.

Naming Directories and Files

You can give your directories and files any names you want, as long as you observe the following rules:

- The name of a directory or file can be from one to fourteen characters long.

- All characters other than / are legal.

- Some characters are best avoided, such as a <SPACE>, <TAB>, <BACKSPACE>, and the following:

    ? @ # $ ˆ & * ( ) ` [ ] \ ¦ ; ' " < >

    If you use a blank or tab in a directory or file name, you must enclose the name in quotation marks on the command line.

- Avoid using a +, – or . as the first character in a file name.

- Uppercase and lowercase characters are distinct to the UNIX System. For example, the system considers a directory or file named **draft** to be different from one named **DRAFT**.

The following are examples of legal directory or file names:

memo	**MEMO**	**section2**	**ref:list**
file.d	**chap3+4**	**item1-10**	**outline**

The rest of this chapter introduces UNIX System commands that enable you to examine the file system.

Organizing a Directory

This section introduces four UNIX System commands that enable you to organize and use a directory structure: **mkdir**, **ls**, **cd**, and **rmdir**.

mkdir   enables you to make new directories and subdirectories within your current directory

ls   lists the names of all the subdirectories and files in a directory

cd   enables you to change your location in the file system from one directory to another

rmdir   enables you to remove an empty directory

These commands can be used with either full or relative path names. Two of the commands, **ls** and **cd**, can also be used without a path name. Each command is described more fully in the four sections that follow.

Creating Directories: the mkdir Command

It is recommended that you create subdirectories in your home directory according to a logical and meaningful scheme that will facilitate the retrieval of information from your files. If you put all files pertaining to one subject together in a directory, you will know where to find them later.

To create a directory, use the **mkdir** command (short for make directory). Simply enter the command name, followed by the name you are giving your new directory or file. For example, in the sample file system, the owner of the **draft** subdirectory created **draft** by issuing the following command from the home directory (**/user1/starship**):

```
$ mkdir draft <CR>
$
```

The second prompt shows that the command has succeeded; the subdirectory **draft** has been created.

Still in the home directory, this user created other subdirectories, such as **letters** and **bin**, in the same way.

    $ mkdir letters<CR>
    $ mkdir bin<CR>
    $

The user could have created all three subdirectories (**draft**, **letters**, and **bin**) simultaneously by listing them all on a single command line.

    $ mkdir draft letters bin<CR>
    $

You can also move to a subdirectory you created and build additional sub-directories within it. When you build directories or create files, you can name them anything you want as long as you follow the guidelines listed earlier under "Naming Directories and Files."

Figure 3-8 summarizes the syntax and capabilities of the **mkdir** command.

Command Recap		
mkdir – makes a new directory		
command	*options*	*arguments*
mkdir	none	*directoryname(s)*
Description:	**mkdir** creates a new directory (subdirectory).	
Remarks:	The system returns a prompt ($ by default) if the directory is successfully created.	

Figure 3-8: Summary of the **mkdir** Command

Listing the Contents of a Directory: the ls Command

All directories in the file system have information about the files and directories they contain, such as name, size, and the date last modified. You can obtain this information about the contents of your current directory and other system directories by executing the **ls** command (short for list).

The **ls** command lists the names of all files and subdirectories in a specified directory. If you do not specify a directory, **ls** lists the names of files and directories in your current directory. To understand how the **ls** command works, consider the sample file system (Figure 3-2) once again.

Say you are logged in to the UNIX System and you run the **pwd** command. The system responds with the path name **/user1/starship**. To display the names of files and directories in this current directory, you then type **ls** and press the <RETURN> key. After this sequence, your terminal will read

```
$ pwd<CR>
$/user1/starship
$ ls<CR>
bin
draft
letters
list
mbox
$
```

As you can see, the system responds by listing, in alphabetical order, the names of files and directories in the current directory **starship**. (If the first character of any of the file or directory names had been a number or an uppercase letter, it would have been printed first.)

To print the names of files and subdirectories in a directory other than your current directory without moving from your current directory, you must specify the name of that directory as follows:

ls *pathname*<**CR**>

The directory name can be either the full or relative path name of the desired directory. For example, you can list the contents of **draft** while you are working in **starship** by entering **ls draft** and pressing the <RETURN> key. Your screen will look like the following:

```
$ ls draft<CR>
outline
table
$
```

Here, **draft** is a relative path name from a parent (**starship**) to a child (**draft**) directory.

You can also use a relative path name to print the contents of a parent directory when you are located in a child directory. The **..** (dot dot) notation provides an easy way to do this. For example, the following command line specifies the relative path name from **starship** to **user1**:

```
$ ls ..<CR>
jmrs
mary2
starship
$
```

You can get the same results by using the full path name from root to **user1**. If you type **ls /user1** and press the <RETURN> key, the system will respond by printing the same list.

Similarly, you can list the contents of any system directory that you have permission to access by executing the **ls** command with a full or relative path name.

The **ls** command is useful if you have a long list of files and you are trying to determine whether one of them exists in your current directory. For example, if you are in the directory **draft** and you want to determine if the files named **outline** and **notes** are there, use the **ls** command as follows:

```
$ ls outline notes<CR>
outline
notes not found
$
```

The system acknowledges the existence of **outline** by printing its name and says that the file **notes** is not found.

The **ls** command does not print the contents of a file. If you want to see what a file contains, use the **cat**, **more**, **pg**, or **pr** command. These commands are described in "Accessing and Manipulating Files," later in this chapter.

Frequently Used ls Options

The **ls** command also accepts options that cause specific attributes of a file or subdirectory to be listed. There are more than a dozen available options for the **ls** commands. Of these, **–a** and **–l** will probably be most valuable in your basic use of the UNIX System. Refer to the *ls*(1) page in the *User's/System Administrator's Reference Manual* for details about other options.

Listing All Files

Some important file names in your home directory, such as **.profile** (pronounced dot-profile), begin with a period. (As you can see from this example, when a period is used as the first character of a file name, it is pronounced dot.) When a file name begins with a dot, it is not included in the list of files reported by the **ls** command. If you want the **ls** to include these files, use the **–a** option on the command line.

For example, to list all the files in your current directory (**starship**), including those that begin with a **.** (dot), type **ls –a** and press the <RETURN> key:

```
$ ls -a<CR>
.

..
.profile
bin
draft
letters
list
mbox
$
```

Listing Contents in Short Format
The **–C** and **–F** options for the **ls** command are frequently used. Together, these options list a directory's subdirectories and files in columns, and identify executable files with an * and directories with a /. Thus, you can list all files in your working directory **starship** by executing the command line shown here:

```
$ ls -CF<CR>
bin/            letters/          mbox
draft/          list*
$
```

NOTE This version of the UNIX System includes the **lc** (short for list in columns) command. Like **ls**, **lc** accepts *pathname* arguments and recognizes several options. When used with no options, **lc** produces output that is identical to the output produced by **ls –C**. For more information about **lc** and a list of available options, see the *ls*(1) entry in the *User's/System Administrator's Reference Manual.*

Listing Contents in Long Format

Probably the most informative **ls** option is **–l**, which displays the contents of a directory in long format, giving mode, number of links, owner, group, size in bytes, and time of last modification for each file. For example, say you run the **ls –l** command while in the **starship** directory:

```
$ ls -l<CR>
total 30
drwxr-xr-x    3 starship      project          96  Oct 27  08:16  bin
drwxr-xr-x    2 starship      project          64  Nov  1  14:19  draft
drwxr-xr-x    2 starship      project          80  Nov  8  08:41  letters
-rwx------    2 starship      project       12301  Nov  2  10:15  list
-rw-------    1 starship      project          40  Oct 27  10:00  mbox
$
```

The first line of output (total 30) shows the amount of disk space used, measured in blocks. Each of the rest of the lines comprises a report on a directory or file in **starship**. The first character in each line (d, –, b, or c) tells you the type of file.

d = directory

– = ordinary disk file

b = block special file

c = character special file

Using this key to interpret the previous screen, you can see that the **starship** directory contains three directories and two ordinary disk files.

The next several characters, which are either letters or hyphens, identify who has permission to read and use the file or directory. (Permissions are discussed in the description of the **chmod** command under "Accessing and Manipulating Files" later in this chapter.)

The following number is the link count. For a file, this equals the number of users linked to that file. For a directory, this number shows the number of directories immediately under it plus two (for the directory itself and its parent directory).

Next, the login name of the file's owner appears (here it is **starship**), followed by the group name of the file or directory (**project**).

The following number shows the length of the file or directory entry measured in units of information (or memory) called bytes. The month, day, and time that the file was last modified is given next. Finally, the last column shows the name of the directory or file.

Figure 3-9 identifies each column in the rows of output from the **ls -l** command.

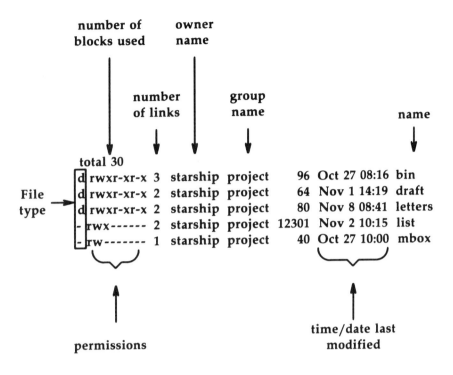

Figure 3-9: Description of Output Produced by the **ls –l** Command

Figure 3-10 summarizes the syntax and capabilities of the **ls** command and two available options.

Command Recap
ls – lists the contents of a directory

command	*options*	*arguments*
ls	**–a, –l,** and others*	*directoryname(s)*

Description:	**ls** lists the names of the files and subdirectories in the specified directories. If no directory name is given as an argument, the contents of your working directory are listed.
Options:	**–a** lists all entries, including those beginning with **.** (dot)
	–l lists contents of a directory in long format, furnishing mode, permissions, size in bytes, and time of last modification
Remarks:	If you want to read the contents of a file, use the **cat** or **more** command.
	The **lc** command is similar to this command, except **lc** lists a directory's contents in multiple columns by default.

*   See the *ls*(1) page in the *User's/System Administrator's Reference Manual* for all available options and an explanation of their capabilities.

Figure 3-10: Summary of the **ls** Command

Changing Your Current Directory: the cd Command

When you first log in on the UNIX System, you are placed in your home directory. As long as you do work in it, it is also your current working directory. However, by using the **cd** command (short for change directory), you can work in other directories as well. To use this command, enter **cd**, followed by a path name to the directory to which you want to move:

cd *pathname_of_newdirectory*<**CR**>

Any valid path name (full or relative) can be used as an argument to the **cd** command. If you do not specify a path name, the command will move you to your home directory. Once you have moved to a new directory, it becomes your current directory.

For example, to move from the **starship** directory to its child directory **draft** (in the sample file system), type **cd draft** and press the <RETURN> key. (Here **draft** is the relative path name to the desired directory.) When you get a prompt, verify your new location by typing **pwd** and pressing the <RETURN> key. Your terminal screen will look like the following:

```
$ cd draft<CR>
$ pwd<CR>
/user1/starship/draft
$
```

Now that you are in the **draft** directory, you can create subdirectories in it by using the **mkdir** command and new files by using the **ed** and **vi** editors. (See Chapters 5 and 6 for tutorials on the **ed** and **vi** commands, respectively.)

It is not necessary to be in the **draft** directory to access files within it. You can access a file in any directory by specifying a full path name for it. For example, to **cat** the **sanders** file in the **letters** directory (**/user1/starship/letters**) while you are in the **draft** directory (**/user1/starship/draft**), specify the full path name of **sanders** on the command line:

      cat /user1/starship/letters/sanders<CR>

You may also use full path names with the **cd** command. For example, to move to the **letters** directory from the **draft** directory, specify **/user1/starship/letters** on the command line as follows:

      cd /user1/starship/letters<CR>

Also, because **letters** and **draft** are both children of **starship**, you can use the relative path name **../letters** with the **cd** command. The **..** notation moves you to the directory **starship**, and the rest of the path name moves you to **letters**.

Figure 3-11 summarizes the syntax and capabilities of the **cd** command.

Command Recap		
cd – changes your working directory		
command	*options*	*arguments*
cd	none	*directoryname*

Description:	**cd** changes your position in the file system from the current directory to the directory specified. If no directory name is given as an argument, the **cd** command places you in your home directory.
Remarks:	When the shell places you in a specified directory, the prompt ($ by default) is returned to you. To access a directory that is not in your working directory, you must use the full or relative path name in place of a simple directory name.

Figure 3-11: Summary of the **cd** Command

Removing Directories: the rmdir **Command**

If you no longer need a directory, you can remove it with the **rmdir** command (short for remove a directory). The standard syntax for this command is

> **rmdir** *directoryname(s)*<**CR**>

You can specify more than one directory name on the command line.

The **rmdir** command will not remove a directory if you are not the owner of it or if the directory is not empty. If you want to remove a file in another user's directory, the owner must give you write permission for the parent directory of the file you want to remove.

If you try to remove a directory that still contains subdirectories and files (that is, it is not empty), the **rmdir** command prints the message *directoryname not empty.* You must remove all subdirectories and files; only then will the command succeed.

For example, say you have a directory called **memos** that contains one subdirectory, **tech**, and two files, **june.30** and **july.31**. (Create this directory in your home directory now so you can see how the **rmdir** command works.) If you try to remove the directory **memos** (by issuing the **rmdir** command from your home directory), the command responds as follows:

```
$ rmdir memos<CR>
rmdir:  memos not empty
$
```

To remove the directory **memos**, you must first remove its contents: the sub-directory **tech** and the files **june.30** and **july.31**. You can remove the **tech** subdirectory by executing the **rmdir** command. For instructions on removing files, see "Accessing and Manipulating Files" later in this chapter.

Once you have removed the contents of the **memos** directory, **memos** itself can be removed. First, however, you must move to its parent directory (your home directory). The **rmdir** command will not work if you are still in the directory you want to remove. From your home directory, type

      rmdir memos<CR>

If **memos** is empty, the command will remove it and return a prompt.

Figure 3-12 summarizes the syntax and capabilities of the **rmdir** command.

Command Recap
rmdir – removes a directory

command	*options*	*arguments*
rmdir	none	*directoryname(s)*

Description:	**rmdir** removes specified directories if they do not contain files and/or subdirectories.
Remarks:	If the directory is empty, it is removed and the system returns a prompt. If the directory contains files or subdirectories, the command returns the message, `rmdir:` *directoryname* `not empty`.

Figure 3-12: Summary of the **rmdir** Command

Accessing and Manipulating Files

This section introduces several UNIX System commands that access and manipulate files in the file system structure. Information in this section is organized into two parts: basic and advanced. The part devoted to basic commands is fundamental to using the file system; the advanced commands offer more sophisticated information processing techniques for working with files.

Basic Commands

This section discusses UNIX System commands that are necessary for accessing and using the files in the directory structure. Figure 3-13 lists these commands.

Command	Function
cat	prints the contents of a specified file on a terminal
more	prints the contents of a specified file on a terminal, one screenful at a time
pg	prints the contents of a specified file on a terminal in chunks or pages
pr	prints a partially formatted version of a specified file on the terminal
lp	requests a paper copy of a file from a line printer
cp	makes a duplicate copy of an existing file
copy	copies groups of files (including directories and subdirectories) to another directory
mv	moves and renames a file
rm	removes a file
wc	reports the number of lines, words, and characters in a file
chmod	changes permission modes for a file (or a directory)

Figure 3-13: Basic Commands for Using Files

Each command is discussed in detail and summarized in a table that you can easily reference later. These tables will allow you to review the syntax and capabilities of these commands at a glance.

Displaying a File's Contents: the cat, more, pg, and pr Commands

The UNIX System provides four commands for displaying and printing the contents of a file or files: **cat, more, pg,** and **pr**. The **cat** command (short for concatenate) displays the contents of the file(s) specified. This output is displayed on your terminal screen unless you tell **cat** to direct it to another file or a new command.

The **more** command displays the contents of a file on the terminal, one screenful at a time. While the **cat** command causes the entire file to scroll quickly on the screen, **more** causes the scrolling to pause at the end of each screenful, until you instruct **more** to display the next screenful. This feature is helpful if you think the file you wish to view is larger than one screenful.

The **pg** command is particularly useful when you want to read the contents of a long file because it displays the text of a file in pages a screenful at a time. Unlike **more**, **pg** lets you scroll through the file backward, as well as forward. The **pr** command formats specified files and displays them on your terminal or, if you request, directs the formatted output to a printer. See the section "Printing Files" in this chapter for more information on using the **pr** command.

The following sections describe how to use the **cat, more, pg,** and **pr** commands.

Concatenate and Print Contents of a File: the cat Command

The **cat** command displays the contents of a file or files. For example, say you are located in the directory **letters** (in the sample file system) and you want to display the contents of the file **johnson**. Type the command line shown on the screen, and you will receive the following output:

```
$ cat johnson<CR>
March 5, 1986

Mr. Ron Johnson
Layton Printing
52 Hudson Street
New York, N.Y.

Dear Mr. Johnson:

I enjoyed speaking with you this morning
about your company's plans to automate
your business.
Enclosed please find
the material you requested
about AB&C's line of computers
and office automation software.

If I can be of further assistance to you,
please don't hesitate to call.

Yours truly,

John Howe
$
```

To display the contents of two (or more) files, simply type the names of the files you want to see on the command line. For example, to display the contents of the files **johnson** and **sanders**, type

$ **cat johnson sanders**<CR>

The **cat** command reads **johnson** and **sanders** and displays their contents in that order on your terminal.

```
$ cat johnson sanders<CR>
March 5, 1986

Mr. Ron Johnson
Layton Printing
52 Hudson Street
New York, N.Y.

Dear Mr. Johnson:

I enjoyed speaking with you this morning
.

.


Yours truly,

John Howe

March 5, 1986

Mrs. D.L. Sanders
Sanders Research, Inc.
43 Nassau Street
Princeton, N.J.

Dear Mrs. Sanders:

My colleagues and I have been following, with great interest,
.

.


Sincerely,

John Howe
$
```

To direct the output of the **cat** command to another file or to a new command, see the sections in Chapter 7 that discuss input and output redirection.

Figure 3-14 summarizes the syntax and capabilities of the **cat** command.

Command Recap		
cat – concatenates and prints a file's contents		
command	*options*	*arguments*
cat	available*	*filename(s)*

Description:	The **cat** command reads the name of each file specified on the command line and displays its contents.
Remarks:	If a specified file exists and is readable, its contents are displayed on the terminal screen; otherwise, the message `cat: cannot open` *filename* appears on the screen.
	To display the contents of a directory, use the **ls** command.

* See the *cat*(1) page in the *User's/System Administrator's Reference Manual* for all available options and an explanation of their capabilities.

Figure 3-14: Summary of the **cat** Command

Display Contents of a File: the more Command

The **more** command lets you examine the contents of a file or group of files, one screenful at a time. At the end of each screenful, **more** tells you what percentage of the file you have viewed so far and awaits your instruction to continue viewing the file or to quit **more**. In general, **more** has the following form:

> **more** *filename(s)* <**CR**>

For example, suppose you are located in the **letters** directory (in the sample file system). If you wish to display the contents of the file **johnson**, type the command line shown on the screen and you will receive the following output:

```
$ more johnson<CR>
March 5, 1986

Mr. Ron Johnson
Layton Printing
52 Hudson Street
New York, N.Y.


Dear Mr. Johnson:


I enjoyed speaking with you this morning
about your company's plans to automate
your business.
Enclosed please find
the material you requested
about AB&C's line of computers
and office automation software.


If I can be of further assistance to you,
please don't hesitate to call.


Yours truly,


John Howe
$
```

The first screenful of **johnson** is displayed on your screen. In this example, **johnson** is a small file, so the text fits on one screen. If **johnson** had contained enough text to fill two screens, **more** would have prompted you to continue or quit, by displaying a prompt at the end of the first screenful, as shown in the following example:

```
$ more johnson<CR>
March 5, 1986

Mr. Ron Johnson
Layton Printing
52 Hudson Street
New York, N.Y.

Dear Mr. Johnson:

I enjoyed speaking with you this morning
about your company's plans to automate
your business.
Enclosed please find
the material you requested
about AB&C's line of computers
and office automation software.

If I can be of further assistance to you,
please don't hesitate to call.

Yours truly,

John Howe

--More--(50%)
```

At this **more** prompt, you could choose either to view the remainder of **johnson** or to quit **more**. To view the next screenful of the file, press the SPACEBAR key. To view the file one line at a time, press <CR>. To quit **more** and return to the system prompt, type **q**.

Figure 3-15 summarizes the syntax and capabilities of the **more** command.

<table>
<tr><td colspan="3" align="center">**Command Recap**</td></tr>
<tr><td colspan="3" align="center">**more** – prints a file's contents, one screenful at a time</td></tr>
<tr><td align="center">*command*</td><td align="center">*options*</td><td align="center">*arguments*</td></tr>
<tr><td align="center">**more**</td><td align="center">available*</td><td align="center">*filename(s)*</td></tr>
<tr><td>**Description:**</td><td colspan="2">The *more* command reads the name of each file specified on the command line and displays its contents, one screenful at a time.</td></tr>
<tr><td>**Remarks:**</td><td colspan="2">If a specified file exists and is readable, its contents are displayed on the terminal screen. If the file exists, but you do not have read permission for it, the message more: Permission denied appears on the screen. If the file does not exist, the message more: no such file or directory appears on the screen.

To display the contents of a directory, use the **ls** or **lc** command.</td></tr>
</table>

---

*   See the *more*(1) page in the *User's/System Administrator's Reference Manual* for all available options and an explanation of their capabilities.

Figure 3-15: Summary of the **more** Command

Paging Through the Contents of a File: the pg Command

The **pg** command (short for page) allows you to examine the contents of a file or files, page by page, on a terminal. The **pg** command displays the text of a file in pages (chunks) followed by a colon prompt (:), a signal that the program is waiting for your instructions. Possible instructions you can then issue include requests for the command to continue displaying the file's contents a page at a time or a request that the command search through the file(s) to locate a specific character pattern. Figure 3-16 summarizes some of the available instructions.

Command*	Function
h	help; displays list of available **pg**† commands
q or Q	quits **pg** mode
<CR>	displays next page of text
l	displays next line of text
d or ^d	displays additional half page of text
. or ^l	redisplays current page of text
f	skips next page of text and displays following one
n	begins displaying next file you specified on command line
p	displays previous file specified on command line
$	displays last page of text in file currently displayed
/pattern	searches forward in file for specified character pattern
?pattern	searches backward in file for specified character pattern

* Most commands can be typed with a number preceding them. For example, +1 (display next page), −1 (display previous page), or 1 (display first page of text).

† See the *User's/System Administrator's Reference Manual* for a detailed explanation of all available **pg** commands.

Figure 3-16: Summary of Commands to Use with **pg**

Like **more**, the **pg** command is useful when you want to read a long file or a series of files because the program pauses after displaying each page, allowing you time to examine it. The size of the page displayed depends on the terminal. For example, on a terminal capable of displaying twenty-four lines, one page is defined as twenty-three lines of text and a line containing a colon. However, if a file is less than twenty-three lines long, its page size will be the number of lines in the file plus one (for the colon).

To look at the contents of a file with **pg**, use the following command line format:

> **pg** *filename(s)*<**CR**>

For example, to display the contents of the file **outline** in the sample file system, type

> **pg outline**<**CR**>

The first page of the file will appear on the screen. Because the file has more lines in it than can be displayed on one page, a colon appears at the bottom of the screen. This is a reminder to you that there is more of the file to be seen. When you are ready to read more, press the <RETURN> key, and **pg** will print the next page of the file.

The following screen summarizes our discussion of the **pg** command this far:

```
$ pg outline<CR>
After you analyze the subject for your
report, you must consider organizing and
arranging the material you want to use in
writing it.

        .

        .

        .

An outline is an effective method of
organizing the material.  The outline
is a type of blueprint or skeleton,
a framework for you the builder-writer
of the report; in a sense it is a recipe
:<CR>
```

After you press the <RETURN> key, **pg** will resume printing the file's contents on the screen:

```
that contains the names of the
ingredients and the order in which
to use them.
            .

            .

            .

Your outline need not be elaborate or
overly detailed; it is simply a guide you
may consult as you write, to be varied,
if need be, when additional important
ideas are suggested in the actual writing.
(EOF):
```

Notice the line at the bottom of the screen containing the string (EOF):. This expression (EOF) means you have reached the end of the file. The colon prompt is a cue for you to issue another command.

When you have finished examining the file, press the <RETURN> key; a prompt will appear on your terminal. (Typing **q** or **Q** and pressing the <RETURN> key also gives you a prompt.) Or you can use one of the other available commands, depending on your needs. In addition, there are a number of options that can be specified on the **pg** command line (see the *pg*(1) page in the *User's/System Administrator's Reference Manual*).

Proper execution of the **pg** command depends on specifying the type of terminal you are using because the **pg** program was designed to be flexible enough to run on many different terminals; how it is executed differs from terminal to terminal. By specifying one type, you are telling this command

- how many lines to print
- how many columns to print

■ how to clear the screen

■ how to highlight prompt signs or other words

■ how to erase the current line

To specify a terminal type, assign the code for your terminal to the TERM variable in your **.profile** file. (For more information about TERM and **.profile**, see Chapter 7; for instructions on setting the TERM variable, see Appendix F.)

Figure 3-17 summarizes the syntax and capabilities of the **pg** command.

Command Recap

pg – displays a file's contents in chunks or pages

command	*options*	*arguments*
pg	available*	*filename(s)*

Description:	The **pg** command displays the contents of the specified file(s) in pages.
Remarks:	After displaying a page of text, the **pg** command awaits instructions from you to do one of the following: continue to display text, search for a pattern of characters, or exit the **pg** mode. In addition, a number of options are available. For example, you can display a section of a file, beginning at a specific line or at a line containing a certain sequence or pattern. You can also opt to go back and review text that has already been displayed.

---

* See the *pg*(1) page in the *User's/System Administrator's Reference Manual* for all available options and an explanation of their capabilities.

Figure 3-17: Summary of the **pg** Command

Making a Duplicate Copy of a File: the cp Command

When using the UNIX System, you may want to make a copy of a file. For example, you might want to revise a file while leaving the original version intact. The **cp** command (short for copy) copies the complete contents of one file into another. The **cp** command also allows you to copy one or more files from one directory into another while leaving the original file or files in place.

To copy the file named **outline** to a file named **new.outline** in the sample directory, simply type **cp outline new.outline** and press the <RETURN> key. The system returns the prompt when the copy is made. To verify the existence of the new file, you can type **ls** and press the <RETURN> key. This command lists the names of all files and directories in the current directory, in this case **draft**. The following screen summarizes these activities:

```
$ cp outline new.outline<CR>
$ ls<CR>
new.outline
outline
table
$
```

The UNIX System does not allow you to have two files with the same name in a directory. In this case, because there was no file called **new.outline** when the **cp** command was issued, the system created a new file with that name. However, if a file called **new.outline** had already existed, it would have been replaced by a copy of the file **outline**; the previous version of **new.outline** would have been deleted.

If you had tried to copy the file **outline** to another file named **outline** in the same directory, the system would have told you the file names were identical and returned the prompt to you. If you had then listed the contents of the directory to determine exactly how many copies of **outline** existed, you would have received the following output on your screen:

```
$ cp outline outline<CR>
cp: outline and outline are identical
$ ls<CR>
outline
table
$
```

The UNIX System does allow you to have two files with the same name as long as they are in different directories. For example, the system would let you copy the file **outline** from the **draft** directory to another file named **outline** in the **letters** directory. If you were in the **draft** directory, you could use any one of four command lines. In the following two command lines, you specify the name of the new file you are creating by making a copy:

■ cp outline /user1/starship/letters/outline<CR> (full path name specified)

■ cp outline ../letters/outline<CR> (relative path name specified)

However, the **cp** command does not require that you specify the name of the new file. If you do not include a name for it on the command line, **cp** gives your new file the same name as the original one, by default. Therefore, you could also use either of these command lines:

■ cp outline /user1/starship/letters<CR> (full path name specified)

■ cp outline ../letters<CR> (relative path name specified)

In any of these four cases, **cp** will make a copy of the **outline** file in the **letters** directory and call it **outline**, too.

Of course, if you want to give your new file a different name, you must specify it. For example, to copy the file **outline** in the **draft** directory to a file named **outline.vers2** in the **letters** directory, you can use either of the following command lines:

- **cp outline /user1/starship/letters/outline.vers2**<CR> (full path name)

- **cp outline ../letters/outline.vers2**<CR> (relative path name)

When assigning new names, keep in mind the conventions for naming directories and files described in "Naming Directories and Files" in this chapter.

Figure 3-18 summarizes the syntax and capabilities of the **cp** command.

Command Recap		
cp – makes a copy of a file		
command	*options*	*arguments*
cp	none	*file1 file2* *file(s) directory*
Description:		**cp** allows you to make a copy of *file1* and call it *file2* leaving *file1* intact or to copy one or more files into a different directory.
Remarks:		When you are copying *file1* to *file2* and a file called *file2* already exists, the **cp** command overwrites the first version of *file2* with a copy of *file1* and calls it *file2*. The first version of *file2* is deleted.
		You cannot copy directories with the **cp** command.

Figure 3-18: Summary of the **cp** Command

Copying a Group of Files: the copy **Command**

The **copy** command lets you copy groups of files to another directory, while leaving the original (source) files intact. To copy a group of files from your current directory to another directory, follow this format:

    copy *source destination* <CR>

You can use full or relative path names for the *source* and *destination* arguments. The *source* argument can consist of a single file name, or a combination of file names and directory names. If *source* is a single file name, **copy** behaves like **cp**. If files or subdirectories do not exist at the destination, **copy** creates them with the same modes as the source.

The **copy** command lets you easily reorganize your directories without having to copy individual files from one directory to another. For example, suppose you are in the **/user1/starship** directory. This directory contains the subdirectories **draft** and **letters**. You can use the **copy** command to copy the contents of **draft** into **letters**. The following sample screen shows your input and the system's output:

```
$ copy draft letters<CR>
$ lc letters<CR>
johnson new.outline outline
sanders table
$
```

The files in the **/user1/starship/draft** directory (**new.outline**, **outline**, and **table**) have been copied into **/user1/starship/letters**. Note that there is no "draft" subdirectory under **letters**. The **copy** command duplicated the contents of **draft** into **letters**, without copying the actual "draft" directory name.

If you want these files to be in a subdirectory called **draft** under the **/user1/starship/letters** directory, add "draft" to the destination path, as shown in the following example:

```
$ copy draft letters/draft<CR>
$ lc letters<CR>
draft johnson sanders
```

The new **draft** subdirectory appears among the contents of **letters**. Now, if you list the contents of **letters**, you will see a new subdirectory called **draft** that has the same contents as **/user1/starship/draft**:

```
$ lc letters/draft<CR>
new.outline outline table
$
```

Frequently Used copy **Options**

The **copy** command accepts several options that let you copy files and directories in many ways. This section describes four frequently used **copy** options. You can use these options together or separately to customize a specific **copy** session.

Copying Files and Directories Interactively

By default, the **copy** program copies the specified source files quickly to their destination, returning you to the system prompt when it has finished duplicating the files. However, suppose you wish to copy most (but not all) of the files in *source* to another directory. In this case, you would like to see the name of each source file before it is copied, so that you can decide whether to copy it to *destination*. To copy files in this interactive manner, use the **-a** option. With the **-a** option, you can reply **y** (yes) or **n** (no) each time **copy** asks you whether it should copy a specific file.

For example, suppose you are working in the **/user1/starship** directory and wish to copy the contents of the **letters** subdirectory, except for the file **sanders**, to the **draft** subdirectory. To do this, type the **copy** command as it appears in the following example:

```
$ copy -a letters draft <CR>
copy file sanders? n <CR>
copy file johnson? y <CR>
$
```

For each file in *source*, **copy** asks you whether you wish to put a copy in *destination*. Only the files you answer **y** to are copied. In this example, **copy** copied **johnson**, but not **sanders**, into the **draft** directory.

Maintaining Original File Settings

When **copy** duplicates a file, it sets the owner and group IDs of the copy in *destination* to that of the user who invoked **copy**. The owner and group of files in *source* remain intact. If you want a copied file to have the same owner and group IDs as its source file, use the **-o** option. This option is helpful when you are reorganizing your directories and wish to maintain original file statistics.

Similarly, **copy** automatically sets the modification time of each file it copies to the time of the copy. If you want the copied files to have the same modification time as their corresponding source files, use the **-m** option. Like the **-o** option, **-m** is convenient when you wish to reorganize your directories, while maintaining previous modification times.

Copying Directories Recursively

By default, **copy** duplicates only files (not subdirectories) even when *source* contains subdirectories. If you want **copy** to duplicate subdirectories and their contents, as well as just files, you must specify a *recursive* copy process. A recursive copy process duplicates all files and subdirectories in *source* to *destination*, creating subdirectories at the destination as they are needed, and maintaining the same directory hierarchy as in *source*. To recursively copy the contents of *source* to *destination*, use the **-r** option with the following syntax:

copy -r *source destination* **<CR>**

Figure 3-19 summarizes the syntax and capabilities of the **copy** command.

Command Recap		
copy – copies groups of files		
command	*options*	*arguments*
copy	**-a, -r,** and others*	*source, destination*
Description:	**copy** copies the files and/or subdirectories specified in *source* to *destination*. If no *source* argument is given, the contents of your working directory are copied to *destination*.	
Options:	**-a** Asks the user before attempting a copy. **-r** Examines every subdirectory it encounters in *source*, copying each subdirectory and its contents to *destination*. By default, **copy** duplicates only the files in *source*.	
Remarks:	If you want to list the contents of a directory, use the **ls** or **lc** command.	

*   See the *copy*(1) page in the *User's/System Administrator's Reference Manual* for all available options and an explanation of their capabilities.

Figure 3-19: Summary of the **copy** Command

Moving and Renaming a File: the mv **Command**

The **mv** command (short for move) allows you to rename a file in the same directory or to move a file from one directory to another. If you move a file to a different directory, the file can be renamed or it can retain its original name.

To rename a file within a directory, follow this format:

mv *file1 file2*<**CR**>

The **mv** command changes a file's name from *file1* to *file2* and deletes *file1*. Remember that the names *file1* and *file2* can be any valid names, including path names.

For example, if you are in the directory **draft** in the sample file system and you would like to rename the file **table** to **new.table**, simply type **mv table new.table** and press the <RETURN> key. If the command executes successfully, you will receive a prompt. To verify that the file **new.table** exists, you can list the contents of the directory by typing **ls** and pressing the <RETURN> key. The screen shows your input and the system's output as follows:

```
$ mv table new.table<CR>
$ ls<CR>
new.table
outline
$
```

You can also move a file from one directory to another, keeping the same name or changing it to a different one. To move the file without changing its name, use the following command line:

mv *file(s) directory*<**CR**>

The file and directory names can be any valid names, including path names.

For example, say you want to move the file **table** from the current directory named **draft** (whose full path name is **/user1/starship/draft**) to a file with the same name in the directory **letters** (whose relative path name from **draft** is **../letters** and whose full path name is **/user1/starship/letters**), you can use any one of several command lines, including the following:

mv table /user1/starship/letters<CR>

mv table /user1/starship/letters/table<CR>

mv table ../letters<CR>

mv table ../letters/table<CR>

mv /user1/starship/draft/table /user1/starship/letters/table<CR>

Now suppose you want to rename the file **table** as **table2** when moving it to the directory **letters**. Use any of these command lines:

mv table /user1/starship/letters/table2<CR>

mv table ../letters/table2<CR>

mv /user1/starship/draft/table2 /user1/starship/letters/table2<CR>

You can verify that the command worked by using the **ls** command to list the contents of the directory.

Figure 3-20 summarizes the syntax and capabilities of the **mv** command.

Command Recap		
mv – moves or renames files		
command	*options*	*arguments*
mv	none	*file1 file2* *file(s) directory*

Description: **mv** allows you to change the name of a file or to move a file(s) into another directory.

Remarks: When you are moving *file1* to *file2*, if a file called *file2* already exists, the **mv** command overwrites the first version of *file2* with *file1* and renames it *file2*. The first version of *file2* is deleted.

Figure 3-20: Summary of the **mv** Command

Removing a File: the rm Command

When you no longer need a file, you can remove it from your directory by executing the **rm** command (short for remove). The basic format for this command is

     rm *file(s)*<**CR**>

You can remove more than one file at a time by specifying those files you want to delete on the command line with a space separating each filename:

     rm *file1 file2 file3*<**CR**>

The system does not save a copy of a file it removes; once you have executed this command, your file is removed permanently.

After you have issued the **rm** command, you can verify its successful execution by running the **ls** command. Because **ls** lists the files in your directory, you'll immediately be able to see whether or not **rm** has executed successfully.

For example, suppose you have a directory that contains two files, **outline** and **table**. You can remove both files by issuing the **rm** command once. If **rm** is executed successfully, your directory will be empty. Verify this by running the **ls** command:

```
$ rm outline table <CR>
$ ls
$
```

The prompt shows that **outline** and **table** were removed.

Figure 3-21 summarizes the syntax and capabilities of the **rm** command.

Command Recap		
rm – removes a file		
command	*options*	*arguments*
rm	available*	*file(s)*
Description:	rm allows you to remove one or more files.	
Remarks:	Files specified as arguments to the **rm** command are removed permanently.	

* See the *rm*(1) page in the *User's/System Administrator's Reference Manual* for all available options and an explanation of their capabilities.

Figure 3-21: Summary of the **rm** Command

Counting Lines, Words, and Characters in a File: the wc Command

The **wc** command (short for word count) reports the number of lines, words, and characters there are in the file(s) named on the command line. If you name more than one file, the **wc** program counts the number of lines, words, and characters in each specified file and then totals the counts. In addition, you can direct the **wc** program to give you only a line, a word, or a character count by using the –**l**, –**w**, or –**c** options, respectively.

To determine the number of lines, words, and characters in a file, use the following format on the command line:

   wc file1<CR>

The system responds with a line in the following format:

   l   w   c   file1

where

■ *l* represents the number of lines in *file1*.

■ *w* represents the number of words in *file1*.

■ *c* represents the number of characters in *file1*.

For example, to count the lines, words, and characters in the file **johnson** (located in the current directory, **letters**), type the following command line:

   $ wc johnson<CR>
   24   66   406 johnson
   $

The system response means that the file **johnson** has 24 lines, 66 words, and 406 characters.

To count the lines, words, and characters in more than one file, use the following format:

   wc *file1 file2*<**CR**>

The system responds in the following format:

l	*w*	*c*	*file1*
l	*w*	*c*	*file2*
l	*w*	*c*	total

Line, word, and character counts for *file1* and *file2* are displayed on separate lines and the combined counts appear on the last line beside the word total.

For example, ask the **wc** program to count the lines, words, and characters in the files **johnson** and **sanders** in the current directory.

```
$ wc johnson sanders<CR>
    24      66     406 johnson
    28      92     559 sanders
    52     158     965 total
$
```

The first line reports that the **johnson** file has 24 lines, 66 words, and 406 characters. The second line reports 28 lines, 92 words, and 559 characters in the **sanders** file. The last line shows that these two files together have a total of 52 lines, 158 words, and 965 characters.

To get only a line, a word, or a character count, select the appropriate command line format from the following lines:

wc **-l** *file1*<**CR**> (line count)

   wc **-w** *file1*<**CR**> (word count)

   wc **-c** *file1*<**CR**> (character count)

For example, if you use the **-l** option, the system reports only the number of lines in **sanders**:

```
$ wc -l sanders<CR>
    28 sanders
$
```

If the **–w** or **–c** option had been specified instead, the command would have reported the number of words or characters, respectively, in the file.

Figure 3-22 summarizes the syntax and capabilities of the **wc** command.

Command Recap
wc – counts lines, words, and characters in a file

command	options	arguments
wc	**–l, –w, –c**	*file(s)*

Description:	**wc** counts lines, words, and characters in the specified file(s), keeping a total count of all tallies when more than one file is specified.
Options	**–l** counts the number of lines in the specified file(s)
	–w counts the number of words in the specified file(s)
	–c counts the number of characters in the specified file(s)
Remarks:	When a file name is specified in the command line, it is printed with the count(s) requested.

Figure 3-22: Summary of the **wc** Command

Protecting Your Files: the chmod **Command**

The **chmod** command (short for change mode) allows you to decide who can read, write, and use your files and who cannot. Because the UNIX Operating System is a multi-user system, you usually do not work alone in the file system. System users can follow path names to various directories and read and use files belonging to one another, as long as they have permission to do so.

If you own a file, you can decide who has the right to read it, write in it (make changes to it), or, if it is a program, execute it. You can also restrict permissions for directories with the **chmod** command. When you grant execute permission for a directory, you allow the specified users to **cd** to it and list its contents with the **ls** command.

To assign these permissions, use the following three symbols:

r   allows system users to read a file or to copy its contents

w   allows system users to write changes into a file (or a copy of it)

x   allows system users to run an executable file

To specify the users to whom you are granting (or denying) these permissions, use the following three symbols:

u   you, the owner of your files and directories (**u** is short for user)

g   members of the group to which you belong (the group could consist of team members working on a project, members of a department, or a group arbitrarily designated by the person who set up your UNIX System account)

o   all other system users

When you create a file or a directory, the system automatically grants or denies permissions to you, members of your group, and other system users. You can alter this automatic action by modifying your environment (see Chapter 7 for details). Moreover, regardless of how the permissions are granted when a file is created, as the owner of the file or directory, you always have the option of changing them. For example, you may want to keep certain files private and reserve them for your exclusive use. You may want to grant permissions to read and write changes into a file to members of your group and all other system users as well. Or you may share a program with members of your group by granting them permission to execute it.

How to Determine Existing Permissions

You can determine what permissions are currently in effect on a file or a directory by using the command that produces a long listing of a directory's contents: **ls -l**. For example, typing **ls -l** and pressing the <RETURN> key while in the directory named **starship/bin** in the sample file system produces the following output:

```
$ ls -l<CR>
total 35
-rwxr-xr-x   1 starship      project         9346  Nov 1  08:06  display
-rw-r--r--   1 starship      project         6428  Dec 2  10:24  list
drwx--x--x   2 starship      project           32  Nov 8  15:32  tools
$
```

Permissions for the **display** and **list** files and the **tools** directory are shown on the left of the screen under the line total 35, and appear in this format:

       -rwxr-xr-x   (for the **display** file)
       -rw-r--r--   (for the **list** file))
       drwx--x---   (for the **tools** directory)

After the initial character, which describes the file type (for example, a - (dash) symbolizes a regular file and a d, a directory), the other nine characters that set the permissions comprise three sets of three characters. The first set refers to permissions for the owner, the second set, to permissions for group members, and the last set, to permissions for all other system users. Within each set of characters, the r, w, and x show the permissions currently granted to each category. If a dash appears instead of an r, w, or x, permission to read, write, or execute is denied.

The following diagram summarizes this breakdown for the file named **display**:

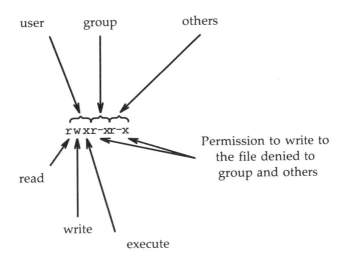

As you can see, the owner has r, w, and x permissions, and members of the group and other system users have r and x permissions.

There are two exceptions to this notation system. Occasionally, the letter s or the letter 1 may appear in the permissions line, instead of an r, w or x. The letter s (short for set user ID or set group ID) represents a special type of permission to execute a file. It appears where you normally see an x (or −) for the user or group (the first and second sets of permissions). From a user's point of view, it is equivalent to an x in the same position; it implies that execute permission exists. It is significant only for programmers and system administrators. (See the *Operations/System Administration Guide* for details about setting the user or group ID.)

The letter 1 is the symbol for lock enabling. It does not mean that the file has been locked. It simply means that the function of locking is enabled, or possible, for this file. The file may or may not be locked; that cannot be determined by the presence or absence of the letter 1.

How to Change Existing Permissions

After you have determined what permissions are in effect, you can change them by executing the **chmod** command in the following format:

> **chmod** *who+permission file(s)*<**CR**>

or

> **chmod** *who=permission file(s)*<**CR**>

The following list defines each component of this command line:

chmod	name of the program
who	one of three user groups (**u, g,** or **o**) **u** = user **g** = group **o** = others
+ or **−**	instruction that grants (+) or denies (−) permission
permission	any combination of three authorizations (**r, w,** and **x**) **r** = read **w** = write **x** = execute
file(s)	file or directory name(s) listed; assumed to be branches from your current directory, unless you use full pathnames

 NOTE The **chmod** command will not work if you type a space(s) between *who*, the instruction that gives (+) or denies (−) permission, and *permission*.

The following examples show a few possible ways to use the **chmod** command. As the owner of **display**, you can read, write, and run this executable file. You can protect the file against being accidentally changed by denying yourself write (**w**) permission. To do this, type the command line

> **chmod u−w display**<**CR**>

After receiving the prompt, type **ls –l** and press the <RETURN> key to verify that this permission has been changed, as shown in the following screen:

```
$ chmod u-w display<CR>
$ ls -l<CR>
total 35
-r-xr-xr-x   1 starship    project    9346 Nov 1  08:06  display
-rw-r--r--   1 starship    project    6428 Dec 2  10:24  list
drwx--x--x   2 starship    project      32 Nov 8  15:32  tools
$
```

As you can see, you no longer have permission to write changes into the file. You will not be able to change this file until you restore write permission for yourself.

Now consider another example. Notice that permission to write into the file **display** has been denied to members of your group and other system users. However, they do have read permission. This means they can copy the file into their own directories and then make changes to it. To prevent all system users from copying this file, you can deny them read permission by typing

chmod go–r display<CR>

The **g** and **o** stand for group members and all other system users, respectively, and the **–r** denies them permission to read or copy the file. Check the results with the **ls –l** command:

```
$ chmod go-r display<CR>
$ ls -l<CR>
total 35
-rwx--x--x   1 starship      project       9346  Nov 1  08:06  display
-rw-r--r--   1 starship      project       6428  Dec 2  10:24  list
drwx--x--x   2 starship      project         32  Nov 8  15:32  tools
$
```

A Note on Permissions and Directories

You can use the **chmod** command to grant or deny permission for directories as well as files. Simply specify a directory name instead of a file name on the command line.

However, consider the impact on various system users of changing permissions for directories. For example, say you grant read permission for a directory to yourself (**u**), members of your group (**g**), and other system users (**o**). Every user who has access to the system will be able to read the names of the files contained in that directory by running the **ls –l** command. Similarly, granting write permission allows the designated users to create new files in the directory and remove existing ones. Granting permission to execute the directory allows designated users to move to that directory (and make it their current directory) by using the **cd** command.

An Alternative Method

There are two methods by which the **chmod** command can be executed. The method described above, in which symbols such as **r**, **w**, and **x** are used to specify permissions, is called the symbolic method.

An alternative method is the octal method. Its format requires you to specify permissions using three octal numbers, ranging from 0 to 7. (The octal number system is different from the decimal system that we typically use on a day-to-day basis.) To learn how to use the octal method, see the *chmod*(1) page in the *User's/System Administrator's Reference Manual*.

Figure 3-23 summarizes the syntax and capabilities of the **chmod** command.

Command Recap		
chmod – changes permission modes for files and directories		
command	*instruction*	*arguments*
chmod	*who + – permission*	*filename(s)* *directoryname(s)*
Description:	**chmod** gives (+) or removes (–) permission to read, write, and execute files for three categories of system users: **user** (you), **group** (members of your group), and **other** (all other users able to access the system on which you are working).	
Remarks:	The instruction set can be represented in either octal or symbolic terms.	

Figure 3-23: Summary of the **chmod** Command

Advanced Commands

Use of the commands already introduced will increase your familiarity with the file system. As this familiarity increases, so might your need for more sophisticated information processing techniques when working with files. This section introduces the following three commands that provide just that:

diff   finds differences between two files

grep   searches for a pattern in a file

sort   sorts and merges files

For additional information about these commands refer to the *User's/System Administrator's Reference Manual.*

Identifying Differences Between Files: the diff Command

The **diff** command locates and reports all differences between two files and tells you how to change the first file so that it is a duplicate of the second. The basic format for the command is

> **diff** *file1* *file2*<**CR**>

If *file1* and *file2* are identical, the system returns a prompt to you. If they are not, the **diff** command instructs you on how to change the first file so it matches the second by using **ed** (line editor) commands. (See Chapter 5 for details about the line editor.) The UNIX System flags lines in *file1* (to be changed) with the < (less than) symbol and lines in *file2* (the model text) with the > (greater than) symbol.

For example, say you execute the **diff** command to identify the differences between the files **johnson** and **mcdonough**. The **mcdonough** file contains the same letter that is in the **johnson** file, with appropriate changes for a different recipient. The **diff** command will identify those changes as follows:

```
3,6c3,6
< Mr. Ron Johnson
< Layton Printing
< 52 Hudson Street
< New York, N.Y.
---
> Mr. J.J. McDonough
> Ubu Press
> 37 Chico Place
> Springfield, N.J.
9c9
< Dear Mr. Johnson:
---
> Dear Mr. McDonough:
```

The first line of output from **diff** is

        3,6c3,6

This means that if you want **johnson** to match **mcdonough**, you must change (c) lines 3 through 6 in **johnson** to lines 3 through 6 in **mcdonough**. The **diff** command then displays both sets of lines.

If you make these changes (using a text editor such as **ed** or **vi**), the **johnson** file will be identical to the **sanders** file. Remember, the **diff** command identifies differences between specified files. If you want to make an identical copy of a file, use the **cp** command.

Figure 3-24 summarizes the syntax and capabilities of the **diff** command.

Command Recap		
diff – finds differences between two files		
command	*options*	*arguments*
diff	available*	*file1 file2*

Description:	The **diff** command reports what lines are different in two files and what you must do to make the first file identical to the second.
Remarks:	Instructions on how to change a file to bring it into agreement with another file are line editor (**ed**) commands: **a** (append), **c** (change), and **d** (delete). Numbers given with **a**, **c**, or **d** show the lines to be modified. Also used are the symbols < (showing a line from the first file) and > (showing a line from the second file).

* See the *diff*(1) page in the *User's/System Administrator's Reference Manual* for all
available options and an explanation of their capabilities.

Figure 3-24: Summary of the **diff** Command

Searching a File for a Pattern: the grep **Command**

You can instruct the UNIX System to search through a file for a specific word, phrase, or group of characters by executing the **grep** command (short for **g**lobally search for a **r**egular **e**xpression and **p**rint). Put simply, a regular expression is any pattern of characters (a word, a phrase, or an equation) that you specify.

The basic format for the command line is

grep *pattern file(s)*<**CR**>

For example, to locate any lines that contain the word automation in the file **johnson**, type

grep automation johnson<**CR**>

The system responds with

```
$ grep automation johnson<CR>
and office automation software.
$
```

The output consists of all the lines in the file **johnson** that contain the pattern for which you were searching (automation).

If the pattern contains multiple words or any character that conveys special meaning to the UNIX System (such as **$, !, *, ?**, and so on), the entire pattern must be enclosed in single quotes. (For an explanation of the special meaning for these and other characters see "Metacharacters" in Chapter 7.) For example, say you want to locate the lines containing the pattern office automation. Your command line and the system's response will read:

```
$ grep 'office automation' johnson<CR>
and office automation software.
$
```

But what if you cannot recall which letter contained a reference to office automation? Was it your letter to Mr. Johnson or the one to Mrs. Sanders? Type the following command line to find out:

```
$ grep 'office automation' johnson sanders<CR>
johnson:and office automation software.
$
```

The output tells you that the pattern office automation is found once in the **johnson** file.

In addition to the **grep** command, the UNIX System provides variations of it called **egrep** and **fgrep**, along with several options that enhance the searching powers of the command. See the *grep*(1), *egrep*(1), and *fgrep*(1) pages in the *User's/System Administrator's Reference Manual* for further information about these commands.

Figure 3-25 summarizes the syntax and capabilities of the **grep** command.

Command Recap		
grep – searches a file for a pattern		
command	*options*	*arguments*
grep	available*	*pattern file(s)*
Description:	The **grep** command searches through specified file(s) for lines containing a pattern and then prints the lines on which it finds the pattern. If you specify more than one file, the name of the file in which the pattern is found is also reported.	
Remarks:	If the pattern you give contains multiple words or special characters, enclose the pattern in single quotes on the command line.	

*   See the *grep*(1) page in the *User's/System Administrator's Reference Manual* for all
       available options and an explanation of their capabilities.

Figure 3-25: Summary of the **grep** Command

───

Sorting and Merging Files: the sort Command

The UNIX System provides an efficient tool called **sort** for sorting and merging files. The format for the command line is

    sort *file(s)*<**CR**>

This command causes lines in the specified files to be sorted and merged in the following order:

■ Lines beginning with numbers are sorted by digit and listed before lines beginning with letters.

■ Lines beginning with uppercase letters are listed before lines beginning with lowercase letters.

■ Lines beginning with symbols, such as *****, **%**, or **@**, are sorted on the basis of the symbol's ASCII representation.

For example, let's say you have two files, **group1** and **group2**, each containing a list of names. You want to sort each list alphabetically and then combine the two lists into one. First, display the contents of the files by executing the **cat** command on each:

```
$ cat group1<CR>
Smith, Allyn
Jones, Barbara
Cook, Karen
Moore, Peter
Wolf, Robert
$ cat group2<CR>
Frank, M. Jay
Nelson, James
West, Donna
Hill, Charles
Morgan, Kristine
$
```

(Instead of printing these two files individually, you could have requested both files on the same command line. If you had typed **cat group1 group2** and pressed the <RETURN> key, the output would have been the same.)

Now sort and merge the contents of the two files by executing the **sort** command. The output of the **sort** program will be printed on the terminal screen unless you specify otherwise.

```
$ sort group1 group2<CR>
Cook, Karen
Frank, M. Jay
Hill, Charles
Jones, Barbara
Moore, Peter
Morgan, Kristine
Nelson, James
Smith, Allyn
West, Donna
Wolf, Robert
$
```

In addition to combining simple lists as in the example, the **sort** command can rearrange lines and parts of lines (called fields) according to a number of other specifications you designate on the command line. The possible specifications are complex and beyond the scope of this text. Refer to the *User's/System Administrator's Reference Manual* for a full description of available options.

Figure 3-26 summarizes the syntax and capabilities of the **sort** command.

Command Recap
sort – sorts and merges files

command	*options*	*arguments*
sort	available*	*file(s)*

Description:	The **sort** command sorts and merges lines from a file or files you specify and displays its output on your terminal screen.
Remarks:	If no options are specified on the command line, lines are sorted and merged in the order defined by the ASCII representations of the characters in the lines.

*   See the *sort*(1) page in the *User's/System Administrator's Reference Manual* for all available options and an explanation of their capabilities.

Figure 3-26: Summary of the **sort** Command

Printing Files

This section introduces the **pr** command, which prepares files to be printed and the **lp** command, which prints files.

Print Partially Formatted Contents of a File: the pr Command

The **pr** command prepares files for printing. It supplies titles and headings, paginates, and prints a file, in any of various page lengths and widths, on your terminal screen.

You have the option of requesting that the command print its output on another device, such as a line printer (read the discussion of the **lp** command in this section). You can also direct the output of **pr** to a different file (see the sections on input and output redirection in Chapter 7).

If you choose not to specify any of the available options, the **pr** command produces output in a single column that contains 66 lines per page and is preceded by a short heading. The heading consists of five lines: two blank lines; a line containing the date, time, file name, and page number; and two more blank lines. The formatted file is followed by five blank lines.

The **pr** command is often used together with the **lp** command to provide a paper copy of text as it was entered into a file. (See the section on the **lp** command for details.) However, you can also use the **pr** command to format and print the contents of a file on your terminal. For example, to review the contents of the file **johnson** in the sample file system, type

    $ pr johnson<CR>

The following screen gives an example of output from this command:

```
$ pr johnson<CR>


Mar  5 15:43 1986 johnson Page 1


March 5, 1986

Mr. Ron Johnson
Layton Printing
52 Hudson Street
New York, N.Y.


Dear Mr. Johnson:

I enjoyed speaking with you this morning
about your company's plans to automate
your business.
Enclosed please find
the material you requested
about AB&C's line of computers
and office automation software.

If I can be of further assistance to you,
please don't hesitate to call.

Yours truly,

John Howe
.
.
$
```

The ellipses after the last line in the file represent the remaining lines (all blank in this case) that **pr** formatted into the output (so that each page contains a total of sixty-six lines). If you are working on a video display terminal, which allows you to view twenty-four lines at a time, the entire sixty-six lines of the formatted file will be printed rapidly without pause. This means that the first forty-two lines will roll off the top of your screen, making it impossible for you to read them unless you have the ability to roll back a screen or two. However, if the file you are examining is particularly long, even this ability may not be sufficient to allow you to read the file.

In such cases, type < ̂s> to interrupt the flow of printing on your screen. When you are ready to continue, type < ̂q> to resume printing.

Figure 3-27 summarizes the syntax and capabilities of the **pr** command.

	Command Recap	
	pr – prints formatted contents of a file	
command	*options*	*arguments*
pr	available*	*filename(s)*

Description: The **pr** command prints a copy of a file(s) on your terminal screen unless you specify otherwise. It prints the text of the file(s) on sixty-six line pages and places five blank lines at the bottom of each page and a five-line heading at the top of each page. The heading includes two blank lines; a line containing the date, time, file name, and page number; and two additional blank lines.

Remarks: If a specified file exists, its contents are formatted and displayed; if not, the message `pr: can't open` *filename* is printed.

The **pr** command is often used with the **lp** command to produce a paper copy of a file. It can also be used to review a file on a video display terminal. To stop and restart the printing of a file on a terminal, type < ^s> and < ^q>, respectively.

* See the *pr*(1) page in the *User's/System Administrator's Reference Manual* for all available options and an explanation of their capabilities.

Figure 3-27: Summary of the **pr** Command

The LP Print Service

You can perform various printing tasks by using a set of UNIX System software tools called the LP print service. You can make requests for print jobs, change or cancel those requests, enable and disable printers, and obtain information about the printers available to you by using five commands associated with the LP print service: **lp**, **cancel**, **lpstat**, **enable**, and **disable**. This section explains how to use these commands to accomplish such tasks.

The function of each print service command is shown in Figure 3-28.

Command	Function
lp	requests a paper copy of a file from a printer
cancel	cancels a request for a paper copy of a file
lpstat	displays information on the screen about the current status of the LP print service
enable	activates the printer(s) specified so jobs that are requested through the **lp** command can be printed
disable	deactivates the printer(s) specified so jobs that are requested through the **lp** command can no longer be printed

Figure 3-28: Print Commands and Their Functions

NOTE

The **enable** and **disable** commands are not always available to users. The system administrator will decide whether to make these commands available to all users.

Requesting a Paper Copy of a File: the lp Command

Some terminals have built-in printers that allow you to get paper copies of files. If you have such a terminal, you can get a paper copy of your file simply by turning on the printer and executing the **cat** or **pr** command.

If you are using a video display terminal, however, you will need a printer to obtain a paper copy of a file. The **lp** command (originally named for "line printer") allows you to request a print job from a printer. To request a simple print job, enter the command line

lp *filename*<**CR**>

where *filename* is the name of the file you want to have printed. For example, to request that the file **johnson** be printed, type

lp johnson<**CR**>

The system will respond with the name (or type) of the printer on which the file is being printed and an identification (ID) number for your request:

```
$ lp johnson<CR>
request id is laser-6885   (1 file)
$
```

This system response shows that your job will be printed on a printer named "laser" (the default printer for this system), has a request ID number of laser-6885, and consists of one file.

Options to lp

The options available with the **lp** command allow you to request the following for your print job: a specific printer or class of printers (referred to here as "print destination"); special print modes (such as landscape or portrait); page size and pitch settings; which pages are to be printed and the number of copies to be made; queue priority; forms (instead of blank paper); character sets and print wheels; content type; continuous printing of files (without breaks between separate files); banner-page options; and messages from the **lp** command. This section explains how to take advantage of these options.

Select a Print Destination

The term "print destination" refers to any device that your system administrator has defined to be a printer (such as "bif2") or class of printers (such as "bif"). The **–d** *dest* (short for destination) option on the command line causes your file to be printed at the destination specified in the *dest* argument, as long as a printer is available and capable of meeting your specifications for the job. In the following example, a request is made to have a file called **memo** printed on printer3:

$ lp –d printer3 memo<CR>

Special Printing Modes

The final appearance of the document you are printing depends not only on its content, but also on certain other features that affect the composition of the page. For example, you might want to print your document on one side of the paper or on both sides. You might want your memo to be marked "draft" or to appear as the final, official version. Or, if you have a chart that will not fit on a page in the usual "portrait" mode, you may want to print it sideways on the page in "landscape" mode. The number of these special printing modes that are available to you depends on the available printer(s).

To request special printing modes for your print job, include the **–y** option on the command line as follows:

$ lp **–y** *list_of_modes filename*<CR>

Each item in the list of modes must be a one-word name; it can be any combination of letters and numbers.

The printer will accept your request if all the modes you requested in the list are known by the "filter" being used as an interface between your print request and the printer. To find out which filters are available on your system and which **–y** options are allowed, check with your system administrator.

Page Size and Pitch Settings

Page size consists of two measurements: length and width. Pitch settings are specifications for the number of lines per inch (vertical measurement) and the number of characters per inch (horizontal measurement). When a file is printed, these dimensions may be determined in one of the following four ways:

■ by the printer's default dimensions

■ by the default dimensions established by your system administrator

■ by the dimensions provided with a particular form which you have selected

■ by your specification for that particular job

To request your own specification for a print job, use the **-o** option to **lp**, and specify the desired sizes in "scaled decimal numbers." The term "scaled decimal number" refers to a non-negative number used to indicate a unit of size. (The type of unit is shown by a "trailing" letter attached to the number.) Three types of scaled decimal numbers are discussed for the LP print service: numbers that show sizes in centimeters (marked with a trailing "c"); numbers that show sizes in inches (marked with a trailing "i"); and numbers that show sizes in units appropriate to use (without a trailing letter), such as lines, columns, lines per inch, or characters per inch. The following command line shows how to request a print job with your own specifications for page size and pitch settings (specifications are shown in *sdn* or scaled decimal numbers):

    $ **lp -o** "**length**=*sdn* **width**=*sdn* **lpi**=*sdn* **cpi**=*sdn*" *filename*<**CR**>

For example, to request pages that are 8-1/2 inches long and 6-1/4 inches wide, type the following command line:

    $ **lp -o length**=*???* **-o width**=*???*<**CR**>

where *???* represents the correct scaled decimal numbers for the printer you are using.

If you do not specify the page dimensions for your print request, are not using a form for which those dimensions are defined, and are not using a printer for which those dimensions have been defined by an administrator, your job will be printed according to the default dimensions for the type of printer you are using. These default dimensions are listed in a database called **Terminfo**; your system administrator is responsible for maintaining this database and can give you details about it.

For example, if you are using an AT&T Model 455 printer, the default dimensions for the printer will be as follows:

Page length: 66 lines
Page width: 132 columns
Line pitch: 6 lines per inch
Character pitch: 12 characters per inch

If, however, you are using an AT&T Model 470 printer, the default dimensions will be slightly different:

Page length: 66 lines
Page width: 80 columns
Line pitch: 6 lines per inch
Character pitch: 10 characters per inch

Pages and Copies to be Printed

Some filters allow you to specify a list of pages to be printed so that you need not print an entire file to obtain a subset of it. Perhaps you want to proofread a section you have edited, give an excerpt of a file to someone, or print the portion of a file that remains unprinted after a print job has been interrupted. With the proper filter, you can limit the printing of a file to a subset of pages by using the –P option of the lp command.

For example, suppose you have a thirty-page business report in a file called **july.sales**. Your boss wants to include a copy of the summary and a few of the charts from your report in a package of materials she's putting together for a new director in your division. Because the charts and summary appear on a total of five pages, you don't want to print a copy of the entire thirty-page report. Fortunately, your printer has a filter that allows you to specify a list of pages to be printed. You request only pages 4-6 (for the charts) and 28-29 (for the summary):

$ **lp –P 4-6,28,29 july.sales**<CR>

If you do not have any filters or if your filters do not accept a list of pages to print, any requests you make with the –P option will be rejected and you will be notified of the failure.

NOTE Your system administrator installs and maintains filters for your system. Check with your administrator to find out if filters are available and whether they will accept the **–P** option and lists of pages to be printed.

By specifying a list of pages with **–P**, you can request that printing be started in the middle of a file and that certain pages be skipped. You can present your list of pages in any order; the pages will be printed in order of ascending page number. Also, the LP print system will drop any duplicate requests for pages so that only one copy of each page will be printed.

If you do not include the **–P** option on the command line, the entire file will be printed.

If you want to have more than one copy made, you can request a multiple printing by issuing the **–n** (for "number") option. For example, to have four copies made, enter a command line such as the following:

lp –n 4 *filename*<**CR**>

When you do not use this option, only one copy is made by default.

Queue Priority

As you and other users send requests for print jobs to the printers on your system, your requests are arranged in a queue that determines the order of printing. Highest priority is given to requests that have been assigned level 0 priority; lowest priority is given to requests with a level of 39. Whether your job is assigned high or low priority depends on several factors.

First, the default value for job priority on your system is 20, unless your system administrator has defined it otherwise. Every job you submit to a printer will be given this medium-level priority. If your administrator has redefined the default priority level so that it is now, for example, 10, all jobs that you send to the printer will be given this higher priority.

You can change this priority level, however, by requesting a level other than default; to do so, use the **–q** option of the **lp** command. For example, if you need a memo printed immediately, you can send it to the front of the queue by assigning it the highest priority: 0.

$ **lp –q 0 urgent.memo**

Note that the system administrator can limit the priority level that you can use. If your administrator has limited the priority level available to you and you request a priority higher than that, the priority level will remain, by default, at the level set by the administrator. Check with your system administrator to find out what the default priority level is and whether there is a limit on the priority level you can request.

Pre-Printed Forms

Pre-printed forms, such as payroll checks, are often used by companies that need to issue a variety of specialized documents. To accommodate users who have this need, the LP print service is capable of printing your files on pre-printed forms. It gives you the option of assigning a form to each print request you make.

To request a particular form, include the **–f** option on the command line, followed by the name of the form. In this example, a request is being made to have a file called **april.payroll** printed on a type of form called paycheck on a printer called printer4:

> $ **lp –d printer4 –f paycheck april.payroll**<**CR**>

The LP print service will assume that you want your job to be printed on the form specified by the printer listed. If the printer you have listed is not capable of handling this form, it will be rejected. To allow your request to print on any printer on which the form is mounted, include the **–d** option, followed by the argument **any**. Your command line would be entered as follows:

> $ **lp –d any –f** *form_name filename*<**CR**>

The LP print service will then send your request to any printer that is capable of printing the type of form required for your job.

Character Sets and Print Wheels

The **lp** command allows you to select a character set or print wheel with which your job will be printed. To do so, include the **–S** option on the command line as follows:

> $ **lp –S** *character_set filename*<**CR**>

If you have no preference and if you haven't chosen a form that defines a particular character set or print-wheel, you can skip this option.

Content Type

To print a file, a printer must be capable of correctly interpreting its contents. Different printers have different capabilities in this sense; not every printer is able to print every type of content. You can make sure that the LP print service assigns your request to a printer capable of printing it by using the **−T** option of the **lp** command.

The **−T** option allows you to specify the type of printer that can interpret the content of your file. For example, suppose you want to print a file containing your monthly report for July (**july.report**) and you know that the AT&T Model 455 printer can interpret its contents. You also know that there is more than one 455 printer in your system, but you don't know the names of any of them. The **−T** option lets you request any Model 455 printer without specifying one by name as follows:

> $ **lp −T 455 july.report**<CR>

Your file will be forwarded to the first available Model 455 for printing.

What happens if there are no Model 455 printers? The answer depends on whether or not your system supports any filters. A filter is a program that converts data from one format to another; in this case, the filter converts data from the format in which it was typed in the file to a format which can be "read" by a printer. If there are no printers that can handle the content type of your file and your system supports filters, your print request will be sent to a filter. The contents of the file will be converted, by the filter, to a content type that the printer can handle. If, however, there are no printers that can handle the content type of your file and there is no filter that will convert the file, your print request will be rejected.

Filters make it possible to have files printed by a variety of printers. There may be situations, however, in which the content type is a critical factor of the job. In such a case, you do not want to have a file printed unless it can be printed with the original content type. If your system supports filters and you do not want your print request to be sent to one, specify the **−r** option after the **−T** option of the **lp** command as follows:

> $ **lp −T 455 −r july.report**<CR>

Note that with the **-r** option, if your print request cannot be handled by any printer on your system (because of content type), your print request will be rejected.

 Filters are installed and maintained on your LP print service by your system administrator. Ask your administrator for a list of content types available to your system.

No File Breaks between Files

Your print request may consist of more than one file. By default, the LP print service will assume that you want each file to be printed separately. If you want the set of files to be printed continuously, without having each file begin on a new page, specify the **-o** option with **nofilebreak** as follows:

$ **lp -o nofilebreak** *filenames*<**CR**>

Banner-Page Options

The LP print service automatically prints a title page (known here as a "banner" page) with every job printed. If you do not want a banner page printed with your job, include the **-o** option with **nobanner** as follows:

$ **lp -o nobanner** *filename*<**CR**>

Your system administrator can turn off this option for particular printers. If your administrator has done so, any request you make for such a printer will be rejected.

Messages from the Print Service

The LP print service does not automatically notify you when your job has been printed. To make sure you will be notified, list the **-w** option on the **lp** command line as follows:

$ **lp -w** *filename*<**CR**>

The print service will display a message on your terminal screen to let you know when your files have been printed. If you are not logged in when the message is ready to be sent, the message will be sent to you via electronic mail instead.

If you want to be notified through electronic mail that your files have been printed, include the **–m** option on your command line as follows:

$ **lp –m** *filename*<**CR**>

Changing a Request

Suppose you have just noticed that when submitting a request to the print service a little while ago, you forgot to request a longer than usual page length for the job, as you had originally planned to do. Don't worry; it may not be too late to change your print request! As long as the job has not actually been printed, you may submit changes to your original request. Simply execute the **lp** command again, this time including the **–i** option, followed by the ID number assigned to your request. The **–i** option signals your intent to change the previous request to the printer.

For example, suppose your original request was for a page length of 50, a width of 70, no banner, and 3 copies:

$ **lp –o "length=50,width=70,nobanner" –n 3 july.report**<**CR**>
request id is printer2-23

When you later remembered to request a longer page, you reissued the command as follows:

$ **lp –i printer2-23 –o "length=60,width=70,nobanner"**<**CR**>

Notice that although there were two options in the original command line (**–o** and **–n**), only one of them (**–o**) is included in the change request. A change request should specify only those options from the original command line for which you want new values.

However, as this example also demonstrates, when changing the values in a **–o** option, you must not only request additional arguments or request different arguments in place of existing ones, but you must also repeat those arguments that you want to preserve. (This requirement also applies to the **–y** option.) Look again at the command lines in the the preceding example. Notice that three arguments are given for the **–o** option: "length," "width," and "nobanner." Although only one argument to **–o** is being changed (from "length=50" to "length=60"), all three arguments are listed in the change request. Repeating the "width" and "nobanner" arguments is necessary; they are not otherwise preserved from the original command line.

Canceling a Request

To cancel a request to a printer, type the **cancel** command and specify the request ID number. For example, to cancel the printing of the file **letters** (request ID laser-6885), type

$ **cancel laser-6885**<CR>

Note that you can only cancel your own requests.

Getting Printer Status and Information: lpstat

At some time after issuing a request for a print job, you may want to find out whether it is proceeding properly or if problems have arisen. You can check the status of all print requests by executing the **lpstat** command. When issued alone, without any options, this command will tell you the status of all requests you have made to the LP print service.

If you do not want to know about all print requests, you can specify a subset of requests by listing the request ID numbers for those jobs on the command line. (Whenever a print request is issued, a request ID number for it is displayed on the screen.)

$ **lpstat "laser-6885, printer-227"**<CR>

In this example, you are asking for the status of two print requests with the ID numbers "laser-6885" and "printer-227."

In addition, by using various options, you can request the following types of information from **lpstat**:

■ the status of local printers

■ a list of available pre-printed forms

■ a list of available character sets and print wheels

■ a list of available printers

The rest of this section contains instructions for getting these types of information by issuing the options of the **lpstat** command.

What is the Status of the Printers?

First, if you do not already know, you may want to find out the names of the printers in your system. Which printers are available to you depends on your UNIX System facility. Ask your system administrator for the names of available line printers, or type the following command line:

$ **lpstat –p all<CR>**

A list of printers will be displayed, showing which printers are enabled and which are disabled, as follows:

```
printer phil_1 enabled since Aug 22 16:00. available.
printer phil_3 disabled since Aug 26 22:00. available.
```

If you already have the names of the printers on your system, you can get a status report on one or more of them by listing the appropriate names in place of the argument **all** in the preceding example:

$ **lpstat –p phil_1,phil_3<CR>**

More detailed status reports can be obtained by adding the **–l** option to the **lpstat** command line as follows:

$ **lpstat –p phil_1,phil_3 –l<CR>**

For each printer you have specified, a status report will be displayed. Each report will include the following: the printer type, the types of forms mounted on it, acceptable content types, the names of users allowed to use the printer, the default dimensions for page size and character pitch, and so on.

The system administrator may restrict access to certain printers. If you are not allowed access to a printer, the phrase not available will appear.

What Forms are Available?

To find out which pre-printed forms are available on your system, issue the **lpstat** command with the **–f** option and the argument **all** as follows:

$ **lpstat –f all**

The command prints a list of all the forms that your system recognizes and can handle. Forms that are mounted on printers in your system are identified as follows:

```
form payroll_check is available to you, mounted on phil_4
```

Forms that are recognized and can be handled by your system but are not mounted on printers are listed as follows:

    form payroll_check is available to you

The system administrator may restrict access to certain forms. If you are not allowed access to a form, the phrase is not available to you will appear.

If you want to know whether specific forms are available on your system, list them after the **-f** option in place of the argument **all**, as in the following example:

    $ lpstat -f bill_1,bill_2

If you want detailed information about any or all the available forms, use the **-l** option with **lpstat -f** as follows:

    $ lpstat -f all -l

A description of each form, including page length, page width, number of pages, ribbon color, and so on, will be displayed.

Which Character Sets or Print Wheels are Available?

First, you may want to find out which character sets and/or print wheels are available on your LP print system. Issue the **lpstat** command with the **-S** option and the argument **all** as follows:

    $ lpstat -S all<CR>

A list of all character sets and print wheels that can be used on printers in your system will be displayed. If you want to check on whether one or more specific character sets or print wheels are available, list it on the command line in place of the argument **all**:

    $ lpstat -S "charset_1 wheel_3"<CR>

Enabling and Disabling a Printer

NOTE Whether or not you, as a computer user, are able to issue the commands to enable and disable printers depends on your system administrator. Because these functions are administrative, it is left to the discretion of the system administrator to decide whether or not to make the **enable** and **disable** commands available to users.

Before a printer is able to start printing files requested through the **lp** command, it must be activated. You can activate a printer by issuing the **enable** command with one argument: a list of printers.

$ **enable** *printer1 printer2 printer3*<**CR**>

You can verify that you have enabled a printer by requesting a status report for it (see "What is the Status of the Printers?" above).

If you do not want a printer to continue taking print requests, you must deactivate it by issuing the **disable** command.

$ **disable printer1**<**CR**>

The printer will stop printing the current job and save it to complete later.

There are other ways to have your current job handled, however. You may have the current job completed immediately, before the printer is disabled, by using the **−W** option. On the other hand, you may not care whether or not it is completed at all (either immediately or later). If so, specify the **−c** option; any requests that are currently being printed will be cancelled and thrown out as the printer is disabled. The **−W** and **−c** options are mutually exclusive.

Finally, when you disable a printer, it is a good idea to record the reason for your action so that other users may understand why a particular printer is unavailable. To record your reason, add the **−r** option, followed by a reason, to the command line. Be sure to enclose the words that make up your reason in double quotes so that they will be treated as a single argument:

$ **disable −r "disabling for reconfiguration" printer42b**<**CR**>

The reason you provide will be displayed by the **lpstat** command when a user requests a status report on that printer. (If you do not supply a reason, **lpstat** will provide a default reason.)

Summary

Figure 3-29 summarizes the syntax and capabilities of the **lp** command.

Command Recap		
lp requests a paper copy of a file from a printer		
command	*options*	*arguments*
lp	*(as listed)*	*file(s)*
Description:	The **lp** command requests that specified files be printed by a printer, thus providing paper copies of the contents.	
Options:	**–d** *dest*	Allows you to choose *dest* as the printer or class of printers to produce the paper copy. You do not have to use this option if the administrator has set a default destination or if you have set the LPDEST environment variable.
	–y *mode*	Requests special printing modes, such as portrait or landscape. (This option requires a special filter; check with your system administrator to find out whether your system has an appropriate filter.)
	–o *option*	Defines page dimensions: length and width, number of lines per inch, and number of characters per inch (**–o** performs other tasks, too; see *lp*(1) in the *User's/System Administrator's Reference Manual*).

Command Recap		
lp requests a paper copy of a file from a printer		
command	*options*	*arguments*
lp	(*as listed*)	*file(s)*
	–P *pages*	Specifies subset of pages to be printed. (This option requires a special filter; check with your system administrator to find out whether your system has an appropriate filter.)
	–n *copies*	Specifies number of copies to be made.
	–f *form*	Specifies pre-printed form on which files are to be printed.
	–S *char_set*	Specifies character set or print wheel to be used.
	–T *type*	Specifies content type of print request.
	–w	Notifies you by screen message when print job is complete.
	–m	Notifies you by mail when print job is complete. ?**–i** *req_id*?T{ Allows you to change a print request already issued (but not yet printed).
	–q *level*	Allows you to specify a priority level for your job request.
Remarks:	You can cancel a request to the printer by typing **cancel** and the request ID given to you by the system when the request was acknowledged.	
	Check with your system administrator for information on additional and/or different commands for printers that may be available at your location.	

Figure 3-29: Summary of the **lp** Command

4 Overview of the Tutorials

Introduction

This chapter serves as a transition between the overview that comprises the first three chapters and the tutorials in the following four chapters. Specifically, it provides an overview of the subjects covered in these tutorials: text editing, working in both the standard shell and the C-shell, and communicating electronically. Text editing is covered in Chapter 5, "Line Editor Tutorial," and Chapter 6, "Screen Editor Tutorial." How to work and program in the standard shell is taught in Chapter 7, "Shell Tutorial," and Chapter 8, "C-Shell Tutorial," illustrates how to work and program in the C-shell. Finally, methods of electronic communication are covered in Chapter 9, "Communication Tutorial."

Text Editing

Using the file system is a way of life in a UNIX System environment. This section will teach you how to create and modify files with a software tool called a text editor. The section begins by explaining what a text editor is and how it works. Then it introduces two types of text editors supported on the UNIX System: the line editor, **ed**, and the screen editor, **vi** (short for visual editor). A comparison of the two editors is also included. For detailed information about **ed** and **vi**, see Chapters 5 and 6.

What is a Text Editor?

Whenever you revise a letter, memo, or report, you must perform one or more of the following tasks: insert new or additional material, delete unneeded material, transpose material (sometimes called cutting and pasting), and, finally, prepare a clean, corrected copy. Text editors perform these tasks at your direction, making writing and revising text much easier and quicker than if done by hand.

The UNIX System text editors, like the UNIX System shell, are interactive programs; they accept your commands and then perform the requested functions. From the shell's point of view, the editors are executable programs.

A major difference between a text editor and the shell, however, is the set of commands that each recognizes. All the commands introduced up to this point belong to the shell's command set. A text editor has its own distinct set of commands that allow you to create, move, add, and delete text in files, as well as acquire text from other files.

How Does a Text Editor Work?

To understand how a text editor works, you need to understand the environment created when you use an editing program and the modes of operation understood by a text editor.

Text Editing Buffers

When you use a text editor to create a new file or modify an existing one, you first ask the shell to put the editor in control of your computing session. As soon as the editor takes over, it allocates a temporary work space called the editing buffer; any information that you enter while editing a file is stored in this buffer where you can modify it.

Because the buffer is a temporary work space, any text you enter and any changes you make to it are also temporary. The buffer and its contents will exist only as long as you are editing. If you want to save the file, you must tell the text editor to write the contents of the buffer into a file. The file is then stored in the computer's memory. If you do not, the buffer's contents will disappear when you leave the editing program. To prevent this from happening, the text editors send you a reminder to write your file if you attempt to end an editing session without doing so.

 If you have made a critical mistake or are unhappy with the edited version, you can choose to leave the editor without writing the file. By doing so, you leave the original file intact; the edited copy disappears.

Regardless of whether you are creating a new file or updating an existing one, the text in the buffer is organized into lines. A line of text is simply a series of characters that appears horizontally across the screen and is ended when you press the <RETURN> key. Occasionally, files may contain a line of text that is too long to fit on the terminal screen. Some terminals automatically display the continuation of the line on the next row of the screen; others do not.

Modes of Operation

Text editors are capable of understanding two modes of operation: command mode and text input mode. When you begin an editing session, you will be placed automatically in command mode. In this mode you can move around in a file, search for patterns in it, or change existing text. However, you cannot create text while you are in command mode. To do this, you must be in text input mode. While you are in this mode, any characters you type are placed in the buffer as part of your text file. When you have finished entering text and want to run editing commands again, you must return to command mode.

Because a typical editing session involves moving back and forth between these two modes, you may sometimes forget which mode you are working in. You may try to enter text while in command mode or a command while in input mode. This is something even experienced users do from time to time. It will not take long to recognize your mistake and determine the solution after you complete the tutorials in Chapters 5 and 6.

Line Editor

The line editor, accessed by the **ed** command, is a fast, versatile program for preparing text files. It is called a line editor because it manipulates text on a line-by-line basis. This means you must specify, by line number, the line containing the text you want to change. Then **ed** prints the line on the screen where you can modify it.

This text editor provides commands with which you can change lines, print lines, read and write files, and enter text. In addition, you can invoke the line editor from a shell program; something you cannot do with the screen editor. (See Chapter 7 for information on basic shell programming techniques.)

The line editor (**ed**) works well on video display terminals and paper printing terminals. It will also accommodate you if you are using a slow-speed telephone line. (The visual editor, **vi**, can be used only on video display terminals.) Refer to Chapter 5, "Line Editor Tutorial," for instructions on how to use **ed**. Also see Appendix C for a summary of line editor commands.

Screen Editor

The screen editor, accessed by the **vi** command, is a display-oriented, interactive software tool. It allows you to view the file you are editing a page at a time. This editor works most efficiently when used on a video display terminal operating at 1200 or higher baud.

For the most part, you modify a file (by adding, deleting, or changing text) by positioning the cursor at the point on the screen where the modification is to be made and then making the change. The screen editor immediately displays the results of your editing; you can see the change you made in the context of the surrounding text. Because of this feature, the screen editor is considered more sophisticated than the line editor.

Furthermore, the screen editor offers a choice of commands. For example, a number of screen editor commands allow you to move the cursor around a file. Other commands scroll the file up or down on the screen. Still other commands allow you to change existing text or to create new text. In addition to its own set of commands, the screen editor can access line editor commands.

The trade-off for the screen editor's speed, visual appeal, efficiency, and power is the heavy demand it places on the computer's processing time. Every time you make a change, no matter how simple, **vi** must update the screen. Refer to Chapter 6, "Screen Editor Tutorial," for instructions on how to use **vi**. Appendix D contains a summary of screen editor commands, and Figure 4-1 compares the features of the line editor (**ed**) and the screen editor (**vi**).

Feature	Line Editor (ed)	Screen Editor (vi)
Recommended terminal type	Video display or paper-printing.	Video display.
Speed	Accommodates high- and low-speed data transmission lines.	Works best via high-speed data transmission lines (1200+ baud).
Versatility	Can be specified to run from shell scripts as well as used during editing sessions.	Must be used interactively during editing sessions.
Sophistication	Changes text quickly. Uses comparatively small amounts of processing time.	Changes text easily. However, can make heavy demands on computer resources.
Power	Provides a full set of editing commands. Standard UNIX System text editor.	Provides its own editing commands and recognizes line editor commands as well.
Advantages	There are fewer commands you must learn to use **ed**.	**vi** allows you to see the effects of your editing in the context of a page of text, immediately. (When you use the **ed** editor, making changes and viewing the results are separate steps.)

Figure 4-1: Comparison of Line and Screen Editors (**ed** and **vi**)

The Shell

Every time you log in to the UNIX System, you start communicating with the shell and continue to do so until you log off the system. However, while you are using a text editor, your interaction with the shell is suspended; it resumes as soon as you stop using the editor.

The shell is much like other programs, except that instead of performing one job, as **cat** or **ls** does, it is central to your interactions with the UNIX System. The shell's primary function is to act as a command interpreter between you and the computer system. As an interpreter, the shell translates your requests into language the computer understands, calls requested programs into memory, and executes them.

This section introduces methods of using the shell that enhance your ability to use system features. In addition to using it to run a single program, you may also use the shell to

- interpret the name of a file or a directory you enter in an abbreviated way using a type of shell shorthand

- redirect the flow of input and output of the programs you run

- execute multiple programs simultaneously or in a pipeline format

- tailor your computing environment to meet your individual needs

In addition to being the command language interpreter, the shell is a programming language. For detailed information on how to use the shell as a command interpreter and a programming language, refer to Chapter 7.

Customizing Your Computing Environment

This section deals with another control provided by the shell: your environment. When you log in to the UNIX System, the shell automatically sets up a computing environment for you. The default environment set up by the shell includes these variables:

HOME your login directory

LOGNAME your login name

PATH route the shell takes to search for executable files or commands (typically **PATH=:/bin:/usr/bin**)

The **PATH** variable tells the shell where to look for the executable program invoked by a command. Therefore, it is used every time you issue a command. If you have executable programs in more than one directory, you will want all of them to be searched by the shell to make sure every command can be found.

You can use the default environment supplied by your system or you can tailor an environment to meet your needs. If you choose to modify any part of your environment, you can use either of two methods to do so. If you want to change a part of your environment only for the duration of your current computing session, specify your changes in a command line (see Chapter 7 for details). However, if you want to use a different environment (not the default environment) regularly, you can specify your changes in a file that will set up the desired environment for you automatically every time you log in. This file must be called **.profile** and must be located in your home directory.

The **.profile** typically performs some or all of the following tasks: checks for mail; sets data parameters, terminal settings, and tab stops; assigns a character or character string as your login prompt; and assigns the erase and kill functions to keys. You can define as few or as many tasks as you want in your **.profile**. You can also change parts of it at any time. For instructions on modifying a **.profile**, see "Modifying Your Login Environment" in Chapter 7.

Now check to see whether or not you have a **.profile**. If you are not already in your home directory, **cd** to it. Then examine your **.profile** by issuing this command:

   cat .profile

If you have a **.profile**, its contents will appear on your screen. If you do not have a **.profile** you can create one with a text editor, such as **ed** or **vi**. (See "Modifying Your Login Environment" in Chapter 7 for instructions.)

Programming in the Shell

The shell is not only the command language interpreter but also a command level programming language. This means that instead of always using the shell strictly as a liaison between you and the computer, you can also program it to repeat sequences of instructions automatically. To do this, you must create executable files containing lists of commands. These files are called shell procedures or shell scripts. Once you have a shell script for a particular task, you can simply request that the shell read and execute the contents of the script whenever you want to perform that task.

Like other programming languages, the shell provides such features as variables, control structures, subroutines, and parameter passing. These features enable you to create your own tools by linking together system commands.

For example, you can combine three UNIX System programs (the **date**, **who**, and **wc** commands) into a simple shell script called **users** that tells you the current date and time, and how many users are working on your system. If you use the **vi** editor (described in Chapter 6) to create your script, you can follow this procedure. First, create the file **users** with the editor by typing

    vi users\<CR\>

The editor will draw a blank page on your screen and wait for you to enter text.

```
  cursor
  ~
  ~
  ~
  ~
  ~
  ~
  ~
  ~
  ~
  "users" [New file]
```

Enter the three UNIX System commands on one line:

       date; who ¦ wc –l

Then write and quit the file:

       :wq

Make **users** executable by adding execute permission with the **chmod** command:

       chmod ug+x users<CR>

Now try running your new command. The following screen shows the kind of output you will get:

```
$ users<CR>
Sat Mar 1 16:40:12 EST 1986
       4
$
```

The output tells you that four users were logged in on the system when you typed the command at 16:40 on Saturday, March 1, 1986.

For step-by-step instructions on writing shell scripts and information about more sophisticated shell programming techniques, see Chapter 7, "Shell Tutorial."

Communicating Electronically

As a UNIX System user, you can send messages or transmit information stored in files to other users who work on your system or another UNIX System. To do so, you must be logged in on a UNIX System that is capable of communicating with the UNIX System to which you want to send information. The command you use to send information depends on what you are sending. This guide introduces you to these communication programs:

mail   This command allows you to send messages or files to other UNIX System users, using their login names as addresses. It also allows you to receive messages sent by other users. **mail** holds messages and lets the recipients read them at their convenience.

mailx   This command is a sophisticated, more powerful version of **mail**. It offers a number of options for managing the electronic mail you send and receive.

uucp   This command is used to send files from one UNIX System to another. (Its name is an acronym for UNIX to UNIX System copy.) You can use **uucp** to send a file to a directory you specify on a remote computer. When the file has been transferred, the owner of the directory is notified of its arrival by **mail**.

uuto/uupick   These commands are used to send and retrieve files. You can use the **uuto** command to send a file(s) to a public directory; when it is available, the recipient is notified by mail that the file(s) has arrived. The recipient then can use the **uupick** command to copy the file(s) from the public directory to a directory of choice.

uux   This command lets you execute commands on a remote computer. It gathers files from various computers, executes the specified command on these files, and sends the standard output to a file on the specified computer.

Chapter 9 offers tutorials on each of these commands.

Programming in the System

The UNIX System provides a powerful and convenient environment for programming and software development, using the C programming language, FORTRAN-77, BASIC, Pascal, and COBOL. As well, the UNIX System provides some sophisticated tools designed to make software development easier and to provide a systematic approach to programming.

For information on available UNIX System programming languages, see the *Product Overview* or *Documentation Roadmap*.

For information on the general topic of programming in the UNIX System environment, see the *Programmer's Guide*, which provides tutorials on the following five tools:

SCCS Source Code Control System

make a program that maintains programs

lex a program that generates programs for simple lexical tasks

yacc a program that generates parser programs

5   Line Editor Tutorial (ed)

Exercise 7

Introducing the Line Editor

This chapter is a tutorial on the line editor, **ed**. **ed** is versatile and requires little computer time to perform editing tasks. It can be used on any type of terminal. The examples of command lines and system responses in this chapter will apply to your terminal, whether it is a video display terminal or a paper printing terminal. The **ed** commands can be typed in at your terminal or they can be used in a shell program (see Chapter 7, "Shell Tutorial").

ed is a line editor; during editing sessions it is always pointing at a single line in the file called the current line. When you access an existing file, **ed** makes the last line the current line so you can start appending text easily. Unless you specify the number of a different line or range of lines, **ed** will perform each command you issue on the current line. In addition to letting you change, delete, or add text on one or more lines, **ed** allows you to add text from another file to the buffer.

During an editing session with **ed**, you are altering the contents of a file in a temporary buffer, where you work until you have finished creating or correcting your text. When you edit an existing file, a copy of that file is placed in the buffer and your changes are made to this copy. The changes have no effect on the original file until you instruct **ed** to move the contents of the buffer into the file by using the write command.

After you have read through this tutorial and tried the examples and exercises, you will have a good working knowledge of **ed**. The following basics are included:

- entering the line editor **ed**, creating text, writing the text to a file, and quitting **ed**

- addressing particular lines of the file and displaying lines of text

- deleting text

- substituting new text for old text

- using special characters as shortcuts in search and substitute patterns

- moving text around in the file, as well as other useful commands and information

Suggestions for Using this Tutorial

The commands discussed in each section are reviewed at the end of that section. A summary of all **ed** commands introduced in this chapter is found in Appendix C, where they are listed by topic.

At the end of some sections, exercises are given so you can experiment with the commands. The answers to all exercises are at the end of this chapter.

The notational conventions used in this chapter are those used throughout this *Guide*. They are described in the Preface.

Getting Started

The best way to learn **ed** is to log in to the UNIX System and try the examples as you read this tutorial. Do the exercises; do not be afraid to experiment. As you experiment and try out **ed** commands, you will learn a fast and versatile method of text editing.

In this section you will learn the commands used to

■ enter **ed**

■ append text

■ move up or down in the file to display a line of text

■ delete a line of text

■ write the buffer to a file

■ quit **ed**

How to Enter ed

To enter the line editor, type **ed** and a file name:

> **ed** *filename*<**CR**>

Choose a name that reflects the contents of the file. If you are creating a new file, the system responds with a question mark and the file name:

> $ **ed new-file**<**CR**>
> ?new-file

If you edit an existing file, **ed** responds with the number of characters in the file:

> $ **ed old-file**<**CR**>
> 235

How to Create Text

The editor receives two types of input from your terminal: editing commands and text. To avoid confusing them, **ed** recognizes two modes of editing work: command mode and text input mode. When you work in command mode, any characters you type are interpreted as commands. In input mode, any characters you type are interpreted as text to be added to a file.

Whenever you enter **ed**, you are put into command mode. To create text in your file, change to input mode by typing **a** (for append) on a line by itself and pressing the <RETURN> key:

    a<CR>

Now you are in input mode; any characters you type from this point will be added to your file as text. Be sure to type **a** on a line by itself; if you do not, the editor will not execute your command.

After you have finished entering text, type a period on a line by itself. This takes you out of text input mode and returns you to command mode. Now you can give **ed** other commands.

The following example shows how to enter **ed**, create text in a new file called **try-me**, and quit text input mode with a period:

```
$ ed try-me<CR>
? try-me
a<CR>
This is the first line of text.<CR>
This is the second line,<CR>
and this is the third line.<CR>
.<CR>
```

Notice that **ed** does not give a response to the period; it just waits for a new command. If **ed** does not respond to a command, you may have forgotten to type a period after entering text and may still be in text input mode. Type a period and press the <RETURN> key at the beginning of a line to return to command mode. Now you can execute editing commands. For example, if you have added some unwanted characters or lines to your text, you can delete them once you have returned to command mode.

How to Display Text

To display a line of a file, type **p** (for print) on a line by itself. The **p** command prints the current line, that is, the last line on which you worked. Continue with the previous example. You have just typed a period to exit input mode. Now type the **p** command to see the current line:

```
$ ed try-me<CR>
? try-me
a<CR>
This is the first line of text.<CR>
This is the second line,<CR>
and this is the third line.<CR>
.<CR>
p<CR>
and this is the third line.
```

You can print any line of text by specifying its line number (also known as the address of the line). The address of the first line is 1; of the second, 2; and so on. For example, to print the second line in the file **try-me**, type

```
2p<CR>
This is the second line,
```

You can also use line addresses to print a span of lines by specifying the addresses of the first and last lines of the section you want to see, separated by a comma. For example, to print the first three lines of a file, type

1,3p<CR>

You can even print the whole file this way. For example, you can display a twenty-line file by typing **1,20p**. If you do not know the address of the last line in your file, you can substitute a **$**, the **ed** symbol for the address of the last line. (These conventions are discussed in detail in the section "Line Addressing.")

```
1,$p<CR>
This is the first line of text.
This is a second line,
and this is the third line.
```

If you forget to quit text input mode with a period, you will add text that you do not want. Try to make this mistake. Add another line of text to your **try-me** file, and then try the **p** command without quitting text input mode. Then quit text input mode and print the entire file:

```
p<CR>
and this is the third line.
a<CR>
This is the fourth line.<CR>
p<CR>
.<CR>
1,$p<CR>
This is the first line of text.
This is the second line,
and this is the third line.
This is the fourth line.
p
```

What did you get? The next section will explain how to delete the unwanted line.

How to Delete a Line of Text

To delete text, you must be in the command mode of **ed**. Typing **d** deletes the current line. Try this command on the last example to remove the unwanted line containing **p**. Display the current line (**p** command), delete it (**d** command), and display the remaining lines in the file (**p** command). Your screen should look like this:

```
p<CR>
p
d<CR>
1,$p<CR>
This is the first line of text.
This is a second line,
and this is the third line.
This is the fourth line.
```

ed does not send you any messages to confirm that you have deleted text. The only way you can verify that the **d** command has succeeded is by printing the contents of your file with the **p** command. To receive verification of your deletion, you can put the **d** and **p** commands together on one command line. If you repeat the previous example with this command, your screen should look like this:

```
p<CR>
p
dp<CR>
This is the fourth line.
```

How to Move Up or Down in the File

To display the line below the current line, press the <RETURN> key while in command mode. If there is no line below the current line, **ed** responds with a ? and continues to treat the last line of the file as the current line. To display the line above the current line, press the minus key (–).

The following screen provides examples of how both of these commands are used:

```
p<CR>
This is the fourth line.
-<CR>
and this is the third line.
-<CR>
This is a second line,
-<CR>
This is the first line of text.
<CR>
This is a second line,
<CR>
and this is the third line.
```

Notice that by typing **–<CR>** or **<CR>**, you can display a line of text without typing the **p** command. These commands are also line addresses. Whenever you type a line address and do not follow it with a command, **ed** assumes that you want to see the line you have specified. Experiment with these commands: create some text, delete a line, and display your file.

How to Save the Buffer Contents in a File

As we discussed earlier, during an editing session, the system holds your text in a temporary storage area called a buffer. When you have finished editing, you can save your work by writing it from the temporary buffer to a permanent file in the computer's memory. By writing to a file, you are simply putting a copy of the contents of the buffer into the file. The text in the buffer is not disturbed, and you can make further changes to it.

 NOTE
It is a good idea to write the buffer text into your file frequently. If an interrupt occurs (such as an accidental loss of power to your terminal), you may lose the material in the buffer, but you will not lose the copy written to your file.

To write your text to a file, enter the **w** command. You do not need to specify a file name; simply type **w** and press the <RETURN> key. If you have just created new text, **ed** creates a file for it with the name you specified when you entered the editor. If you have edited an existing file, the **w** command writes the contents of the buffer to that file by default.

If you prefer, you can specify a new name for your file as an argument on the **w** command line. Be careful not to use the name of a file that already exists unless you want to replace its contents with the contents of the current buffer. **ed** will not warn you about an existing file; it will simply overwrite that file with your buffer contents.

For example, if you decide you would prefer the **try-me** file to be called **stuff**, you can rename it:

```
$ ed try-me<CR>
? try-me
a<CR>
This is the first line of text.<CR>
This is the second line,<CR>
and this is the third line.<CR>
.
w stuff <CR>
85
```

Notice the last line of the screen. This is the number of characters in your text. When the editor reports the number of characters in this way, the write command has succeeded.

How to Quit the Editor

When you have completed editing your text, write it from the buffer into a file with the **w** command. Then leave the editor and return to the shell by typing **q** (for quit):

```
w<CR>
85
q<CR>
$
```

The system responds with a shell prompt. At this point, the editing buffer vanishes. If you have not executed the write command, your text in the buffer has also vanished. If you did not make any changes to the text during your editing session, no harm is done. However, if you did make changes, you could lose your work in this way. Therefore, if you type **q** after changing the file without writing it, **ed** warns you with a ?. You then have a chance to write and quit:

```
q<CR>
?
w<CR>
85
q<CR>
$
```

If, instead of writing, you insist on typing **q** a second time, **ed** assumes you do not want to write the buffer's contents to your file and returns you to the shell. Your file is left unchanged and the contents of the buffer are wiped out.

You now know the basic commands needed to create and edit a file using **ed**. Figure 5-1 summarizes these commands.

Command	Function
ed *file*	enters **ed** to edit *file*
a	appends text after the current line
.	quits text input mode and returns to **ed** command mode
p	prints text on your terminal
d	deletes text
<CR>	displays the next line in the buffer (literally, carriage return)
+	displays the next line in the buffer
−	displays the previous line in the buffer
w	writes the contents of the buffer to the file
q	quits **ed** and returns to the shell

Figure 5-1: Summary of **ed** Editor Commands

Exercise 1

Answers for all the exercises in this chapter are found at the end of the chapter. However, they are not necessarily the only possible correct answers. Any method that enables you to perform a task specified in an exercise is correct, even if it does not match the answer given.

1-1.   Enter **ed** with a file named **junk**. Create a line of text containing **Hello World**, write it to the file, and quit **ed**.

Now use **ed** to create a file called **stuff**. Create a line of text containing two words, **Goodbye world**, write this text to the file, and quit **ed**.

1-2.   Enter **ed** again with the file named **junk**. What was the editor's response? Was the character count for it the same as the character count reported by the **w** command in Exercise 1-1?

Display the contents of the file. Is that your file **junk**?

How can you return to the shell? Try **q** without writing the file. Why do you think the editor allowed you to quit without writing to the buffer?

1-3.   Enter **ed** with the file **junk**. Add a line:

Wendy's horse came through the window.

Since you did not specify a line address, where do you think the line was added to the buffer? Display the contents of the buffer. Try quitting the buffer without writing to the file. Try writing the buffer to a different file called **stuff**. Notice that **ed** does not warn you that a file called **stuff** already exists. You have erased the contents of **stuff** and replaced them with new text.

General Format of ed Commands

ed commands have a simple and regular format:

[address1[,address2]]command[argument]<**CR**>

The brackets around *address1, address2,* and *argument* show that these are optional. The brackets are not part of the command line.

address1,address2

The addresses give the position of lines in the buffer. *Address1* through *address2* gives you a range of lines that will be affected by the *command.* If *address2* is omitted, the command will affect only the line specified by *address1.*

command The *command* is one character and tells the editor what task to perform.

argument The *arguments* to a *command* are those parts of the text that will be modified, a file name, or another line address.

This format will become clearer to you when you begin to experiment with the **ed** commands.

Line Addressing

A line address is a character or group of characters that identifies a line of text. Before **ed** can execute commands that add, delete, move, or change text, it must know the line address of the affected text. Type the line address before the command:

[address1],[address2]command<**CR**>

Both *address1* and *address2* are optional. Specify *address1* alone to request action on a single line of text; specify both *address1* and *address2* to request a span of lines. If you do not specify any *address*, **ed** assumes that the line address is the current line.

The most common ways to specify a line address in **ed** are

- by entering line numbers (assuming that the lines of the files are consecutively numbered from 1 to *n*, beginning with the first line of the file)

- by entering special symbols for the current line, last line, or a span of lines

- by adding or subtracting lines from the current line

- by searching for a character string or word on the desired line

You can access one line or a span of lines, or make a global search for all lines containing a specified character string. (A character string is a set of successive characters, such as a word.)

Numerical Addresses

ed gives a numerical address to each line in the buffer. The first line of the buffer is 1, the second line is 2, and so on, for each line in the buffer. Any line can be accessed by **ed** with its line address number. To see how line numbers address a line, enter **ed** with the file **try-me** and type a number:

```
$ ed try-me<CR>
110
1<CR>
This is the first line of text.
3<CR>
and this is the third line.
```

Remember that **p** is the default command for a line address specified without a command. Because you gave a line address, **ed** assumes you want that line displayed on your terminal.

Numerical line addresses frequently change in the course of an editing session. Later in this chapter you will create lines, delete lines, or move a line to a different position. This will change the line address numbers of some lines. The number of a specific line is always the current position of that line in the editing buffer. For example, if you add five lines of text between line 5 and 6, line 6 becomes line 11. If you delete line 5, line 6 becomes line 5.

Symbolic Addresses

Symbolic Address of the Current Line

The current line is the line most recently acted on by any **ed** command. If you have just entered **ed** with an existing file, the current line is the last line of the buffer. The symbol for the address of the current line is a period. Therefore, you can display the current line simply by typing a period (.) and pressing the <RETURN> key.

Try this command in the file **try-me**:

```
$ ed try-me<CR>
110
.<CR>
This is the fourth line.
```

The . is the address. Because a command is not specified after the period, **ed** executes the default command **p** and displays the line found at this address.

To get the line number of the current line, type the following command:

.=<CR>

ed responds with the line number. For example, in the **try-me** file, the current line is 4:

```
.<CR>
This is the fourth line.
.=<CR>
4
```

Symbolic Address of the Last Line

The symbolic address for the last line of a file is the $ sign. To verify that the $ sign accesses the last line, access the **try-me** file with **ed** and specify this address on a line by itself. (Keep in mind that when you first access a file, your current line is always the last line of the file.)

```
$ ed try-me<CR>
110
.<CR>
This is the fourth line.
$<CR>
This is the fourth line.
```

Remember that the **$** address within **ed** is not the same as the $ prompt from the shell.

Symbolic Address of the Set of All Lines

When used as an address, a comma (,) refers to all the lines of a file, from the first through the last line. It is an abbreviated form of the string mentioned earlier that represents all lines in a file, **1,$**. Try this shortcut to print the contents of **try-me**:

```
,p<CR>
This is the first line of text.
This is the second line,
and this is the third line.
This is the fourth line.
```

Symbolic Address of the Current Line through the Last Line

The semicolon (;) represents a set of lines, beginning with the current line and ending with the last line of a file. It is equivalent to the symbolic address .,$. Try it with the file **try-me**:

```
2p<CR>
This is the second line,
;p<CR>
This is the second line,
and this is the third line.
This is the fourth line.
```

Relative Addresses: Adding or Subtracting Lines from the Current Line

You may often want to address lines with respect to the current line. You can do this by adding or subtracting a number of lines from the current line with a plus (+) or a minus (−) sign. Addresses derived in this way are called relative addresses. To experiment with relative line addresses, add several more lines to your file **try-me**, as shown in the following screen. Also, write the buffer contents to the file so your additions will be saved:

```
$ ed try-me<CR>
110
.<CR>
This is the fourth line.
a<CR>
five<CR>
six<CR>
seven<CR>
eight<CR>
nine<CR>
ten<CR>
.<CR>
w<CR>
140
```

Now try adding and subtracting line numbers from the current line:

```
4<CR>
This is the fourth line.
+3<CR>
seven
-5<CR>
This is a second line,
```

What happens if you ask for a line address that is greater than the last line, or if you try to subtract a number greater than the current line number?

```
5<CR>
five
-6<CR>
?
.=<CR>
5
+7<CR>
?
```

Notice that the current line remains at line 5 of the buffer. The current line changes only if you give **ed** a correct address. The **?** response means there is an error. "Other Useful Commands and Information," at the end of this chapter, explains how to get a help message that describes the error.

Character String Addresses

You can search forward or backward in the file for a line containing a particular character string. To do so, specify a string preceded by a delimiter.

Delimiters mark the boundaries of character strings; they tell **ed** where a string starts and ends. The most common delimiter is **/** (slash) used in the following format:

> */pattern*

When you specify a pattern preceded by a **/** (slash), **ed** begins at the current line and searches forward (down through subsequent lines in the buffer) for the next line containing the *pattern*. When the search reaches the last line of the buffer, **ed** wraps around to the beginning of the file and continues its search from line 1 to the line where you began the search.

The following rectangle represents the editing buffer. The path of the arrows shows the search initiated by a **/** :

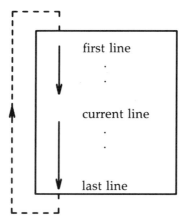

Another useful delimiter is **?**. If you specify a pattern preceded by a **?**, (**?***pattern*), **ed** begins at the current line and searches backward (up through previous lines in the buffer) for the next line containing the *pattern*. If the search reaches the first line of the file, it will wrap around and continue searching upward from the last line of the file to the line where you began the search.

The following rectangle represents the editing buffer. The path of the arrows shows the search initiated by a **?** :

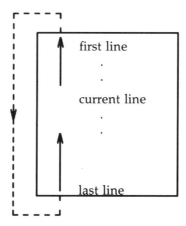

Experiment with these two methods of requesting address searches on the file **try-me**. What happens if **ed** does not find the specified character string?

```
$ ed try-me<CR>
140
.<CR>
ten
?first<CR>
This is the first line of text.
/fourth<CR>
This is the fourth line.
/junk<CR>
?
```

In this example, **ed** found the specified strings **first** and **fourth**. Then, because no command was given with the address, it executed the **p** command by default, displaying the lines it had found. When **ed** cannot find a specified string (such as **junk**), it responds with a ? .

You can also use the **/** (slash) to search for multiple occurrences of a pattern without typing it more than once. First, specify the pattern by typing */pattern*, as usual. After **ed** has printed the first occurrence, it waits for another command. Type **/** and press the <RETURN> key; **ed** will continue to search forward through the file for the last *pattern* specified. Try this command by searching for the word **line** in the file **try-me**:

```
.<CR>
This is the first line of text.
/line<CR>
This is the second line,
/<CR>
and this is the third line.
/<CR>
This is the fourth line.
/<CR>
This is the first line of text.
```

Notice that after **ed** has found all occurrences of the *pattern* between the line where you requested a search and the end of the file, it wraps around to the beginning of the file and continues searching.

Specifying a Range of Lines

There are two ways to request a group of lines. You can specify a range of lines, such as *address1* through *address2*, or you can specify a global search for all lines containing a specified pattern.

The simplest way to specify a range of lines is to use the line numbers of the first and last lines of the range, separated by a comma. Place this address before the command. For example, if you want to display lines 2 through 7 of the editing buffer, give *address1* as 2 and *address2* as 7 in the following format:

2,7p<CR>

Try this on the file **try-me**:

```
2,7p<CR>
This is the second line,
and this is the third line.
This is the fourth line.
five
six
seven
```

Did you try typing **2,7** without the **p**? What happened? If you do not add the **p** command, **ed** prints only *address2*, the last line of the range of addresses.

Relative line addresses can also be used to request a range of lines. Be sure that *address1* precedes *address2* in the buffer. Relative addresses are calculated from the current line, as the following example shows:

```
4<CR>
This is the fourth line
-2,+3p<CR>
This is the second line,
and this is the third line.
This is the fourth line.
five
six
seven
```

Specifying a Global Search

There are two commands that do not follow the general format of **ed** commands: **g** and **v**. These are global search commands that specify addresses with a character string (*pattern*). The **g** command searches for all lines containing the string *pattern* and performs the *command* on those lines. The **v** command searches for all lines that do not contain the *pattern* and performs the *command* on those lines.

The general format for these commands is

g/*pattern*/*command*<**CR**>
v/*pattern*/*command*<**CR**>

Try these commands by using them to search for the word **line** in **try-me**:

```
g/line/p<CR>
This is the first line of text.
This is the second line,
and this is the third line.
This is the fourth line
```

```
v/line/p<CR>
five
six
seven
eight
nine
ten
```

Notice the function of the **v** command: it finds all the lines that do not contain the word specified in the command line (**line**).

Once again, the default command for the lines addressed by **g** or **v** is **p**; you do not need to include a **p** as the last delimiter on your command line.

```
g/line<CR>
This is the first line of text.
This is the second line,
and this is the third line.
This is the fourth line
```

However, if you are giving line addresses to be used by other **ed** commands, you need to include beginning and ending delimiters. You can use any of the methods discussed in this section to specify line addresses for **ed** commands. Figure 5-2 summarizes the symbols and commands available for addressing lines.

Address	Description
n	the number of a line in the buffer
.	the current line (the line most recently acted on by an **ed** command)
.=	the command used to request the line number of the current line
$	the last line of the file
,	the set of lines from line 1 through the last line
;	the set of lines from the current line through the last line
+ *n*	the line that is located *n* lines after the current line
– *n*	the line that is located *n* lines before the current line
/*abc*	the command used to search forward in the buffer for the first line that contains the pattern *abc*
?*abc*	the command used to search backward in the buffer for the first line that contains the pattern *abc*
g/*abc*	the set of all lines that contain the pattern *abc*
v/*abc*	the set of all lines that do not contain the pattern *abc*

Figure 5-2: Summary of Line Addressing

Exercise 2

2-1.   Create a file called **towns** with the following lines:

> My kind of town is
> Chicago
> Like being no where at all in
> Toledo
> I lost those little town blues in
> New York
> I lost my heart in
> San Francisco
> I lost $$ in
> Las Vegas

2-2.   Display line 3.

2-3.   If you specify a range of lines with the relative address −2,+3p, what lines are displayed ?

2-4.   What is the current line number? Display the current line.

2-5.   What does the last line say?

2-6.   What line is displayed by the following request for a search?

> **?town<CR>**

After **ed** responds, type this command alone on a line:

> **?<CR>**

What happened?

2-7.   Search for all lines that contain the pattern "in." Then search for all lines that do not contain the pattern "in."

Displaying Text in a File

ed provides two commands for displaying lines of text in the editing buffer: **p** and **n**.

Displaying Text Alone: the p Command

You have already used the **p** command in several examples. You are probably now familiar with its general format:

[*address1,address2*]**p**<**CR**>

p does not take arguments. However, it can be combined with a substitution command line. This will be discussed later in this chapter.

Experiment with the line addresses shown in Figure 5-3 on a file in your home directory. Try the **p** command with each address and see if **ed** responds as described in the figure.

Specify this Address	Check for this Response
1,$p<CR>	**ed** should display the entire file on your screen.
–5p<CR>	**ed** should move backward five lines from the current line and display the line found there.
+2p<CR>	**ed** should move forward two lines from the current line and display the line found there.
1,/x/p<CR>	**ed** displays the set of lines from line one through the first line after the current line that contains the character x. It is important to enclose the letter x between slashes so that **ed** can distinguish between the search pattern address (x) and the **ed** command (**p**).

Figure 5-3: Sample Addresses for Displaying Text

Displaying Text with Line Addresses: the n Command

The **n** command displays text and precedes each line with its numerical line address. It is helpful when you are deleting, creating, or changing lines. The general command line format for **n** is the same as that for **p**:

[*address1,address2*]n<CR>

Like **p**, **n** does not take arguments, but it can be combined with the substitute command.

Try running **n** on the **try-me** file:

```
$ ed try-me<CR>
140
1,$n<CR>
1        This is the first line of text.
2        This is the second line,
3        and this is the third line.
4        This is the fourth line.
5        five
6        six
7        seven
8        eight
9        nine
10       ten
```

Figure 5-4 summarizes the **ed** commands for displaying text.

Command	Function
p	displays specified lines of text in the editing buffer on your screen
n	displays specified lines of text in the editing buffer with their numerical line addresses on your screen

Figure 5-4: Summary of Commands for Displaying Text

Creating Text

ed has three basic commands for creating new lines of text:

a   append text

i   insert text

c   change text

Appending Text: the a Command

The append command, **a**, allows you to add text AFTER the current line or a specified address in the file. You have already used this command in the "Getting Started" section of this chapter. The general format for the append command line is

[*address1*]**a**<**CR**>

Specifying an address is optional. The default value of *address1* is the current line.

In previous exercises, you used this command with the default address. Now try using different line numbers for *address1*. In the following example, a new file called **new-file** is created. In the first append command line, the default address is the current line. In the second append command line, line 1 is specified as *address1*. The lines are displayed with **n** so that you can see their numerical line addresses. Remember, the append mode is ended by typing a period (**.**) on a line by itself.

```
$ ed new-file<CR>
?new-file
a<CR>
Create some lines
of text in
this file.
.<CR>
1,$n<CR>
1    Create some lines
2    of text in
3    this file.
1a<CR>
This will be line 2<CR>
This will be line 3<CR>
.<CR>
1,$n<CR>
1    Create some lines
2    This will be line 2
3    This will be line 3
4    of text in
5    this file.
```

Notice that after you append the two new lines, the line that was originally line 2 (of text in) becomes line 4.

You can take shortcuts to places in the file where you want to append text by combining the append command with symbolic addresses. The following three command lines allow you to move through and add to the text quickly in this way:

.a<CR>   appends text after the current line

$a<CR>   appends text after the last line of the file

0a<CR>   appends text before the first line of the file (at a symbolic address called line 0)

To try using these addresses, create a one-line file called **lines** and type the examples shown in the following screens. (The examples appear in separate screens for easy reference only; it is not necessary to access the **lines** file three times to try each append symbol. You can access **lines** once and try all three consecutively.)

```
$ ed lines<CR>
?lines
a<CR>
This is the current line.<CR>
.<CR>
p<CR>
This is the current line.
.a<CR>
This line is after the current line.<CR>
.<CR>
-1,.p<CR>
This is the current line.
This line is after the current line.
```

```
$a<CR>
This is the last line now.<CR>
.<CR>
$<CR>
This is the last line now.
```

```
0a<CR>
This is the first line now.<CR>
This is the second line now.<CR>
The line numbers change<CR>
as lines are added.<CR>
.<CR>
1,4n<CR>
1               This is the first line now.
2               This is the second line now.
3               The line numbers change
4               as lines are added.
```

Because the append command creates text after a specified address, the last example refers to the line before line 1 as the line after line 0. To avoid such circuitous references, use another command provided by the editor: the insert command, **i**.

Inserting Text: the i **Command**

The insert command (**i**), allows you to add text BEFORE a specified line in the editing buffer. The general command line format for **i** is the same as that for **a**:

[*address1*]**i**<CR>

As with the append command, you can insert one or more lines of text. To quit input mode, you must type a period (.) alone on a line.

Create a file called **insert** in which you can try the insert command (**i**):

```
$ ed insert<CR>
?insert
a<CR>
Line 1<CR>
Line 2<CR>
Line 3<CR>
Line 4<CR>
.<CR>
w<CR>
69
```

Now insert one line of text above line 2 and another above line 1. Use the **n** command to display all the lines in the buffer:

```
2i<CR>
This is the new line 2.<CR>
.<CR>
1,$n<CR>
1          Line 1
2          This is the new line 2.
3          Line 2
4          Line 3
5          Line 4
1i<CR>
This is the beginning.<CR>
.<CR>
1,$n<CR>
1          In the beginning
2          Line 1
3          Now this is line 2
4          Line 2
5          Line 3
6          Line 4
```

Experiment with the insert command by combining it with symbolic line addresses as follows:

■ .i<CR>

■ $i<CR>

Changing Text: the c **Command**

The change text command (**c**) erases all specified lines and allows you to create one or more lines of text in their place. Because **c** can erase a range of lines, the general format for the command line includes two addresses:

[*address1,address2*]**c**<CR>

The change command puts you in text input mode. To leave input mode, type a period alone on a line.

Address1 is the first and *address2* is the last of the range of lines to be replaced by new text. To erase one line of text, specify only *address1*. If no address is specified, **ed** assumes the current line is the line to be changed.

Now create a file called **change** in which you can try this command. After entering the text shown in the screen, change lines one through four by typing **1,4c**:

```
1,5n<CR>
1          line 1
2          line 2
3          line 3
4          line 4
5          line 5
1,4c<CR>
Change line 1<CR>
and lines 2 through 4<CR>
.<CR>
1,$n<CR>
1          change line 1
2          and lines 2 through 4
3          line 5
```

Now experiment with **c** and try to change the current line:

```
.<CR>
line 5
c<CR>
This is the new line 5.
.<CR>
.<CR>
This is the new line 5.
```

If you are not sure whether you have left text input mode, it is a good idea to type another period. If the current line is displayed, you know you are in the command mode of **ed**.

Figure 5-5 summarizes the **ed** commands for creating text.

Command	Function
a	appends text after the specified line in the buffer
i	inserts text before the specified line in the buffer
c	changes the text on the specified line(s) to new text
.	quits text input mode and returns to **ed** command mode

Figure 5-5: Summary of Commands for Creating Text

Exercise 3

3-1.   Create a new file called **ex3**. Instead of using the append command to create new text in the empty buffer, try the insert command. What happens?

3-2.   Enter **ed** with the file **towns**. What is the current line?

Insert above the third line:

    Illinois\<CR>

Insert above the current line:

    or\<CR>
    Naperville\<CR>

Insert before the last line:

    hotels in\<CR>

Display the text in the buffer preceded by line numbers.

3-3.   In the file **towns**, display lines 1 through 5 and replace lines 2 through 5 with:

    London\<CR>

Display lines 1 through 3.

3-4.   After you have completed exercise 3-3, what is the current line?

Find the line of text containing:

    Toledo

Replace

    Toledo

with

    Peoria

Display the current line.

3-5   With one command line search for and replace:

New York

with:

Iron City

Deleting Text

This section discusses two types of commands for deleting text in **ed**. One type is to be used when you are working in command mode: **d** deletes a line and **u** undoes the last command. The other type of command is to be used in text input mode: **#** (the pound sign) deletes a character and **@** (the at sign) kills a line. The delete keys that are used in input mode are the same keys you use to delete text that you enter after a shell prompt. They are described in detail in "Correcting Typing Errors" in Chapter 2.

Deleting Lines: the d Command

You have already deleted lines of text with the delete command (**d**) in the "Getting Started" section of this chapter.

The general format for the **d** command line is

*[address1,address2]***d**<CR>

You can delete a range of lines (*address1* through *address2*), or you can delete one line only (*address1*). If no address is specified, **ed** deletes the current line.

The next example displays lines one through five and then deletes lines two through four:

```
1,5n<CR>
1            1 horse
2            2 chickens
3            3 ham tacos
4            4 cans of mustard
5            5 bails of hay
2,4d<CR>
1,$n<CR>
1            1 horse
2            5 bails of hay
```

How can you delete only the last line of a file? Using a symbolic line address makes this easy:

$d<CR>

How can you delete the current line? One of the most common errors in **ed** is forgetting to type a period to leave text input mode. When this happens, unwanted text may be added to the buffer. In the next example, a line containing a print command (**1,$p**) is accidentally added to the text before the user leaves input mode. Because this line was the last one added to the text, it becomes the current line. The symbolic address . is used to delete it.

```
a<CR>
Last line of text<CR>
1,$p<CR>
.<CR>
p<CR>
1,$p
.d<CR>
p<CR>
Last line of text.
```

Before experimenting with the delete command, you may first want to learn about the undo command, **u**.

Undoing the Previous Command: the u Command

The **u** command (short for undo) nullifies the last command and restores any text changed or deleted by that command. It takes no addresses or arguments. The format is

u<CR>

One purpose for which the **u** command is useful is to restore text you have mistakenly deleted. If you delete all the lines in a file and then type **p**, **ed** will respond with a ? since there are no more lines in the file. Use the **u** command to restore them:

```
1,$p<CR>
This is the first line.
This is the middle line.
This is the last line.
1,$d<CR>
p<CR>
?
u<CR>
p<CR>
This is the last line.
```

Now experiment with **u**: use it to undo the append command:

```
.<CR>
This is the only line of text
a<CR>
Add this line<CR>
.<CR>
1,$p<CR>
This is the only line of text
Add this line
u<CR>
1,$p<CR>
This is the only line of text
```

NOTE

u cannot be used to undo the write command (**w**) or the quit command (**q**). However, **u** can undo an undo command (**u**).

How to Delete in Text Input Mode

While in text input mode, you can correct the current line of input with the same keys you use to correct a shell command line. By default, there are two keys available to correct text. The @ sign key kills the current line. The # sign key backs up over one character on the current line so you can retype it, thus effectively erasing the original character. (See "Correcting Typing Errors" in Chapter 2 for details.)

As mentioned in Chapter 2, you can reassign the line kill and character erase functions to other keys if you prefer. (See "Modifying Your Login Environment" in Chapter 7 for instructions.) If you have reassigned these functions, you must use the keys you chose while working in **ed**; the default keys (@ and #) will no longer work.

Escaping the Delete Function

You may want to include an @ sign or a # sign as a character of text. To avoid having these characters interpreted as delete commands, you must precede them with a \ (backslash), as shown in the following example:

```
a<CR>
leave San Francisco \@ 20:15 on flight \#347 <CR>
.<CR>
p<CR>
leave San Francisco @ 20:15 on flight #347
```

Figure 5-6 summarizes the **ed** commands and shell commands for deleting text in **ed**.

Command	Function
In command mode:	
<d>	deletes one or more lines of text
<u>	undoes the previous command
<@>	deletes the current command line
In text input mode:	
<@>	deletes the current line
<#> or <BACKSPACE>	deletes the last character typed in

Figure 5-6: Summary of Commands for Deleting Text

Substituting Text

You can modify text with the substitute command. This command replaces the first occurrence of a string of characters with new text. The general command line format is

[*address1,address2*]**s**/*old_text*/*new_text*/[*command*]<**CR**>

Each component of the command line is described below:

address1,address2
The range of lines being addressed by **s**. The address can be one line (*address1*), a range of lines (*address1* through *address2*), or a global search address. If no address is given, **ed** makes the substitution on the current line.

s   The substitute command.

/old_text   The argument specifying the text to be replaced. It is usually delimited by slashes but can be delimited by other characters such as a **?** or a period. It consists of the words or characters to be replaced. The command replaces the first occurrence of these characters that it finds in the text.

/new_text   The argument specifying the text to replace *old_text*. It is delimited by slashes or the same delimiters used to specify the *old_text*. It consists of the words or characters that are to replace the *old_text*.

/command   Any one of the following four commands:

g	Changes all occurrences of *old_text* on the specified lines.
l	Displays the last line of substituted text, including non-printing characters. (See the last section of this chapter, "Other Useful Commands and Information.")
n	Displays the last line of the substituted text preceded by its numerical line address.
p	Displays the last line of substituted text.

Substituting on the Current Line

The simplest example of the substitute command is making a change to the current line. You do not need to give a line address for the current line, as shown in the following example:

s/*old_text*/*new_text*/<**CR**>

The next example contains a typing error. While the line that contains it is still the current line, you make a substitution to correct it. The old text is the **ai** of **airor** and the new text is **er**:

```
a<CR>
In the beginning, I made an airor.
.<CR>
.p<CR>
In the beginning, I made an airor.
s/ai/er<CR>
```

Notice that **ed** gives no response to the substitute command. To verify that the command has succeeded in this case, you either have to display the line with **p** or **n**, or include **p** or **n** as part of the substitute command line. In the following example, **n** is used to verify that the word **file** has been substituted for the word **toad**:

```
.p<CR>
This is a test toad
s/toad/file/n<CR>
1        This is a test file
```

However, **ed** allows you one shortcut: it prints the results of the command automatically if you omit the last delimiter after the *new_text* argument:

```
.p<CR>
This is a test file
s/file/frog<CR>
This is a test frog
```

Substituting on One Line

To substitute text on a line that is not the current line, include an address in the command line as follows:

[*address1*]**s**/*old_text*/*new_text*/<**CR**>

For example, in the following screen the command line includes an address for the line to be changed (line 1) because the current line is line 3:

```
1,3p<CR>
This is a pest toad
testing testing
come in toad
.<CR>
come in toad
1s/pest/test<CR>
This is a test toad
```

As you can see, **ed** printed the new line automatically after the change was made because the last delimiter was omitted.

Substituting on a Range of Lines

You can make a substitution on a range of lines by specifying the first address (*address1*) through the last address (*address2*):

[*address1,address2*]**s**/*old_text*/*new_text*/<**CR**>

If **ed** does not find the pattern to be replaced on a line, no changes are made to that line.

In the following example, all the lines in the file are addressed for the substitute command; however, only the lines that contain the string **es** (the *old_text* argument) are changed:

```
1,$p<CR>
This is a test toad
testing testing
come in toad
testing 1, 2, 3
1,$s/es/ES/n<CR>
4        tESting 1, 2, 3
```

When you specify a range of lines and include **p** or **n** at the end of the substitute line, only the last line changed is printed.

To display all the lines in which text was changed, use the **n** or **p** command with the address **1,$**:

```
1,$n<CR>
1        This is a tESt toad
2        tESting testing
3        come in toad
4        tESting 1, 2, 3
```

Notice that only the first occurrence of **es** (on line 2) has been changed. To change every occurrence of a pattern, use the **g** command, described in the next section.

Global Substitution

One of the most versatile tools in **ed** is global substitution. By placing the **g** command after the last delimiter on the substitute command line, you can change every occurrence of a pattern on the specified lines. Try changing every occurrence of the string es in the last example. If you are following along, doing the examples as you read this, remember you can use **u** to undo the last substitute command.

```
u<CR>
1,$p<CR>
This is a test toad
testing, testing
come in toad
testing 1, 2, 3
1,$s/es/ES/g<CR>
1,$p<CR>
This is a tESt toad
tESting tESting
come in toad
tESting 1, 2, 3
```

Another method is to use a global search pattern as an address instead of the range of lines specified by **1,$**:

```
1,$p<CR>
This is a test toad
testing testing
come in toad
testing 1, 2, 3
g/test/s/es/ES/g<CR>
1,$p<CR>
This is a tESt toad
tESting tESting
come in toad
tESting 1, 2, 3
```

If the global search pattern is unique and matches the argument *old_text* (text to be replaced), you can use an **ed** shortcut: specify the pattern once as the global search address and do not repeat it as an *old_text* argument. **ed** will remember the pattern from the search address and use it again as the pattern to be replaced:

g/*old_text***/s//***new_text***/g<CR>**

NOTE

Whenever you use this shortcut, be sure to include two slashes (//) after the **s**.

```
1,$p<CR>
This is a test toad
testing testing
come in toad
testing 1, 2, 3
g/es/s//ES/g<CR>
1,$p<CR>
This is a tESt toad
tESting tESting
come in toad
tESting 1, 2, 3
```

Experiment with other search pattern addresses:

> /*pattern*<**CR**>
> ?*pattern*<**CR**>
> **v**/*pattern*<**CR**>

See what they do when combined with the substitute command. In the following example, the **v**/*pattern* search format is used to locate lines that do not
contain the pattern testing. Then the substitute command (**s**) is used to
replace the existing pattern (in) with a new pattern (**out**) on those lines:

```
v/testing/s/in/out<CR>
This is a test toad
come out toad
```

Note that the line This is a test toad was also printed, even though no substitution was made on it. When the last delimiter is omitted, all lines found with the search address are printed, regardless of whether or not substitutions have been made on them.

Now search for lines that do contain the pattern testing with the **g** command:

```
g/testing/s//jumping<CR>
jumping testing
jumping 1, 2, 3
```

Notice that this command makes substitutions only for the first occurrence of the *pattern* (testing) in each line. Once again, the lines are displayed on your terminal because the last delimiter has been omitted.

Exercise 4

4-1. In your file **towns** change `town` to **city** on all lines but the line with
`little town` on it.

> The file should read:

> **My kind of city is**
> **London**
> **Like being no where at all in**
> **Peoria**
> **I lost those little town blues in**
> **Iron City**
> **I lost my heart in**
> **San Francisco**
> **I lost $$ in**
> **hotels in**
> **Las Vegas**

4-2. Try using **?** as a delimiter. Change the current line

> `Las Vegas`

to

> **Toledo**

Because you are changing the whole line, you can also do this by
using the change command, **c**.

4-3. Try searching backward in the file for the word

> `lost`

and substitute

> **found**

using the **?** as the delimiter. Did it work?

4-4.   Search forward in the file for

      no

and substitute

     NO

for it. What happens if you try to use **?** as a delimiter?

Experiment with the various command combinations available for addressing a range of lines and doing global searches.

What happens if you try to substitute something for the **$$** ? Try to substitute **Big $** for **$** on line 9 of your file. Type:

    9s/$/Big $<CR>

What happened?

Special Characters

If you try to substitute the **$** sign in the line

```
I lost my $ in Las Vegas
```

you will find that instead of replacing the **$**, the new text is placed at the end of the line. The **$** is a special character in **ed** that is symbolic for the end of the line.

ed has several special characters that give you a shorthand for search patterns and substitution patterns. The characters act as wild cards. If you have tried to type in any of these characters, the result was probably different than what you had expected.

The special characters are as follows:

.	matches any one character
*	matches zero or more occurrences of the preceding character
.*	matches zero or more occurrences of any character following the period
ˆ	matches the beginning of the line
$	matches the end of the line
\	takes away the special meaning of the special character that follows
&	repeats the old text to be replaced in the new text of the replacement pattern
[...]	matches the first occurrence of a character in the brackets
[ˆ...]	matches the first occurrence of a character that is not in the brackets

In the following example, **ed** searches for any three-character sequence ending in the pattern at:

```
1,$p<CR>
rat
cat
turtle
cow
goat
g/.at<CR>
rat
cat
goat
```

Notice that the word goat is included because the string oat matches the string .at.

The * (asterisk) represents zero or more occurrences of a specified character in a search or substitute pattern. This can be useful in deleting repeated occurrences of a character that have been inserted by mistake. For example, suppose you hold down the "r" key too long while typing the word broke. You can use the * to delete every unnecessary "r" with one substitution command:

```
p<CR>
brrroke
s/br*/br<CR>
broke
```

Notice that the substitution pattern includes the b before the first r. If the b were not included in the search pattern, the * would interpret it during the search as a zero occurrence of r, make the substitution on it, and quit. (Remember, only the first occurrence of a pattern is changed in a substitution unless you request a global search with **g**.) The following screen shows how the substitution would be made if you did not specify both the b and the r before the *:

```
p<CR>
brrroke
s/r*/r<CR>
rbrrroke
```

If you combine the period and the *, the combination will match all characters. With this combination, you can replace all characters in the last part of a line:

```
p<CR>
Toads are slimy, cold creatures
s/are.*/are wonderful and warm<CR>
Toads are wonderful and warm
```

The .* can also replace all characters between two patterns:

```
p<CR>
Toads are slimy, cold creatures
s/are.*cre/are wonderful and warm cre<CR>
Toads are wonderful and warm creatures
```

If you want to insert a word at the beginning of a line, use the ^ (circumflex) for the old text to be substituted. This is very helpful when you want to insert the same pattern in the front of several lines. The next example places the word **all** at the beginning of each line:

```
1,$p<CR>
creatures great and small
things wise and wonderful
things bright and beautiful
1,$s/^/all /<CR>
1,$p<CR>
all creatures great and small
all things wise and wonderful
all things bright and beautiful
```

The $ sign is useful for adding characters at the end of a line or a range of lines:

```
1,$p<CR>
I love
I need
I use
The IRS wants my
1,$s/$/ money.<CR>
1,$p<CR>
I love money.
I need money.
I use money.
The IRS wants my money.
```

In these examples, you must remember to put a space after the word `all` or before the word money because **ed** adds the specified characters to the very beginning or the very end of the sentence. If you forget to leave a space before the word money, your file will look like this:

```
1,$s/$/money/<CR>
1,$p<CR>
I lovemoney
I needmoney
I usemoney
The IRS wants mymoney
```

The **$** sign also provides a handy way to add punctuation to the end of a line:

```
1,$p<CR>
I love money
I need money
I use money
The IRS wants my money
1,$s/$/./<CR>
1,$p/<CR>
I love money.
I need money.
I use money.
The IRS wants my money.
```

Because **.** is not matching a character (old text), but replacing a character (new text), it does not have a special meaning. To change a period in the middle of a line, you must take away the special meaning of the period in the old text. To do this, simply precede the period with a \ (backslash). This is how you take away the special meaning of some special characters that you want to treat as normal text characters in search or substitute arguments. For example, the following screen shows how to take away the special meaning of the period:

```
p<CR>
Way to go.  Wow!
s/\./!<CR>
Way to go!  Wow!
```

The same method can be used with the backslash character itself. If you want to treat a \ as a normal text character, be sure to precede it with a \. For example, if you want to replace the \ symbol with the word backslash, use the substitute command line shown in the following screen:

```
1,2p<CR>
This chapter explains
how to use the \.
s/\\/backslash<CR>
how to use the backslash.
```

If you want to add text without changing the rest of the line, the & provides a useful shortcut. The & (ampersand) repeats the old text in the replacement pattern so that you do not have to type the pattern twice. For example:

```
p<CR>
The neanderthal skeletal remains
s/thal/& man's/<CR>
p<CR>
The neanderthal man's skeletal remains
```

ed automatically remembers the last string of characters in a search pattern or the old text in a substitution. However, you must prompt **ed** to repeat the replacement characters in a substitution with the % sign. The % sign allows you to make the same substitution on multiple lines without requesting a global substitution. For example, to change the word money to the word gold, repeat the last substitution from line 1 on line 3, but not on line 4:

```
1,$n<CR>
 1        I love money
 2        I need food
 3        I use money
 4        The IRS wants my money
1s/money/gold<CR>
I love gold
3s//%<CR>
I use gold
1,$n<CR>
 1        I love gold
 2        I need food
 3        I use gold
 4        The IRS wants my money
```

ed automatically remembers the word money (the old text to be replaced) so that string does not have to be repeated between the first two delimiters. The **%** sign tells **ed** to use the last replacement pattern, **gold**.

ed tries to match the first occurrence of one of the characters enclosed in brackets and substitute the specified old text with new text. The brackets can be at any position in the pattern to be replaced.

In the following example, **ed** changes the first occurrence of the numbers 6, 7, 8, or 9 to 4 on each line in which it finds one of those numbers:

```
1,$p<CR>
Monday          33,000
Tuesday         75,000
Wednesday       88,000
Thursday        62,000
1,$s/[6789]/4<CR>
Monday          33,000
Tuesday         45,000
Wednesday       48,000
Thursday        42,000
```

The next example deletes the Mr or Ms from a list of names:

```
1,$p<CR>
Mr Arthur Middleton
Mr Matt Lewis
Ms Anna Kelley
Ms M. L. Hodel
1,$s/M[rs] //<CR>
1,$p<CR>
Arthur Middleton
Matt Lewis
Anna Kelley
M. L. Hodel
```

If a ^ (circumflex) is the first character in brackets, **ed** interprets it as an instruction to match characters that are not within the brackets. However, if the circumflex is in any other position within the brackets, **ed** interprets it literally, as a circumflex:

```
1,$p<CR>
grade  A   Computer Science
grade  B   Robot Design
grade  A   Boolean Algebra
grade  D   Jogging
grade  C   Tennis
1,$s/grade [^AB]/grade A<CR>
1,$p<CR>
grade  A   Computer Science
grade  B   Robot Design
grade  A   Boolean Algebra
grade  A   Jogging
grade  A   Tennis
```

Whenever you use special characters as wild cards in the text to be changed, remember to use a unique pattern of characters. In the above example, if you had used only

   1,$s/[^AB]/A<CR>

you would have changed the g in the word grade to A. Try it.

Experiment with these special characters. Find out what happens (or does not happen) if you use them in different combinations.

Figure 5-7 summarizes the special characters for search or substitute patterns.

Command	Function
.	matches any one character in a search or substitute pattern
*	matches zero or more occurrences of the preceding character in a search or substitute pattern
.*	matches zero or more occurrences of any characters following the period
^	matches the beginning of the line in the substitute pattern to be replaced or in a search pattern
$	matches the end of the line in the substitute pattern to be replaced
\	takes away the special meaning of the special character that follows in the substitute or search pattern
&	repeats the old text to be replaced in the new text replacement pattern
%	matches the last replacement pattern
[...]	matches the first occurrence of a character in the brackets
[^...]	matches the first occurrence of a character that is not in the brackets

Figure 5-7: Summary of Special Characters

Exercise 5

5-1.   Create a file that contains the following lines of text:

A   **Computer Science**
D   **Jogging**
C   **Tennis**

What happens if you try this command line:

1,$s/[^AB]/A/<CR>

Undo the above command. How can you make the C and D unique? (Hint: they are at the beginning of the line, in the position shown by the ^.) Do not be afraid to experiment!

5-2.   Insert the following line above line 2:

These are not really my grades.

Using brackets and the ^ character, create a search pattern that you can use to locate the line you inserted. There are several ways to address a line. When you edit text, use the way that is quickest and easiest for you.

5-3.   Add the following lines to your file:

I love money
I need money
The IRS wants my money

Now use one command to change them to:

It's my money
It's my money
The IRS wants my money

Using two command lines, do the following: change the word on the first line from **money** to **gold**, and change the last two lines from **money** to **gold** without using the words **money** or **gold** themselves.

5-4.   How can you change the line

1020231020

to

10202031020

without repeating the old digits in the replacement pattern?

5-5.   Create a line of text containing the following characters:

* . \ & % ^ *

Substitute a letter for each character. Do you need to use a backslash for every substitution?

Moving Text

You have now learned to address lines, create and delete text, and make substitutions. **ed** has one more set of versatile and important commands. You can move, copy, or join lines of text in the editing buffer. You can also read in text from a file that is not in the editing buffer or write lines of the file in the buffer to another file in the current directory. The commands that move text are

m	moves lines of text
t	copies lines of text
j	joins contiguous lines of text
w	writes lines of text to a file
r	reads in the contents of a file

Move Lines of Text

The **m** command allows you to move blocks of text to another place in the file. The general format is

[*address1,address2*]**m**[*address3*]<**CR**>

The components of this command line include

address1,address2
> The range of lines to be moved. If only one line is moved, only *address1* is given. If no address is given, the current line is moved.

m   The move command.

address3   The new location of the lines to be moved. Note that the new lines will follow *address3*.

Try the following example to see how the command works. Create a file that contains these three lines of text:

I want to move this line.
I want the first line
below this line.

Type

1m3<CR>

ed will move line 1 below line 3.

```
                    ┌──────────────────────────────┐
                  ┌─│ I want to move this line.     │
                  │ └──────────────────────────────┘
                  │
                  │   I want the first line
                  │   below this line.
                  └─▶ I want to move this line.
```

The next screen shows how this will appear on your terminal:

```
 1,$p<CR>
 I want to move this line.
 I want the first line
 below this line.
 1m3<CR>
 1,$p<CR>
 I want the first line
 below this line.
 I want to move this line.
```

If you want to move a paragraph of text, have *address1* and *address2* define the range of lines of the paragraph.

In the following example, a block of text (lines 8 through 12) is moved below line 65. Notice the **n** command that prints the line numbers of the file:

```
8,12n<CR>
8              This is line 8.
9              It is the beginning of a
10             very short paragraph.
11             This paragraph ends
12             on this line.
64,65n<CR>
64             Move the block of text
65             below this line.
8,12m65<CR>
59,65n<CR>
59             Move the block of text
60             below this line.
61             This is line 8.
62             It is the beginning of a
63             very short paragraph.
64             This paragraph ends
65             on this line.
```

How can you move lines above the first line of the file? Try the following command:

   3,4m0<CR>

When *address3* is 0, the lines are placed at the beginning of the file.

Copy Lines of Text

The copy command, **t** (short for transfer), acts like the **m** command except that the block of text is not deleted at the original address of the line. A copy of that block of text is placed after a specified line of text.

The general format of the **t** command also looks like the **m** command:

[*address1,address2*]**t**[*address3*]<**CR**>

address1,address2
> The range of lines to be copied. If only one line is copied, only *address1* is given. If no address is given, the current line is copied.

t
> The copy command.

address3
> The new location of the lines to be copied. Note that the new lines will follow *address3*.

The next example shows how to copy three lines of text below the last line:

```
                     Safety procedures:

          If there is a fire in the building:
          Close the door of the room to seal off the fire
```

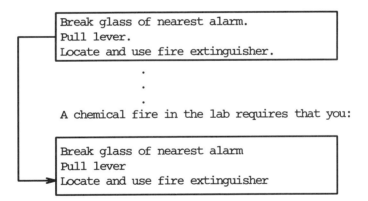

```
          Break glass of nearest alarm.
          Pull lever.
          Locate and use fire extinguisher.

                        .
                        .
                        .

          A chemical fire in the lab requires that you:

          Break glass of nearest alarm
          Pull lever
          Locate and use fire extinguisher
```

The commands and **ed**'s responses to them are displayed in the next screen. Again, the **n** command displays the line numbers:

```
5,8n<CR>
5          Close the door of the room, to seal off the fire.
6          Break glass of nearest alarm.
7          Pull lever.
8          Locate and use fire extinguisher.
30n<CR>
30         A chemical fire in the lab requires that you:
6,8t30<CR>
30,$n<CR>
30         A chemical fire in the lab requires that you:
31         Break glass of nearest alarm
32         Pull lever
33         Locate and use fire extinguisher
6,8n<CR>
6          Break glass of nearest alarm
7          Pull lever
8          Locate and use fire extinguisher
```

The text in lines 6 through 8 remains in place. A copy of those three lines is placed after line 50.

Experiment with **m** and **t** on one of your files.

Joining Contiguous Lines

The **j** command (short for join) joins the current line with the following line. The general format is

[*address1,address1*]**j**<**CR**>

The next example shows how to join several lines together. An easy way of doing this is to display the lines you want to join using **p** or **n**:

```
1,2p<CR>
Now is the time to join
the team.
p<CR>
the team.
1p<CR>
Now is the time to join
j<CR>
p<CR>
Now is the time to jointhe team.
```

Notice that there is no space between the last word (join) and the first word of the next line (the). You must place a space between them by using the **s** command.

Write Lines of Text to a File

The **w** command (short for write) writes text from the buffer into a file. The general format is

[*address1,address2*]**w** [*filename*]<**CR**>

address1,address2

> The range of lines to be placed in another file. If you do not use *address1* or *address2*, the entire file is written into a new file.

w   The write command.

filename   The name of the new file that contains a copy of the block of text.

In the following example, the body of a letter is saved in a file called **memo** so that it can be sent to other people:

```
1,$n<CR>
1                   March 17, 1986
2              Dear Kelly,
3              There will be a meeting in the
4              green room at 4:30 P.M. today.
5              Refreshments will be served.
3,6w  memo<CR>
87
```

The **w** command places a copy of lines three through six into a new file called **memo**. **ed** responds with the number of characters in the new file.

Problems

The **w** command overwrites pre-existing files; it erases the current file and puts the new block of text in the file without warning you. If, in our example, a file called **memo** had existed before we wrote our new file to that name, the original file would have been erased.

In "Other Useful Commands and Information," later in this chapter, you will learn how to execute shell commands from **ed**. Then you can list the file names in the directory to make sure that you are not overwriting a file.

Another potential problem is that you cannot write other lines to the file **memo**. If you try to add lines 13 through 16, the existing lines (3 through 6) will be erased and the file will contain only the new lines (13 through 16).

Read in the Contents of a File

The **r** command (short for read) appends text from a file to a buffer. The general format for the **r** command is

[*address1*]**r** *filename*<**CR**>

address1 The location where the new text will be placed. Note that the new text will follow *address1*. If *address1* is not given, the file is added to the end of the buffer.

r   The read command.

filename The name of the file to be copied into the editing buffer.

Using the example from the **w** command, the next screen shows a file being edited and new text being read into it:

```
1,$n<CR>
1                    March 17, 1986
2          Dear Michael,
3          Are you free later today?
           Hope to see you there.
3r memo<CR>
87
3,$n<CR>
3          Are you free later today?
4          There is a meeting in the
5          green room at 4:30 P.M. today.
6          Refreshments will be served.
7          Hope to see you there.
```

ed responds to the read command with the number of characters in the file being added to the buffer (in the **memo** file).

It is a good idea to display new or changed lines of text to be sure that they are correct.

Figure 5-8 summarizes the **ed** commands for moving text.

Command	Function
m	moves lines of text
t	copies lines of text
j	joins contiguous lines
w	writes text into a new file
r	reads in text from another file

Figure 5-8: Summary of **ed** Commands for Moving Text

Exercise 6

6-1.   There are two ways to copy lines of text in a buffer: by issuing the **t** command or by using the **w** and **r** commands to first write text to a file and then read the file into a buffer.

Writing to a file and then reading the file into a buffer is a longer process. Can you think of an example where this method would be more practical?

What commands can you use to copy lines 10 through 17 of the **exer** file into the **exer6** file at line 7?

6-2.   Lines 33 through 46 give an example that you want placed after line 3, not after line 32. What command performs this task?

6-3.   Say you are on line 10 of a file and you want to join lines 13 and 14. What commands can you issue to do this?

Other Useful Commands and Information

There are four other commands and a special file that will be useful to you during editing sessions:

h or H   accesses the help commands, which provide error messages

l   displays characters that are not normally displayed

f   displays the current file name

!   temporarily escapes **ed** to execute a shell command

ed.hup   saves a copy of the **ed** buffer when a system interrupt occurs

Help Commands

You may have noticed when you were editing a file that **ed** responds to some of your commands with a ?. The ? is a diagnostic message issued by **ed** when it has found an error. The help commands give you a short message to explain the reason for the most recent diagnostic.

There are two help commands:

h   Displays a short error message that explains the reason for the most recent ?.

H   Places **ed** in help mode so that a short error message is displayed every time the ? appears. (To cancel this request, type **H**.)

If you try to quit **ed** without writing the changes in the buffer to a file, you will get a ?. Do this now. When the ? appears, type **h**:

```
q<CR>
?
h<CR>
warning: expecting 'w'
```

The ? is also displayed when you specify a new file name on the **ed** command line. Give **ed** a new file name. When the ? appears, type **h** to find out
what the error message means:

```
ed newfile<CR>
? newfile
h<CR>
cannot open input file
```

This message means one of two things: either there is no file called **newfile**
or there is such a file but **ed** is not allowed to read it.

As explained earlier, the **H** command responds to the ? and then turns on
the help mode of **ed** so that **ed** gives you a diagnostic explanation every time
the ? is subsequently displayed. To turn off help mode, type **H** again. The
next screen shows **H** being used to turn on help mode. Sample error messages are also displayed in response to some common mistakes:

```
$ ed newfile<CR>
e newfile<CR>
?newfile
H<CR>
cannot open input file
/hello<CR>
?
illegal suffix
1,22p<CR>
?
line out of range
a<CR>
I am appending this line to the buffer.
.<CR>
s/$ tea party<CR>
?
illegal or missing delimiter
,$s/$/ tea party<CR>
?
unknown command
H<CR>
q<CR>
?
h<CR>
warning: expecting 'w'
```

You may have encountered the following error messages during previous editing sessions:

illegal suffix
> **ed** cannot find an occurrence of the search pattern **hello** because the buffer is empty.

line out of range
> **ed** cannot print any lines because the buffer is empty or the line specified is not in the buffer.

A line of text is appended to the buffer to show you some error messages associated with the **s** command:

illegal or missing delimiter
>The delimiter between the old text to be replaced and the new text is missing.

unknown command
>*address1* was not typed in before the comma; **ed** does not recognize ,**$**.

Help mode is then turned off, and **h** is used to determine the meaning of the last ? . While you are learning **ed**, you may want to leave help mode turned on. If so, use the **H** command. However, once you become adept at using **ed**, you will only need to see error messages occasionally. Then you can use the **h** command.

Display Nonprinting Characters

If you are typing a tab character, the terminal will normally display up to eight spaces (covering the space up to the next tab setting). (Your tab setting may be more or less than eight spaces. See Chapter 7, "Shell Tutorial," on settings using **stty**.)

If you want to see how many tabs you have inserted into your text, use the **l** (list) command. The general format for the **l** command is the same as for **n** and **p**:

>[*address1,address2*]l<**CR**>

The components of this command line are

address1,address2
>The range of lines to be displayed. If no address is given, the current line will be displayed. If only *address1* is given, only that line will be displayed.

l
>The command that displays the nonprinting characters along with the text.

The **l** command denotes tabs with a > (greater than) character. To type control characters, hold down the CONTROL key and press the appropriate alphabetic key. The key that sounds the bell is < ^g> (CTRL-g). It is displayed as \07 which is the octal representation (the computer's code) for < ^g>.

Type in two lines of text that contain a < ^g> (CTRL-g) and a tab. Then use the **l** command to display the lines of text on your screen:

```
a<CR>
Add a <^g> (CTRL-g) to this line.<CR>
Add a <tab> (tab) to this line.<CR>
.<CR>
1,2l<CR>
Add a \07 (CTRL-g) to this line.<CR>
Add a > (tab) to this line.<CR>
```

Did the bell sound when you typed < ^g>?

The Current File Name

In a long editing session, you may forget the file name. The **f** command will remind you which file is currently in the buffer. Or, you may want to preserve the original file that you entered into the editing buffer and write the contents of the buffer to a new file. In a long editing session, you may forget and accidentally overwrite the original file with the customary **w** and **q** command sequence. You can prevent this by telling the editor to associate the contents of the buffer with a new file name while you are in the middle of the editing session. This is done with the **f** command and a new file name.

The format for displaying the current file name is **f** alone on a line:

   f<CR>

To see how **f** works, enter **ed** with a file. For example, if your file is called **oldfile**, **ed** will respond as shown in the following screen:

```
ed oldfile<CR>
323
f<CR>
oldfile
```

To associate the contents of the editing buffer with a new file name use this general format:

f newfile<CR>

If no file name is specified with the write command, **ed** remembers the file name given at the beginning of the editing session and writes to that file. If you do not want to overwrite the original file, you must either use a new file name with the write command or change the current file name using the **f** command followed by the new file name. Because you can use **f** at any point in an editing session, you can change the file name immediately. You can then continue with the editing session without worrying about overwriting the original file.

The next screen shows the commands for entering the editor with **oldfile** and then changing its name to **newfile**. A line of text is added to the buffer and then the **w** and **q** commands are issued:

```
ed oldfile<CR>
323
f<CR>
oldfile
f newfile<CR>
newfile
a<CR>
Add a line of text.<CR>
.<CR>
w<CR>
343
q<CR>
```

Once you have returned to the shell, you can list your files and verify the existence of the new file, **newfile**. **newfile** should contain a copy of the contents of **oldfile** plus the new line of text.

Escape to the Shell

How can you make sure you are not overwriting an existing file when you write the contents of the editor to a new file name? You need to return to the shell to list your files. The ! allows you to temporarily return to the shell, execute a shell command, and then return to the current line of the editor.

The general format for the escape sequence is

!*shell command line*<CR>
shell response to the command line
!

When you type the ! as the first character on a line, the shell command must follow on that same line. The program's response to your command will appear as the command is running. When the command has finished executing, the ! will be appear alone on a line. This means that that you are back in the editor at the current line.

For example, if you want to return to the shell to find out the correct date, type **!** and the shell command **date**:

```
p<CR>
This is the current line
! date<CR>
Tue  Apr  1   14:24:22   EST   1986

!
p<CR>
This is the current line.
```

The screen first displays the current line. Then the command is given to temporarily leave the editor and display the date. After the date is displayed, you are returned to the current line of the editor.

If you want to execute more than one command on the shell command line, see the discussion on **;** in the section called "Special Characters" in Chapter 7.

Recovering From System Interrupts

What happens if you are creating text in **ed** and there is an interrupt to the system, you are accidentally hung up on the system, or your terminal is unplugged? When an interrupt occurs, the UNIX System tries to save the contents of the editing buffer in a special file named **ed.hup**. Later you can retrieve your text from this file in one of two ways. First, you can use a shell command to move **ed.hup** to another file name, such as the name the file had while you were editing it (before the interrupt). Second, you can enter **ed** and use the **f** command to rename the contents of the buffer. An example of the second method is shown in the following screen:

```
ed ed.hup<CR>
928
f myfile<CR>
myfile
```

If you use the second method to recover the contents of the buffer, be sure to remove the **ed.hup** file afterward.

Conclusion

You now are familiar with many useful commands in **ed**. The commands that were not discussed in this tutorial, such as **G**, **P**, **Q** and the use of **( )** and **{ }**, are discussed on the *ed*(1) page of the *User's/System Administrator's Reference Manual*. You can experiment with these commands and try them to see what tasks they perform.

Figure 5-9 summarizes the functions of the commands introduced in this section.

Command	Function
h	Displays a short error message for the preceding diagnostic ?.
H	Turns on help mode. An error message will be given with each diagnostic ?. The second **H** turns off help mode.
l	Displays nonprinting characters in the text.
f	Displays the current file name.
f *newfile*	Changes the current file name associated with the editing buffer to *newfile*.
!cmd	Temporarily escapes to the shell to execute a shell command *cmd*.
ed.hup	Saves the editing buffer if the terminal is hung up before a write command.

Figure 5-9: Summary of Other Useful Commands

Exercise 7

7-1.   Create a new file called **newfile1**. Access **ed** and change the file's name to **current1**. Then create some text and write and quit **ed**. Run the **ls** command to verify that there is not a file called **newfile1** in your directory. If you type the shell command **ls**, you will see that the directory does not contain a file called **newfile1**.

7-2.   Create a file called **file1**. Append some lines of text to the file. Leave append mode but do not write the file. Turn off your terminal. Then turn on your terminal and log in again. Issue the **ls** command in the shell. Is there a new file called **ed.hup**? Place **ed.hup** in **ed**. How can you change the current file name to **file1**? Display the contents of the file. Are the lines the same lines you created before you turned off your terminal?

7-3.   While you are in **ed**, temporarily escape to the shell and send a mail message to yourself.

Answers to Exercises

Exercise 1

1-1.

```
$ ed junk<CR>
? junk
a<CR>
Hello world.<CR>
.<CR>
w<CR>
12
q<CR>
$
```

1-2.

```
$ ed junk<CR>
12
1,$p<CR>
Hello world.<CR>
q<CR>
$
```

The system did not respond with the warning question mark because you did not make any changes to the buffer.

1-3.

```
$ ed junk<CR>
12
a<CR>
Wendy's horse came through the window.<CR>
.<CR>
1,$p<CR>
Hello world.
Wendy's horse came through the window.
q<CR>
?
w stuff<CR>
60
q<CR>
$
```

Exercise 2

2-1.

```
$ ed towns<CR>
? towns
a<CR>
My kind of town is<CR>
Chicago<CR>
Like being no where at all in<CR>
Toledo<CR>
I lost those little town blues in<CR>
New York<CR>
I lost my heart in<CR>
San Francisco<CR>
I lost $$ in<CR>
Las Vegas<CR>
.<CR>
w<CR>
164
```

2-2.

```
3<CR>
Like being no where at all in
```

2-3.

```
-2,+3p<CR>
My kind of town is
Chicago
Like being no where at all in
Toledo
I lost those little town blues in
New York
```

2-4.

```
.=<CR>
6
6<CR>
New York
```

2-5.

```
$<CR>
Las Vegas
```

2-6.

```
?town<CR>
I lost those little town blues in
?<CR>
My kind of town is
```

2-7.

```
g/in<CR>
My kind of town is
Like being no where at all in
I lost those little town blues in
I lost my heart in
I lost $$ in

v/in<CR>
Chicago
Toledo
New York
San Francisco
Las Vegas
```

Exercise 3

3-1.

```
$ ed ex3<CR>
?ex3
i<CR>
?
q<CR>
```

The **?** after the **i** means there is an error in the command. There is no current line before which text can be inserted.

3-2.

```
$ ed towns<CR>
164
.n<CR>
10              Las Vegas
3i<CR>
Illinois<CR>
.<CR>
.i<CR>
or<CR>
Naperville<CR>
.<CR>
$i<CR>
hotels in<CR>
1,$n<CR>
 1  my kind of town is
 2  Chicago
 3  or
 4  Naperville
 5  Illinois
 6  Like being no where at all in
 7  Toledo
 8  I lost those little town blues in
 9  New York
10  I lost my heart in
11  San Francisco
12  I lost $$ in
13  hotels in
14  Las Vegas
```

3-3.

```
1,5n<CR>
1   My kind of town is
2   Chicago
3   or
4   Naperville
5   Illinois
2,5c<CR>
London<CR>
.<CR>
1,3n<CR>
1   My kind of town is
2   London
3   Like being no where at all
```

3-4.

```
.<CR>
Like being no where at all
/Tol<CR>
Toledo
c<CR>
Peoria<CR>
.<CR>
.<CR>
Peoria
```

3-5.

```
.<CR>
/New Y/c<CR>
Iron City<CR>
.<CR>
.<CR>
Iron City
```

Your search string need not be the entire word or line. It only needs to be unique.

Exercise 4

4-1.

```
v/little town/s/town/city<CR>
My kind of city is
London
Like being no where at all in
Peoria
Iron City
I lost my heart in
San Francisco
I lost $$ in
hotels in
Las Vegas
```

The line

    `I lost those little town blues in`

was not printed because it was NOT addressed by the **v** command.

4-2.

```
.<CR>
Las Vegas
s?Las Vegas?Toledo<CR>
Toledo
```

4-3.

```
?lost?s??found<CR>
I found $$ in
```

4-4.

```
/no?s??NO<CR>
?
/no/s//NO<CR>
Like being NO where at all in
```

You cannot mix delimiters such as / and ? in a command line.

The substitution command on line 9 produced this output:

```
I found $$ inBig $
```

It did not work correctly because the $ sign is a special character in **ed**.

Exercise 5

5-1.

```
$ ed file1<CR>
? file1
a<CR>
A  Computer Science<CR>
D  Jogging<CR>
C  Tennis<CR>
.<CR>
1,$s/[^AB]/A/<CR>
1,$p<CR>
A  Computer Science
A  Jogging
A  Tennis
u<CR>
```

```
1,$s/^[^AB]/A<CR>
1,$p<CR>
A  Computer Science
A  Jogging
A  Tennis
```

5-2.

```
2i<CR>
These are not really my grades.<CR>
1,$p<CR>
A  Computer Science
These are not really my grades.
A  Tennis
A  Jogging
/^[^A]<CR>
These are not really my grades
?^[T]<CR>
These are not really my grades
```

5-3.

```
1,$p<CR>
I love money
I need money
The IRS wants my money
g/^I/s/I.*m /It's my m<CR>
It's my money
It's my money
```

```
/s/money/gold<CR>
It's my gold
2,$s//%<CR>
The IRS wants my gold
```

5-4.

```
s/10202/&0<CR>
102020031020
```

5-5.

```
a<CR>
* . \ & % ^ *<CR>
.<CR>
s/*/a<CR>
a . \ & % ^ *
s/*/b<CR>
a . \ & % ^ b
```

Because there were no preceding characters, * substituted for itself.

```
s/ \./c<CR>
a c \ & % ^ b
s/ \\/d<CR>
a c d & % ^ b
s/&/e<CR>
a c d e % ^ b
s/%/f<CR>
a c d e f ^ b
```

The **&** and **%** are only special characters in the replacement text.

```
s/ \ˆ/g<CR>
a c d e f g b
```

Exercise 6

6-1.   Any time you have lines of text that you may want to have repeated several times, it may be easier to write those lines to a file and read in the file at those points in the text.

If you want to copy the lines into another file you must write them to a file and then read that file into the buffer containing the other file.

```
ed exer<CR>
725
10,17 w temp<CR>
210
q<CR>
ed exer6<CR>
305
7r temp<CR>
210
```

The file **temp** can be called any file name.

6-2.

```
33,46m3<CR>
```

6-3.

```
.=<CR>
10
13p<CR>
This is line 13.
j<CR>
.p<CR>
This is line 13.and line 14.
```

Remember that .= gives you the current line.

Exercise 7

7-1.

```
$ ed newfile1<CR>
? newfile1
f current1<CR>
current1
a<CR>
This is a line of text<CR>
Will it go into newfile1<CR>
or into current1<CR>
.<CR>
w<CR>
66
q<CR>
$ ls<CR>
bin
current1
```

7-2.

```
ed file1<CR>
? file1
a<CR>
I am adding text to this file.<CR>
Will it show up in ed.hup?<CR>
.<CR>
```

Turn off your terminal.

Log in again.

```
ed ed.hup<CR>
58
f file1<CR>
file1
1,$p<CR>
I am adding text to this file.
Will it show up in ed.hup?
```

7-3.

```
$ ed file1<CR>
58
! mail mylogin<CR>
You will get mail when<CR>
you are done editing!<CR>
.<CR>
!
```

6   Screen Editor Tutorial (vi)

Introduction

This chapter is a tutorial on the screen editor, **vi** (short for visual editor). The **vi** editor is a powerful and sophisticated tool for creating and editing files. It is designed for use with a video display terminal that is used as a window through which you can view the text of a file. A few simple commands allow you to make changes to the text that are quickly reflected on the screen.

The **vi** editor displays from one to many lines of text. It allows you to move the cursor to any point on the screen or in the file (by specifying places such as the beginning or end of a word, line, sentence, paragraph, or file) and create, change, or delete text from that point. You can also use some line editor commands, such as the powerful global commands that allow you to change multiple occurrences of the same character string by issuing one command. To move through the file, you can scroll the text forward or backward, revealing the lines below or above the current window, as shown in Figure 6-1.

 Not all terminals have text scrolling capability; whether or not you can take advantage of **vi**'s scrolling feature depends on what type of terminal you have.

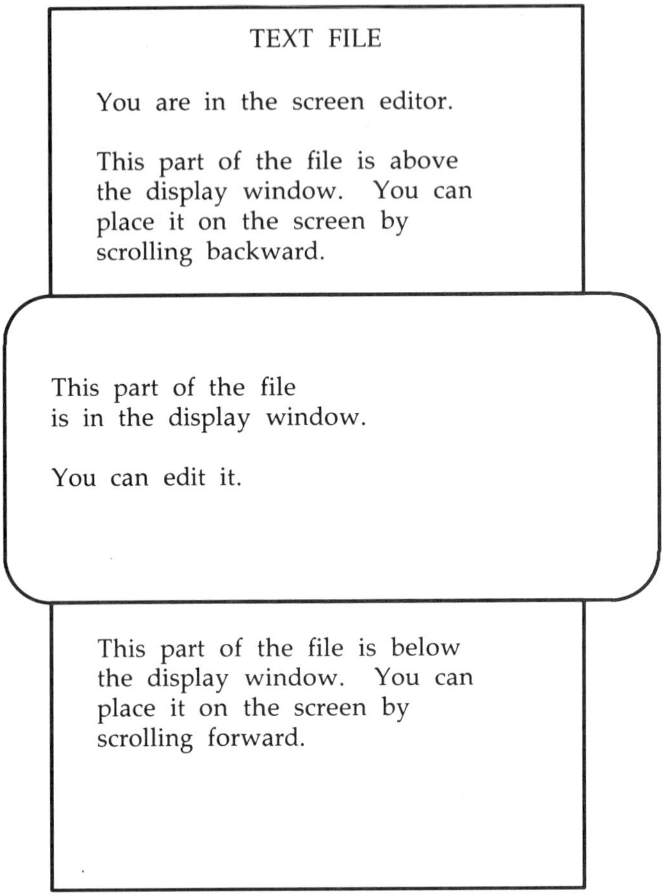

TEXT FILE

You are in the screen editor.

This part of the file is above
the display window. You can
place it on the screen by
scrolling backward.

This part of the file
is in the display window.

You can edit it.

This part of the file is below
the display window. You can
place it on the screen by
scrolling forward.

Figure 6-1: Displaying a File with a **vi** Window

There are more than 100 commands in **vi**. This chapter covers the basic commands that will enable you to use **vi** simply but effectively. Specifically, it explains how to do the following tasks:

- change your shell environment to set your terminal configuration and an automatic carriage return

- set up your terminal so that **vi** is accessible

- enter **vi**, create text, delete mistakes, write the text to a file, and quit

- move text within a file

- electronically cut and paste text

- use special commands and shortcuts

- use line editing commands available within **vi**

- temporarily escape to the shell to execute shell commands

- recover a file lost by an interruption to an editing session

- edit several files in the same session

Suggestions for Reading this Tutorial

As you read this tutorial, keep in mind the notational conventions described in the Preface. In the screens in this chapter, arrows are used to show the position of the cursor.

The commands discussed in each section are reviewed at the end of the section. A summary of **vi** commands is found in Appendix D, where they are listed by topic. At the end of some sections, exercises are given so you can experiment. The answers to all the exercises are at the end of this chapter. The best way to learn **vi** is by doing the examples and exercises as you read the tutorial. Log in on the UNIX System when you are ready to read this chapter.

Getting Started

The UNIX System is flexible; it can run on many types of computers and can be accessed from many kinds of terminals. However, because it is internally structured to be able to operate in so many ways, it needs to know what kind of hardware is being used in a given situation.

In addition, the UNIX System offers various optional features for using your terminal that you may or may not want to incorporate into your computing session routine. Your choice of these options, together with your hardware specifications, comprise your login environment. Once you have set up your login environment, the shell implements these specifications and options automatically every time you log in.

This section describes two parts of the login environment: setting the terminal configuration, which is essential for using **vi** properly, and setting the wrapmargin, or automatic (carriage) <RETURN>, which is optional.

Setting the Terminal Configuration

Before you enter **vi**, you must set your terminal configuration. This simply means that you tell the UNIX System what type of terminal you are using. This is necessary because the software for the **vi** editor is executed differently on different terminals.

Each type of terminal has several code names that are recognized by the UNIX System. Appendix F, "Setting Up the Terminal," tells you how to find a recognized name for your terminal. Keep in mind that many computer installations add terminal types to the list of terminals supported by default in your UNIX System. It is a good idea to check with your local system administrator for the most up-to-date list of available terminal types.

To set your terminal configuration, type

TERM=*terminal_name*<**CR**>
export TERM<**CR**>
tput init<**CR**>

The first line puts a value (a terminal type) in a variable called TERM. The second line exports this value; it conveys the value to all UNIX System programs whose execution depends on the type of terminal being used.

The **tput** command on the third line initializes (sets up) the software in your terminal so that it functions properly with the UNIX System. It is essential to run the **tput init** command when you are setting your terminal configuration because terminal functions such as tab settings will not work properly unless you do.

For example, if your terminal is a Teletype 5425 this is how your commands will appear on the screen:

```
$ TERM=5425<CR>
$ export TERM<CR>
$ tput init<CR>
```

Do not experiment by entering names for terminal types other than your terminal. This might confuse the UNIX System, and you may have to log off, hang up, or get help from your system administrator to restore your login environment.

Changing Your Environment

If you are going to use **vi** regularly, you should change your login environment permanently so you do not have to configure your terminal each time you log in. Your login environment is controlled by a file in your home directory called **.profile**.

If you specify the setting for your terminal configuration in your **.profile**, your terminal will be configured automatically every time you log in. You can do this by adding the three lines shown in the last screen (the **TERM** assignment, **export** command, and **tput** command) to your **.profile**. (For detailed instructions, see Chapter 7.)

Setting the Automatic <RETURN

 NOTE To set an automatic <RETURN> you must know how to create a file. If you are familiar with another text editor, such as **ed**, follow the instructions in this section. If you do not know how to use an editor but would like to have an automatic <RETURN> setting, skip this section for now and return to it when you have learned the basic skills taught in this chapter.

If you want the <RETURN> key to be entered automatically, create a file called **.exrc** in your home directory. You can use the **.exrc** file to contain options that control the **vi** editing environment.

To create a **.exrc** file, enter an editor with that file name. Then type in one line of text: a specification for the wrapmargin (automatic carriage return) option. The format for this option specification is

wm=n**<CR>**

n represents the number of characters from the righthand side of the screen where you want an automatic carriage return to occur. For example, say you want a carriage return at twenty characters from the righthand side of the screen. Type

wm=20<CR>

Finally, write the buffer contents to the file and quit the editor (see "Text Editing Buffers" in Chapter 4). The next time you log in, this file will give you the wrapmargin feature as you enter text in a file.

To check your settings for the terminal and wrapmargin when you are in **vi**, enter the command

:set<CR>

vi will report the terminal type and the wrapmargin, as well as any other options you may have specified. You can also use the **:set** command to create or change the wrapmargin option. Try experimenting with it.

Creating a File

First, enter the editor by typing **vi** and the name of the file you want to create or edit:

vi *filename*<**CR**>

For example, say you want to create a file called **stuff**. When you type the **vi** command with the file name **stuff**, **vi** clears the screen and displays a window in which you can enter and edit text:

```
__
~
~
~
~
~
~
~
~
"stuff" [New file]
```

The __ (underscore) on the top line shows the cursor waiting for you to enter a command there. (On video display terminals, the cursor may be a blinking underscore or a reverse color block.) Every other line is marked with a ~ (tilde), the symbol for an empty line.

If, before entering **vi**, you have forgotten to set your terminal configuration or have set it to the wrong type of terminal, you will see an error message instead:

```
$ vi stuff<CR>
terminal_name: unknown terminal type

[Using open mode]
"stuff" [New file]
```

You cannot set the terminal configuration while you are in the editor; you must be in the shell. Leave the editor by typing

> **: q<CR>**

Then set the correct terminal configuration.

How to Create Text: the Append Mode

If you have successfully entered **vi**, you are in command mode and **vi** is waiting for your commands. How do you create text?

- Press the A key (<**a**>) to enter the append mode of **vi**. (Do not press the <RETURN> key.) You can now add text to the file. (An A is not printed on the screen.)

- Type in some text.

- To begin a new line, press the <RETURN> key.

  If you have specified the wrapmargin option in a **.exrc** file, you will get a new line whenever you get an automatic <RETURN> (see "Setting the Automatic <RETURN>").

How to Leave Append Mode

When you finish creating text, press the <ESC> key to leave append mode and return to command mode. Then you can edit any text you have created or write the text in the buffer to a file:

```
<a>Create some text<CR>
in the screen editor<CR>
and return to<CR>
command mode.<ESC>
```

If you press the <ESC> key and a bell sounds, you are already in command mode. The text in the file is not affected by this, even if you press the <ESC> key several times.

Editing Text: the Command Mode

To edit an existing file, you must be able to add, change, and delete text. However, before you can perform those tasks, you must be able to move to the part of the file you want to edit. **vi** offers an array of commands for moving from page to page, between lines, and between specified points inside a line. These commands, along with commands for deleting and adding text, are introduced in this section.

How to Move the Cursor

To edit your text, you need to move the cursor to the point on the screen where you will begin the correction. This is easily done with four keys that are grouped together on the keyboard: h, j, k, and l.

<h>   moves the cursor one character to the left

<j>   moves the cursor down one line

<k>   moves the cursor up one line

<l>   moves the cursor one character to the right

The <j> and <k> commands maintain the column position of the cursor. For example, if the cursor is on the seventh character from the left, when you type <j> or <k> it goes to the seventh character on the new line. If there is no seventh character on the new line, the cursor moves to the last character on the line.

Many people who use **vi** find it helpful to mark these four keys with arrows showing the direction in which each key moves the cursor.

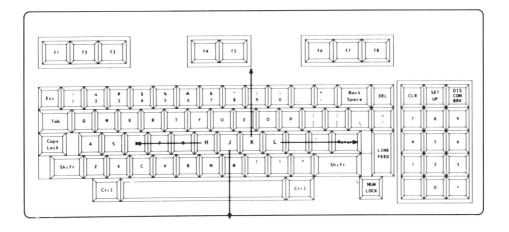

NOTE   Some terminals have special cursor control keys that are marked with arrows. Use them in the same way you use the <**h**>, <**j**>, <**k**>, and <**l**> commands.

Watch the cursor on the screen while you press the <**h**>, <**j**>, <**k**>, and <**l**> keys. Instead of pressing a motion command key a number of times to move the cursor a corresponding number of spaces or lines, you can precede the command with the desired number. For example, to move two spaces to the right, press <**l**> twice or enter <**2l**>. To move up four lines, press <**k**> four times or enter <**4k**>. If you cannot go any farther in the direction you have requested, **vi** will sound a bell.

Now experiment with the <**j**> and <**k**> motion commands. First, move the cursor up seven lines. Type

   <**7k**>

The cursor will move up seven lines above the current line. If there are less than seven lines above the current line, a bell will sound and the cursor will remain on the current line.

Now move the cursor down thirty-five lines. Type

   <**35j**>

vi will clear and redraw the screen. The cursor will be on the thirty-fifth line below the current line, appearing in the middle of the new window. If there are less than thirty-five lines below the current line, the bell will sound and the cursor will remain on the current line. Watch what happens when you type the next command:

   <**35k**>

Like most **vi** commands, the <**h**>, <**j**>, <**k**>, and <**l**> motion commands are silent; they do not appear on the screen as you enter them. The only time you should see characters on the screen is when you are in append mode and are adding text to your file. If the motion command letters appear on the screen, you are still in append mode. Press the <ESC> key to return to command mode and try the commands again.

Moving the Cursor to the Right or Left

In addition to the motion command keys <**h**> and <**l**>, the space bar and the <BACKSPACE> key can be used to move the cursor right or left to a character on the current line.

<**space bar**>	moves the cursor one character to the right
<*n***space bar**>	moves the cursor *n* characters to the right
<**BACKSPACE**>	moves the cursor one character to the left
<*n***BACKSPACE**>	moves the cursor *n* characters to the left

Try typing in a number before the command key. Notice that the cursor moves the specified number of characters to the left or right. In the example below, the cursor movement is shown by the arrows.

To move the cursor quickly to the right or left, prefix a number to the command. For example, suppose you want to create four columns on your screen. After you've finished typing the headings for the first three columns, you notice a typing mistake:

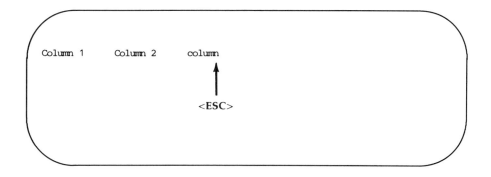

You want to correct your mistake before continuing. Exit insert mode and return to command mode by pressing the <ESC> key; the cursor will move to the n. Then use the <h> command to move back five spaces:

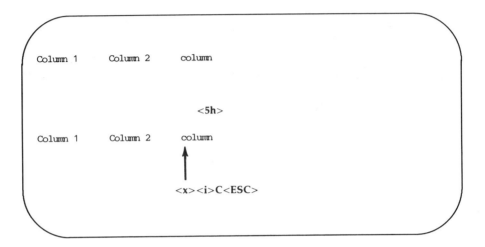

Erase the c by typing <x>. Then change to insert mode (<i>) and enter a C, followed by the <ESC> key. Use the <l> motion command to return to your earlier position:

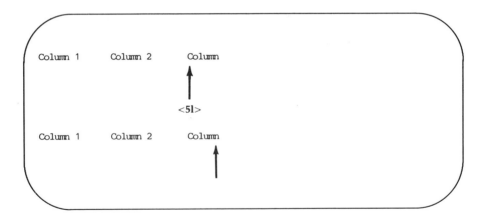

Again, you can specify a multiple space movement by typing a number before pressing the space bar or <BACKSPACE> key. The cursor will move the number of characters you request to the left or right.

How to Delete Text

If you want to delete a character, move the cursor to that character and press <**x**>. Watch the screen as you do so; the character will disappear and the line will readjust to the change. To erase three characters in a row, press <**x**> three times. In the following example, the arrows under the letters show the positions of the cursor.

<**x**>   deletes one character

<*n***x**>   deletes *n* characters, where *n* is the number of charac-
                                     ters you want to delete

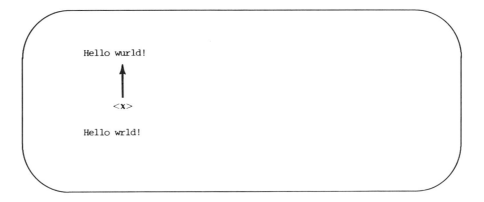

Now try preceding <**x**> with the number of characters you want to delete. For example, delete the second occurrence of the word deep from the text shown in the following screen. Put the cursor on the first letter of the string you want to delete, and delete five characters (for the four letters of deep plus an extra space):

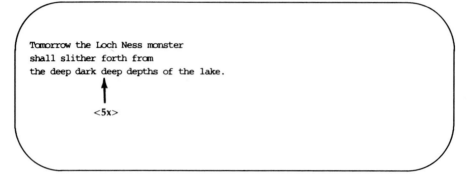

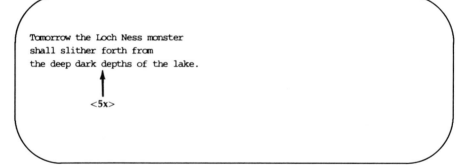

Notice that **vi** adjusts the text so that no gap appears in place of the deleted string. If, as in this case, the string you want to delete happens to be a word, you can also use the **vi** command for deleting a word. This command is described later in the section "Word Positioning."

How to Add Text

There are two basic commands for adding text: the insert (**<i>**) and append (**<a>**) commands. To add text with the insert command at a point in your file that is visible on the screen, move the cursor to that point by using **<h>**, **<j>**, **<k>**, and **<l>**. Then press **<i>** and start entering text. As you type, the new text will appear on the screen to the left of the character on which you put the cursor. That character and all characters to the right of the cursor will move right to make room for your new text. The **vi** editor will continue to accept the characters you type until you press the <ESC> key. If necessary, the original characters will even wrap around onto the next line:

You can use the append command in the same way. The only difference is that the new text will appear to the right of the character on which you put the cursor.

Later in this tutorial you will learn how to move around on the screen or scroll through a file to add or delete characters, words, or lines.

Quitting vi

When you have finished entering text, you will want to write the buffer contents to a file and return to the shell. To do this, hold down the <SHIFT> key and press **Z** twice (**<ZZ>**). The editor remembers the file name you specified with the **vi** command at the beginning of the editing session and moves the buffer text to the file of that name. A notice at the bottom of the screen gives the file name and the number of lines and characters in the file. Then the shell gives you a prompt:

```
<a>This is a test file.<CR>
I am adding text to<CR>
a temporary buffer and<CR>
now it is perfect.<CR>
I want to write this file,<CR>
and return to the shell.<ESC><ZZ>
~
~
~
~
"stuff" [New file] 7 lines, 151 characters
$
```

You can also use the **:w** and **:q** line editor commands for writing and quitting a file. (Line editor commands begin with a colon and appear on the bottom line of the screen.)   The **:w** command writes the buffer to a file. The **:q**
command leaves the editor and returns you to the shell. You can type these
commands separately or combine them into the single command **:wq**. It is
easier to combine them:

```
<a>This is a test file.<CR>
I am adding text to<CR>
a temporary buffer and<CR>
now it is perfect.<CR>
I want to write this file,<CR>
and return to the shell.<ESC>
~
~
~
~
~
:wq<CR>
```

Figure 6-2 summarizes the basic commands you need to enter and use **vi**.

Command	Function
TERM=*terminal_name* **export TERM**	sets the terminal configuration
tput init	initializes the terminal as defined by *terminal_name*
vi *filename*	enters the **vi** editor to edit the file called *filename*
\<a\>	adds text after the cursor
\<h\>	moves one character to the left
\<j\>	moves down one line
\<k\>	moves up one line
\<l\>	moves one character to the right
\<x\>	deletes a character
\<CR\>	enters a carriage return
\<ESC\>	leaves append mode and returns to **vi** command mode
:w	writes to a file
:q	quits **vi**
:wq	writes to a file and quits **vi**
\<ZZ\>	writes to a file and quits **vi**

Figure 6-2: Summary of Commands for the **vi** Editor

Exercise 1

Answers to the exercises are given at the end of this chapter. However, keep in mind that there is often more than one way to perform a task in **vi**. If your method works, it is correct.

As you give commands in the following exercises, watch the screen to see how it changes or how the cursor moves.

1-1.   If you have not logged in yet, do so now. Then set your terminal configuration.

1-2.   Enter **vi** and append the following five lines of text to a new file called **exer1**.

> **This is an exercise!**
> **Up, down,**
> **left, right,**
> **build your terminal's**
> **muscles bit by bit**

1-3.   Move the cursor to the first line of the file and the seventh character from the right. Notice that as you move up the file, the cursor moves in to the last letter of the file, but it does not move out to the last letter of the next line.

1-4.   Delete the seventh and eighth characters from the right.

1-5.   Move the cursor to the last character on the last line of text.

1-6.   Append the following new line of text:

> **and byte by byte**

1-7.   Write the buffer to a file and quit **vi**.

1-8.   Re-enter **vi** and append two more lines of text to the file **exer1**. What does the notice at the bottom of the screen say once you have re-entered **vi** to edit **exer1**?

Moving the Cursor Around the Screen

Until now you have been moving the cursor with the <**h**>, <**j**>, <**k**>, <**l**>, <BACKSPACE> key, and space bar. There are several other commands that can help you move the cursor quickly around the screen. This section explains how to position the cursor in the following ways:

- by characters on a line
- by lines
- by text objects
    - □ words
    - □ sentences
    - □ paragraphs
- in the window

There are also commands that position the cursor within parts of the **vi** editing buffer that are not visible on the screen. These commands will be discussed in the next section, "Positioning the Cursor in Undisplayed Text."

To follow this section of the tutorial, you should enter **vi** with a file that contains at least forty lines. If you do not have a file of that length, create one now. Remember that to execute the commands described here, you must be in **vi** command mode. Press the <ESC> key to make sure that you are in command mode rather than append mode.

Positioning the Cursor on a Character

There are three ways to position the cursor on a character in a line:

- by moving the cursor right or left to a character
- by specifying the character at either end of the line
- by searching for a character on a line

The first method was discussed earlier in this chapter under "Moving the Cursor to the Right or Left." The following sections describe the other two methods.

Moving the Cursor to the Beginning or End of a Line

The second method of positioning the cursor on a line is by using one of three commands that put the cursor on the first or last character of a line.

<$>	puts the cursor on the last character of a line
<0> (zero)	puts the cursor on the first character of a line
< ^ >	puts the cursor on the first nonblank character of a line

The following examples show the movement of the cursor produced by each of these three commands:

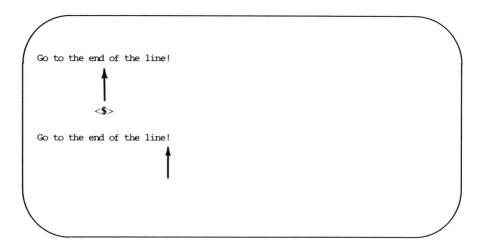

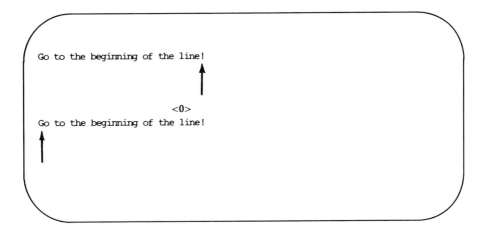

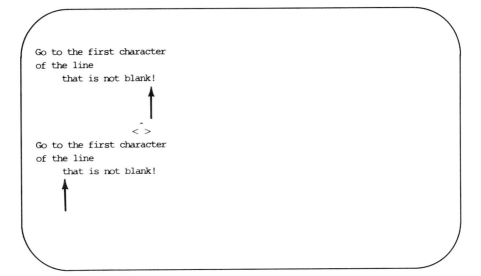

Searching for a Character on a Line

The third way to position the cursor on a line is to search for a specific character on the current line. If the character is not found on the current line, a bell sounds and the cursor does not move. (There is also a command that searches a file for patterns. This is discussed in "Searching for a Pattern of Characters.") There are six commands you can use to search within a line: <**f**>, <**F**>, <**t**>, <**T**>, <**n**>, and <**N**>. You must specify a character after all of them except the <**n**> and <**N**> commands.

<**f***x*>   Moves the cursor to the right to the specified character *x*.

<**F***x*>   Moves the cursor to the left to the specified character *x*.

<**t***x*>   Moves the cursor right to the character just before the specified character *x*.

<**T***x*>   Moves the cursor left to the character just after the specified character *x*.

<**n**>   Continues to search in the same direction for the character specified in the last command. The **n** remembers the character and seeks out the next occurrence of that character on the current line.

<**N**>   Continues to search in the opposite direction for the character specified in the last command. The **N** remembers the character and seeks out the previous occurrence of that character on the current line.

For example, in the following screen **vi** searches to the right for the first occurrence of the letter A on the current line:

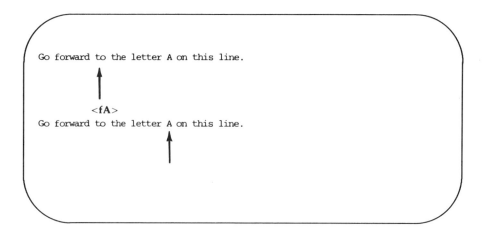

Try the search commands on one of your files.

Line Positioning

Besides the <**j**> and <**k**> commands that you have already used, the <**+**>, <**-**>, and <**CR**> commands can be used to move the cursor to other lines.

The Minus Sign Motion Command

The <**-**> command moves the cursor up a line, positioning it at the first nonblank character on the line. To move more than one line at a time, specify the number of lines you want to move before the <**-**> command. For example, to move the cursor up thirteen lines, type

> <**13-**>

The cursor will move up thirteen lines. If some of those lines are above the current window, the window will scroll up to reveal them. This is a rapid way to move quickly up a file.

Now try to move up 100 lines. Type

> <**100-**>

What happened to the window? If there are less then 100 lines above the current line a bell will sound, telling you that you have made a mistake, and the cursor will remain on the current line.

The Plus Sign Motion Command

The <**+**> or the <**CR**> command moves the cursor down a line. Specify the number of lines you want to move before the <**+**> command. For example, to move the cursor down nine lines, type

> <**9+**>

The cursor will move down nine lines. If some of those lines are below the current screen, the window will scroll down to reveal them.

Now try to do the same thing by pressing the <RETURN> key. Were the results the same as when you pressed the <**+**> key?

Word Positioning

The **vi** editor considers a word to be a string of characters that can include letters, numbers, or underscores (_). There are six word positioning commands: <w>, <b>, <e>, <W>, <B>, and <E>. The lowercase commands (<w>, <b>, and <e>) treat any character other than a letter, digit, or underscore as a delimiter, signifying the beginning or end of a word. Punctuation before or after a blank is considered a word. The beginning or end of a line is also a delimiter.

The uppercase commands (<W>, <B>, and <E>) treat punctuation as part of the word; words are delimited by blanks and newlines only.

The following is a summary of the word positioning commands:

<w>   Moves the cursor forward to the first character in the next word. You may press <w> as many times as you want to reach the word you want.

<nw>   Moves the cursor forward *n* number of words to the first character of that word. The end of the line does not stop the movement of the cursor; instead, the cursor wraps around and continues counting words from the beginning of the next line.

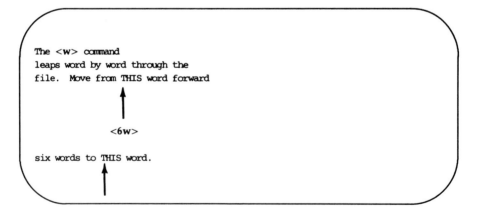

```
The <w> command
leaps word by word through the
file.  Move from THIS word forward
six words to THIS word.
             ↑
```

<W>   Ignores all punctuation and moves the cursor forward to the word after the next blank.

<e>   Moves the cursor forward in the line to the last character in the next word.

```
Go forward one word to the end of
the next word in this line
    ↑
<e>
```

```
Go forward one word to the end of
the next word in this line
      ↑
```

```
Go to the end of the third word after the current word.
      ↑
   <3e>
```

```
Go to the end of the third word after the current word.
          ↑
```

<E>   Moves the cursor forward in the line, delimiting words only by blanks.

<b>   Moves the cursor backward in the line to the first character of the previous word.

<*n*b> Moves the cursor backward *n* number of words to the first character of the *n*th word. The <b> command does not stop at the beginning of a line but moves to the end of the line above and continues moving backward.

<B>   Moves the cursor backward in the line, delimiting words only by blank spaces and newlines. It treats all other punctuation as letters of a word.

```
Leap backward word by word through
the file. Go back four words from here.
                    ↑

            <4b>
```

```
the file. Go back four words from here.
   ↑
```

Positioning the Cursor by Sentences

The **vi** editor also recognizes sentences. In **vi** a sentence ends in ! , . , or ?. If these delimiters appear in the middle of a line, they must be followed by two blanks for **vi** to recognize them. You should get used to the **vi** convention of recognizing two blanks after a period as the end of a sentence because it is often useful to be able to operate on a sentence as a unit.

You can move the cursor from sentence to sentence in the file with the <(> (open parenthesis) and <)> (close parenthesis) commands.

< **(** > moves the cursor to the beginning of the current sentence

< *n*(> moves the cursor to the beginning of the *n*th sentence above the current sentence

< **)** > moves the cursor to the beginning of the next sentence

< *n*) > moves the cursor to the beginning of the *n*th sentence below the current sentence

The example in the following screens shows how the open parenthesis moves the cursor around the screen:

```
Suddenly we spotted whales in the
distance.  Daniel was the first to see them.


              ↑
              |
              |
         <(>
```

```
distance.  Daniel was the first to see them.

↑
```

Now repeat the command, preceding it with a number. For example, type

<**3**(>   (or)
<**5**)>

Did the cursor move the correct number of sentences?

Positioning the Cursor by Paragraphs

Paragraphs are recognized by **vi** if they begin after a blank line. If you want to be able to move the cursor to the beginning of a paragraph (or later in this tutorial, to delete or change a whole paragraph), then make sure each paragraph ends in a blank line.

<{>   moves the cursor to the beginning of the current para-graph, which is delimited by a blank line above it

<**n**{>   moves the cursor to the beginning of the *n*th paragraph above the current paragraph

<}>   moves the cursor to the beginning of the next paragraph

<**n**}>   moves the cursor to the *n*th paragraph below the current line

The following two screens show how the cursor can be moved to the beginning of another paragraph:

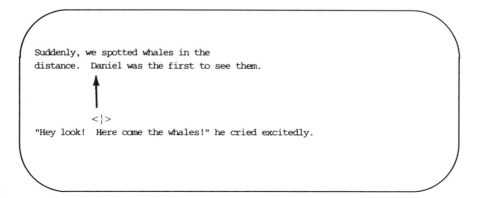

Positioning in the Window

The **vi** editor also provides three commands that help you position yourself in the window. Try out each command. Be sure to type them in uppercase.

<H>   moves the cursor to the first line on the screen

<M>   moves the cursor to the middle line on the screen

<L>   moves the cursor to the last line on the screen

This part of the file is
above the display window.

Type <H> (HOME) to move the cursor here.

Type <M> (MIDDLE) to move the cursor here.

Type <L> (LAST line on screen) to move
the cursor here.

This part of the file is
below the display window.

Figures 6-3 through 6-6 summarize the **vi** commands for moving the cursor by positioning it on a character, line, word, sentence, paragraph, or position on the screen. (Additional **vi** commands for moving the cursor are summarized in Figure 6-7, later in the chapter.)

Positioning on a Character	
\<h\>	Moves the cursor one character to the left.
\<l\>	Moves the cursor one character to the right.
\<BACKSPACE\>	Moves the cursor one character to the left.
\<space bar\>	Moves the cursor one character to the right.
\<fx**\>**	Moves the cursor to the right to the specified character *x*.
\<Fx**\>**	Moves the cursor to the left to the specified character *x*.
\<tx**\>**	Moves the cursor to the right to the character just before the specified character *x*.
\<Tx**\>**	Moves the cursor to the left to the character just after the specified character *x*.
\<n\>	Continues searching in the same direction on the line for the last character requested with \<f\>, \<F\>, \<t\>, or \<T\>. The **n** remembers the character and finds the next occurrence of it on the current line.
\<N\>	Continue searching in opposite direction on the line for the last character requested with \<f\>, \<F\>, \<t\>, or \<T\>. The **N** remembers the character and finds the next occurrence of it on the current line.

Figure 6-3: Summary of **vi** Motion Commands (Sheet 1 of 4)

Positioning on a Line	
<k>	Moves the cursor up one line to the same column in the previous line (if a character exists in that column).
<j>	Moves the cursor down one line to the same column in the next line (if a character exists in that column).
<->	Moves the cursor up one line to the beginning of the previous line.
<+>	Moves the cursor down one line to the beginning of the next line.
<CR>	Moves the cursor down one line to the beginning of the next line.

Figure 6-4: Summary of **vi** Motion Commands (Sheet 2 of 4)

Positioning on a Word	
\<w\>	Moves the cursor forward to the first character in the next word.
\<W\>	Ignores all punctuation and moves the cursor forward to the next word delimited only by blanks.
\<b\>	Moves the cursor backward one word to the first character of that word.
\<B\>	Ignores all punctuation and moves the cursor backward one word, delimited only by blanks.
\<e\>	Moves the cursor to the end of the current word.
\<E\>	Moves the cursor to the last character of a word before the next blank space or end of the line.

Figure 6-5: Summary of **vi** Motion Commands (Sheet 3 of 4)

Positioning on a Sentence	
<(>	Moves the cursor to the beginning of the current sentence.
<)>	Moves the cursor to the beginning of the next sentence.
Positioning on a Paragraph	
<{>	Moves the cursor to the beginning of the current paragraph.
<}>	Moves the cursor to the beginning of the next paragraph.
Positioning in the Window	
<H>	Moves the cursor to the first line on the screen (the home position).
<M>	Moves the cursor to the middle line on the screen.
<L>	Moves the cursor to the last line on the screen.

Figure 6-6: Summary of **vi** Motion Commands (Sheet 4 of 4)

Positioning the Cursor in Undisplayed Text

How do you move the cursor to text that is not shown in the current editing window? One option is to use the <*n*j> or <*n*k> command. However, if you are editing a large file, you need to move quickly and accurately to another place in the file. This section covers those commands that can help you move around within the file in the following ways:

- by scrolling forward or backward in the file

- by going to a specified line in the file

- by searching for a pattern in the file

Scrolling the Text

Four commands allow you to scroll the text of a file. The <^f> (CTRL-f) and <^d> (CTRL-d) commands scroll the screen forward. The <^b> (CTRL-b) and <^u> (CTRL-u) commands scroll the screen backward.

The CTRL-f Command

The <^f> (CTRL-f) command scrolls the text forward one full window of text below the current window. **vi** clears the screen and redraws the window. The three lines that were at the bottom of the current window are placed at the top of the new window. If there are not enough lines left in the file to fill the window, the screen displays a ~ (tilde) to show that there are empty lines.

vi clears and redraws the screen as follows:

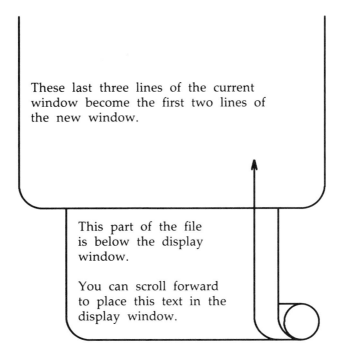

These last three lines of the current window become the first two lines of the new window.

This part of the file is below the display window.

You can scroll forward to place this text in the display window.

The CTRL-d Command

The < ˆ**d**> (CTRL-d) command scrolls down a half screen to reveal text below the window. When you type < ˆ**d**>, the text appears to be rolled up at the top and unrolled at the bottom. This allows the lines below the screen to appear on the screen, while the lines at the top of the screen disappear. If there are not enough lines in the file, a bell will sound.

The CTRL-b Command

The <^**b**> (CTRL-b) command scrolls the screen back a full window to reveal the text above the current window. **vi** clears the screen and redraws the window with the text that is above the current screen. Unlike the <^**f**> command, <^**b**> does not leave any reference lines from the previous window. If there are not enough lines above the current window to fill a full new window, a bell will sound and the current window will remain on the screen.

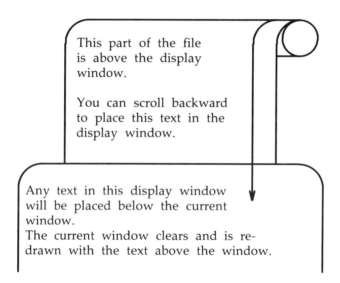

This part of the file
is above the display
window.

You can scroll backward
to place this text in the
display window.

Any text in this display window
will be placed below the current
window.
The current window clears and is redrawn with the text above the window.

Now try scrolling backward. Type

<^**b**>

vi clears the screen and draws a new screen.

This part of the file
is above the display window.

You can scroll backward
to place this text in the
display window.

Any text in this display window
will be placed below the current
window.
The current window clears and is
redrawn with the text above the
window.

Any text that was in the display window is placed below the current window.

The CTRL-u Command

The $<\hat{}\mathbf{u}>$ (CTRL-u) command scrolls up a half screen of text to reveal the lines just above the window. The lines at the bottom of the window are erased. Now scroll down in the text, moving the portion below the screen into the window. Type

$<\hat{}\mathbf{u}>$

When the cursor reaches the top of the file, a bell sounds to notify you that the file cannot scroll further.

Go to a Specified Line

The <G> command positions the cursor on a specified line in the window; if that line is not currently on the screen, <G> clears the screen and redraws the window around it. If you do not specify a line, <G> goes to the last line of the file.

     <G>   goes to the last line of the file

     <*n*G> goes to the *n*th line of the file

Line Numbers

Each line of the file has a line number corresponding to its position in the buffer. To get the number of a particular line, position the cursor on it and type < ˆ**g**>. The < ˆ**g**> command gives you a status notice at the bottom of the screen which tells you

- ■ the name of the file

- ■ if the file has been modified

- ■ the line number on which the cursor rests

- ■ the total number of lines in the buffer

- ■ the percentage of the total lines in the buffer represented by the current line

```
This line is the 35th line of the buffer.
The cursor is on this line.



              ↑
              |
              |
          < ˆg>


There are several more lines in the
buffer.
The last line of the buffer is line 116.
```

```
This line is the 35th line of the buffer.
The cursor is on this line.



There are several more lines in the
buffer.
The last line of the buffer is line 116.

"file.name" [modified] line 36 of 116 --34%--
```

Searching for a Pattern of Characters: the / and ? Commands

The fastest way to reach a specific place in your text is by using one of the search commands: /, ?, <n>, or <N>. These commands allow you to search forward or backward in the buffer for the next occurrence of a specified character pattern. The / and ? commands are not silent; they appear as you type them, along with the search pattern, on the bottom of the screen. The <n> and <N> commands, which allow you to repeat the requests you made for a search with a / or ? command, are silent.

The /, followed by a pattern (/*pattern*), searches forward in the buffer for the next occurrence of the characters in *pattern* and puts the cursor on the first of those characters. For example, the command line

>   **/Hello world<CR>**

finds the next occurrence in the buffer of the words **Hello world** and puts the cursor under the **H**.

The ?, followed by a pattern (?*pattern*), searches backward in the buffer for the first occurrence of the characters in *pattern* and puts the cursor on the first of those characters. For example, the command line

>   **?data set design<CR>**

finds the last occurrence in the buffer (before your current position) of the words **data set design** and puts the cursor under the **d** in **data**.

These search commands do not wrap around the end of a line while searching for two words. For example, say you are searching for the words Hello world. If Hello is at the end of one line and world is at the beginning of the next, the search command will not find that occurrence of Hello World.

However, the search commands do wrap around the end or the beginning of the buffer to continue a search. For example, if you are near the end of the buffer and the pattern for which you are searching (with the */pattern* command) is at the top of the buffer, the command will find the pattern.

The **<n>** and **<N>** commands allow you to continue searches you have requested with */pattern* or *?pattern* without retyping them.

<n>   repeats the last search command

<N>   repeats the last search command in the opposite direction

For example, say you want to search backward in the file for the three-letter pattern the. Initiate the search with **?the** and continue it with **<n>**. The following screens offer a step-by-step illustration of how the **<n>** searches backward through the file and finds four occurrences of the character string the:

```
Suddenly, we spotted whales in the
distance.  Daniel was the first to see them.

"Hey look!  Here come the whales!" he cried excitedly.




?the
```

```
Suddenly, we spotted whales in the
distance.  Daniel was the first to see them.
.P
"Hey look!  Here come the whales!" he cried excitedly.


                    ↑


                   (1)
```

```
Suddenly, we spotted whales in the
distance.  Daniel was the first to see them.

"Hey look!  Here come the whales!" he cried excitedly.


                    ↑


                  <n>
```

Suddenly, we spotted whales in the
distance. Daniel was the first to see them.

(2)

"Hey look! Here come the whales!" he cried excitedly.

Suddenly, we spotted whales in the
distance. Daniel was the first to see them.

\<n\>

"Hey look! Here come the whales!" he cried excitedly.

```
Suddenly, we spotted whales in the
distance.  Daniel was the first to see them.




                (3)


"Hey look!  Here come the whales!" he cried excitedly.
```

```
Suddenly, we spotted whales in the
distance.  Daniel was the first to see them.




                <n>
.P
"Hey look!  Here come the whales!" he cried excitedly.
```

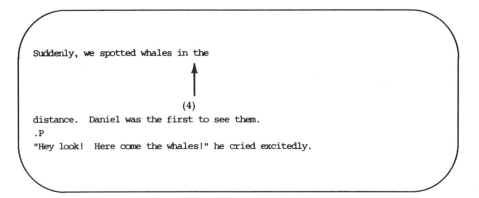

```
Suddenly, we spotted whales in the


                             ↑


                            (4)
distance.  Daniel was the first to see them.
.P
"Hey look!  Here come the whales!" he cried excitedly.
```

The / and **?** search commands do not allow you to specify particular occurrences of a pattern with numbers. You cannot, for example, request the third occurrence (after your current position) of a pattern.

Figure 6-7 summarizes the **vi** commands for moving the cursor by scrolling the text, specifying a line number, and searching for a pattern.

Scrolling	
<ˆf>	scrolls the screen forward a full window, revealing the window of text below the current window
<ˆd>	scrolls the screen down a half window, revealing lines below the current window
<ˆb>	scrolls the screen back a full window, revealing the window of text above the current window
<ˆu>	scrolls the screen up a half window, revealing the lines of text above the current window
Positioning on a Numbered Line	
<1G>	goes to the first line of the file
<G>	goes to the last line of the file
<ˆg>	gives the line number and file status
Searching for a Pattern	
/*pattern*	searches forward in the buffer for the next occurrence of *pattern* and positions the cursor on the first character of *pattern*
?*pattern*	searches backward in the buffer for the first occurrence of *pattern* and positions the cursor under the first character of *pattern*
<n>	repeats the last search command
<N>	repeats the search command in the opposite direction

Figure 6-7: Summary of Additional **vi** Motion Commands

Exercise 2

2-1. Create a file called **exer2**. Type a number on each line, numbering the lines from 1 to 50. Your file should look similar to the following:

```
1
2
3
.
.
.
48
49
50
```

2-2. Use each of the scroll commands, noticing how many lines scroll through the window. Try the following:

$$<\hat{f}>$$
$$<\hat{b}>$$
$$<\hat{u}>$$
$$<\hat{d}>$$

2-3. Go to the end of the file. Append the following line of text:

123456789 123456789

What number does the command <7h> place the cursor on? What number does the command <3l> place the cursor on?

2-4. Try the command <$> and the command <0> (number zero).

2-5. Go to the first character on the line that is not a blank. Move to the first character in the next word. Move back to the first character of the word to the left. Move to the end of the word.

2-6. Go to the first line of the file. Try the commands that place the cursor in the middle of the window, on the last line of the window, and on the first line of the window.

2-7. Search for the number 8. Find the next occurrence of the number 8. Find 48.

Creating Text

There are three basic commands for creating text:

<a> appends text

<i> inserts text

<o> opens a new line on which text can be entered

After you finish creating text with any one of these commands, you can return to the command mode of **vi** by pressing the <ESC> key.

Appending Text

<a> appends text after the cursor

<A> appends text at the end of the current line

You have already experimented with the <a> command in the "Creating a File" section. Make a new file named **junk2**. Append some text using the <a> command. To return to command mode of **vi**, press the <ESC> key. Then compare the <a> command to the <A> command.

Inserting Text

<i> inserts text before the cursor

<I> inserts text at the beginning of the current line before the first character that is not a blank

To return to the command mode of **vi**, press the <ESC> key.

In the following examples you can compare the append and insert commands. The arrows show the position of the cursor, where new text will be added:

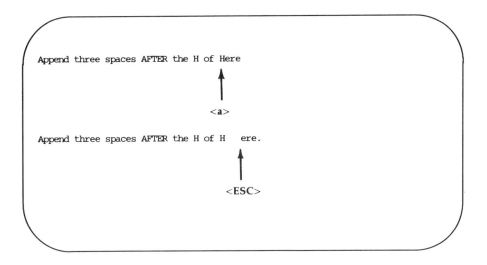

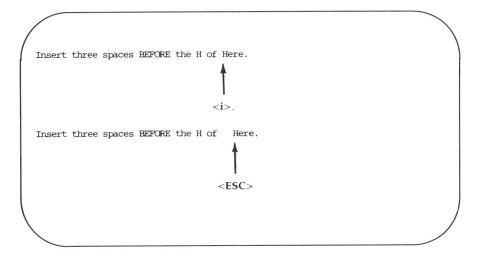

Notice that in both cases, the user has left text input mode by pressing the
<ESC> key.

Opening a Line for Text

<o>   Creates text from the beginning of a new line below the current line. You can issue this command from any point in the current line.

<O>   Creates text from the beginning of a new line above the current line. This command can also be issued from any position in the current line.

The open command creates an opening directly above or below the current line and puts you into text input mode. For example, in the following screens, the <O> command opens a line above the current line, and the <o> command opens a line below the current line. In both cases, the cursor waits for you to enter text at the beginning of the new line:

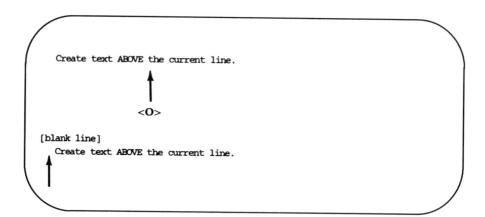

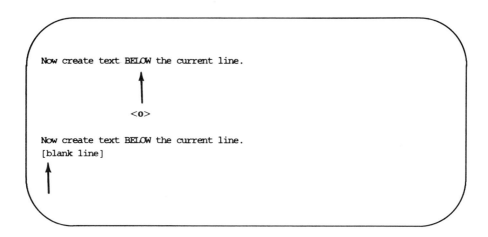

Figure 6-8 summarizes the commands for creating and adding text with the **vi** editor.

Command	Function
\<a\>	appends text after the cursor
\<A\>	appends text at the end of the current line
\<i\>	inserts text in front of the cursor
\<I\>	inserts text before the first character on the current line that is not a blank
\<o\>	opens up a new line for text input below the current line
\<O\>	opens up a new line for text input above the current line
\<ESC\>	returns **vi** to command mode from any of the above text input modes

Figure 6-8: Summary of **vi** Commands for Creating Text

Exercise 3

3-1.   Create a text file called **exer3**.

3-2.   Insert the following four lines of text:

Append text
Insert text
a computer's
job is boring.

3-3.   Add the following line of text above the last line:

financial statement and

3-4.   Using a text insert command, add the following line of text above the third line:

Delete text

3-5.   Add the following line of text below the current line:

byte of the budget

3-6.   Using an append command, add the following line of text below the last line:

But, it is an exciting machine.

3-7.   Move to the first line and add the word **some** before the word **text**.

Now practice using each of the six commands for creating text.

3-8.   Leave **vi** and go on to the next section to find out how to delete any mistakes you made in creating text.

Deleting Text

You can delete text with various commands in command mode and undo the entry of small amounts of text in text input mode. In addition, you can entirely undo the effects of your most recent command.

Undoing Entered Text in Text Input Mode

To delete a character when in text input mode, use the <BACKSPACE> key.

<BACKSPACE>   deletes the current character (the character shown by the cursor)

The <BACKSPACE> key backs up the cursor in text input mode and deletes each character that the cursor backs across. However, the deleted characters are not erased from the screen until you type over them or press the <ESC> key to return to command mode.

In the following example, the arrows represent the cursor:

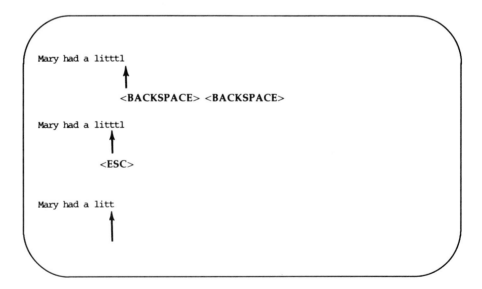

Notice that the characters are not erased from the screen until you press the <ESC> key.

There are two other keys that delete text in text input mode. Although you may not use them often, you should be aware that they are available. To remove the special meanings of these keys so that they can be typed as text, see the section on special commands.

< ^w>   undoes th entry of the current word

<@>   deletes all text entered on current line since text input mode was entered

When you type < ^w>, the cursor backs up over the word last typed and waits on the first character. It does not literally erase the word until you press the <ESC> key or enter new characters over the old ones. The <@> sign behaves in a similar manner except that it removes all text you have typed on the current line since you last entered input mode.

Undo the Last Command

Before you experiment with the delete commands, you should try the **u** command. This command undoes the last command you issued.

<u>   undoes the last command

<U>   restores the current line to its state before you changed it

If you delete lines by mistake, type <u>; your lines will reappear on the screen. If you type the wrong command, type <u> and it will be nullified. The <U> command will nullify all changes made to the current line as long as the cursor has not been moved from it.

If you type <u> twice in a row, the second command will undo the first; your undo will be undone! For example, say you delete a line by mistake and restore it by typing <u>. Typing <u> a second time will delete the line again. Knowing this command can save you a lot of trouble.

Delete Commands in Command Mode

You know that you can precede a command by a number. Many of the commands in **vi**, such as the delete and change commands, also allow you to enter a cursor movement command after another command. The cursor movement command can specify a text object such as a word, line, sentence, or paragraph. The general format of a **vi** command is

[*number*][*command*]*text_object*

The brackets around some components of the command format show that those components are optional.

All delete commands issued in command mode immediately remove unwanted text from the screen and redraw the affected part of the screen.

The delete command follows the general format of a **vi** command:

[*number*]**d***text_object*

Deleting Words

You can delete a word or part of a word with the <**dw**> command. Move the cursor to the first character to be deleted and type <**dw**>. The character under the cursor and all subsequent characters in that word will be erased:

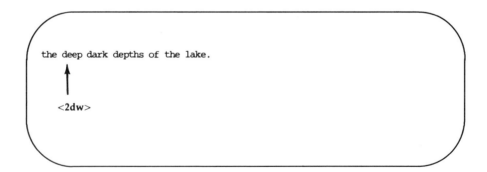

```
the deep dark depths of the lake.



<2dw>
```

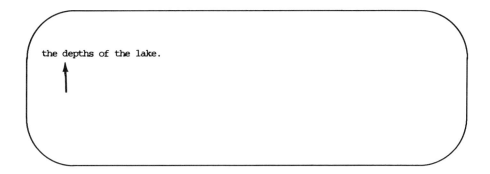

The <**dw**> command deletes one word or punctuation mark and the space(s) that follow it. You can delete several words or marks at once by specifying a number before the command. For example, to delete three words and two commas, type <**5dw**>:

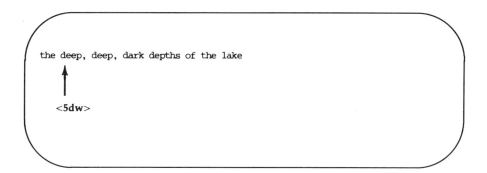

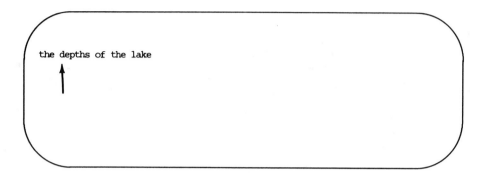

Deleting Paragraphs

To delete paragraphs, use the following commands:

<d{>   or   **<d}>**

Observe what happens to your file. Remember, you can restore the deleted text with **<u>**.

Deleting Lines

To delete a line, type **<dd>**. To delete multiple lines, specify a number before the command. For example, typing

<10dd>

will erase ten lines. If you delete more than a few lines, **vi** will display this notice on the bottom of the screen:

    10 lines deleted

If there are less than ten lines below the current line in the file, a bell will sound and no lines will be deleted.

Deleting Text After the Cursor

To delete all text on a line after the cursor, put the cursor on the first character to be deleted and type

> **<D> or <d$>**

Neither of these commands allows you to specify a number of lines; they can be used only on the current line.

Figure 6-9 summarizes the **vi** commands for deleting text.

Command	Function
For INSERT Mode:	
<BACKSPACE>	deletes the current character
<^h>	deletes the current character
<^W>	deletes the current word
<@>	deletes the current line of new text or deletes all new text on the current line
For COMMAND Mode:	
<u>	undoes the last command
<U>	restores the current line to its previous state
<x>	deletes the current character
<ndx>	deletes n number of text objects of type x
<dw>	deletes the word at the cursor through the next space or to the next punctuation mark
<dW>	deletes the word and punctuation at the cursor through the next space
<dd>	deletes the current line
<D>	deletes the portion of the line to the right of the cursor
<d)>	deletes the current sentence
<d}>	deletes the current paragraph

Figure 6-9: Summary of Delete Commands

Exercise 4

4-1.   Create a file called **exer4** and put the following four lines of text in it:

> **When in the course of human events**
> **there are many repetitive, boring**
> **chores, then one ought to get a**
> **robot to perform those chores.**

4-2.   Move the cursor to line two and append to the end of that line:

> **tedious and unsavory**

Delete the word unsavory while you are in append mode.

Delete the word boring while you are in command mode.

What is another way you could have deleted the word boring?

4-3.   Insert at the beginning of line four:

> **congenial and computerized**

Delete the line.

How can you delete the contents of the line without removing the line itself?

Delete all the lines with one command.

4-4.   Leave the screen editor and remove the empty file from your directory.

Modifying Text

The delete commands and text input commands provide one way for you to modify text. Another way you can change text is by using a command that lets you delete and create text simultaneously. There are three basic change commands: <r>, <s>, and <c>.

Replacing Text

<r>   Replaces the current character (the character shown by the cursor). This command does not initiate text input mode, and so does not need to be followed by pressing the <ESC> key.

<*n*r>   Replaces *n* characters with the same letter. This command automatically terminates after the *n*th character is replaced. It does not need to be followed by pressing the <ESC> key.

<R>   Replaces only those characters typed over until the <ESC> command is given. If the end of the line is reached, this command will append the input as new text.

The <r> command replaces the current character with the next character that is typed in. For example, suppose you want to change the word acts to ants in the following sentence:

    The circus has many acts.

Place the cursor under the c of acts and type

    <r>n

The sentence becomes

    The circus has many ants.

To change many to 7777, place the cursor under the m of many and type

    <4r7>

The <r> command changes the four letters of many to four occurrences of the number seven:

    The circus has 7777 ants.

Substituting Text

The substitute command replaces characters and then allows you to insert additional text from that point until you press the <ESC> key.

<s>   Deletes the character shown by the cursor and appends text. End the text input mode by pressing the <ESC> key.

<ns>   Deletes *n* characters and appends text. End the text input mode by pressing the <ESC> key.

<S>   Replaces all characters in the line.

When you enter the <s> command, the last character in the string of characters to be replaced is overwritten by a $ sign. The characters are not erased from the screen until you type over them, or leave text input mode by pressing the <ESC> key.

Notice that you cannot use an argument with either <r> or <s>. Did you try?

Suppose you want to substitute the word million for the word hundred in the sentence My salary is one hundred dollars. Put the cursor under the h of hundred and type <7s>. Notice where the $ sign appears:

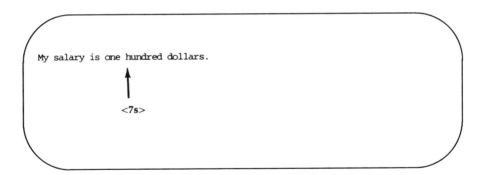

```
My salary is one hundred dollars.


              ↑

           <7s>
```

Then type **million**:

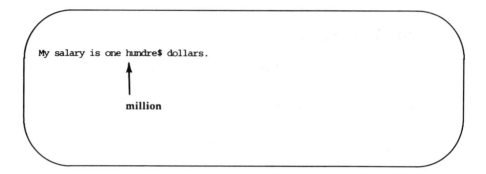

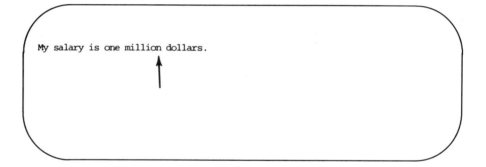

Changing Text

The substitute command replaces characters. The change command replaces text objects and then continues to append text from that point until you press the <ESC> key. To end the change command, press the <ESC> key.

The change command can take an argument. You can replace a character, word, or an entire line with new text.

    <*ncx*>   Replaces *n* number of text objects of type *x*, such as sentences (shown by <)>) and paragraphs (shown by <}>).

<cw>   Replaces a word or the remaining characters in a word with new text. The **vi** editor prints a $ sign to show the last character to be changed.

<*n*cw>   Replaces *n* words.

<cc>   Replaces all the characters in the line.

<*n*cc>   Replaces all characters in the current line and up to *n* lines of text.

<C>   Replaces the remaining characters in the line, from the cursor to the end of the line.

<*n*C>   Replaces the remaining characters from the cursor in the current line and replaces all the lines following the current line up to *n* lines.

The change commands <cw> and <C> use a $ sign to mark the last letter to be replaced. Notice how this works in the following example:

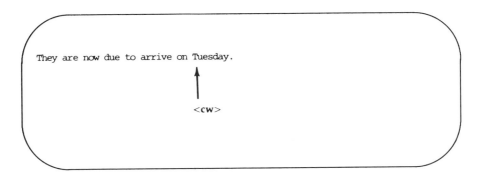

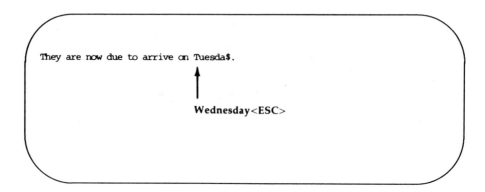

Notice that the new word (Wednesday) has more letters than the word it replaced (Tuesday). Once you have executed the change command you are in text input mode and can enter as much text as you want. The buffer will accept text until you press the <ESC> key.

The <C> command, when used to change the remaining text on a line, works in the same way. When you enter the command it uses a $ sign to mark the end of the text that will be deleted, puts you in text input mode, and waits for you to type new text over the old. The following screens offer an example of the <C> command:

```
This is line 1.
Oh, I must have the wrong number.


<C>
This is line 3.
This is line 4.
```

```
This is line 1.
Oh, I must have the wrong number$


This is line 2.<ESC>
This is line 3.
This is line 4.
```

```
This is line 1.
This is line 2.
This is line 3.
This is line 4.
```

Now try combining arguments. For example, type

<c{>

Because you know the undo command, do not hesitate to experiment with different arguments or to precede the command with a number. You must press the <ESC> key before using the <**u**> command, since <**c**> places you in text input mode.

Compare <**S**> and <**cc**>. The two commands should produce the same results.

Figure 6-10 summarizes the **vi** commands for changing text.

Command	Function
<r>	Replaces the current character.
<R>	Replaces only those characters typed over with new characters until the <ESC> key is pressed.
<s>	Deletes the character the cursor is on and appends text. End the append mode by pressing the <ESC> key.
<S>	Replaces all the characters in the line.
<cc>	Replaces all the characters in the line.
<*n*c*x*>	Replaces *n* number of text objects of type *x*, such as sentences (shown by <)>) and paragraphs (shown by <}>).
<cw>	Replaces a word or the remaining characters in a word with new text.
<C>	Replaces the remaining characters in the line, from the cursor to the end of the line.

Figure 6-10: Summary of **vi** Commands for Changing Text

Cutting And Pasting Text Electronically

vi provides a set of commands that cut and paste text in a file. Another set of commands copies a portion of text and places it in another section of a file.

Moving Text

You can move text from one place to another in the **vi** buffer by deleting the lines and then placing them at the required point. The last text that was deleted is stored in a temporary buffer. If you move the cursor to that part of the file where you want the deleted lines to be placed and press <**p**>, the deleted lines will be added below the current line.

<**p**>   places the contents of the temporary buffer after the cursor

A partial sentence that was deleted by the <**D**> command can be placed in the middle of another line. Position the cursor in the space between the two words, then press <**p**>. The partial line is placed after the cursor.

Characters deleted by <*n***x**> also go into a temporary buffer. Any text object that was just deleted can be placed somewhere else in the text with <**p**>.

The <**p**> command should be used right after a delete command since the temporary buffer only stores the results of one command at a time. The <**p**> command is also used to copy text placed in the temporary buffer by the yank command. The yank command (<**y**>) is discussed in "Copying Text."

Fixing Transposed Letters

A quick way to fix transposed letters is to combine the <**x**> and the <**p**> commands as <**xp**>. <**x**> deletes the letter. <**p**> places it after next character.

Notice the error in the next line:

    A line of tetx

This error can be changed quickly by placing the cursor under the t in tx and pressing the <**x**> and <**p**> keys, in that order. The result is

    A line of text

Try this. Make a typing error in your file and use the <**xp**> command to correct it. Why does this command work?

Copying Text

You can yank (copy) one or more lines of text into a temporary buffer and then put a copy of that text anywhere in the file. To put the text in a new position type <**p**>; the text will appear on the next line.

The yank command follows the general format of a **vi** command:

    [*number*]**y**[*text_object*]

Yanking lines of text does not delete them from their original position in the file. If you want the same text to appear in more than one place, this provides a convenient way to avoid typing the same text several times. However, if you do not want the same text in multiple places, be sure to delete the original text after you have put the text into its new position.

Figure 6-11 summarizes the ways you can use the yank command.

Command	Function
<*n***y***x*>	yanks *n* number of text objects of type *x* (such as sentences and paragraphs)
<**yw**>	yanks a copy of a word
<**yy**>	yanks a copy of the current line
<*n***yy**>	yanks *n* lines
<**y)**>	yanks all text up to the end of a sentence
<**y}**>	yanks all text up to the end of the paragraph

Figure 6-11: Summary of the Yank Command

Notice that this command allows you to specify the number of text objects to be yanked.

Try the following command lines and see what happens on your screen. (Remember, you can always undo your last command.) Type

> **<5yw>**

Move the cursor to another spot. Type

> **<p>**

Now try yanking a paragraph **<y}>** and placing it after the current paragraph. Then move to the end of the file **<G>** and place that same paragraph at the end of the file.

Copying or Moving Text Using Registers

Moving or copying several sections of text to a different part of the file is tedious work. **vi** provides a shortcut for this: named registers in which you can store text until you want to move it. To store text you can either yank or delete the text you wish to store.

Using registers is useful if a piece of text must appear in many places in the file. The extracted text stays in the specified register until you either end the editing session, or yank or delete another section of text to that register.

The general format of the command is

> *[number][* **"** *x]command[text_object]*

The *x* is the name of the register and can be any single letter. It must be preceded by a double quotation mark. For example, place the cursor at the beginning of a line. Type

> **<3 " ayy>**

Type in more text and then go to the end of the file. Type

> **< " ap>**

Did the lines you saved in register **a** appear at the end of the file?

Figure 6-12 summarizes the cut and paste commands.

Command	Function
<p>	places the contents of the temporary buffer containing the text obtained from the most recent delete or yank command into the text after the cursor
<yy>	yanks a line of text and places it into a temporary buffer
<*n*y*x*>	yanks a copy of n number of text objects of type x and places them in a temporary buffer
<"xy*n*>	places a copy of a text object of type n in the register named by the letter x
<"xp>	places the contents of the register x after the cursor

Figure 6-12: Summary of **vi** Commands for Cutting and Pasting Text

Exercise 5

5-1.   Enter **vi** with the file called **exer2** that you created in Exercise 2.

Go to line eight and change its contents to **END OF FILE**

5-2.   Yank the first eight lines of the file and place them in register **z**. Put the contents of register **z** after the last line of the file.

5-3.   Go to line eight and change its contents to **eight is great**.

5-4.   Go to the last line of the file. Substitute **EXERCISE** for FILE Replace OF with TO.

Special Commands

Here are some special commands that you will find useful:

        `<.>`   repeats the last command

        `<J>`   joins two lines together

        `<^l>`   clears the screen and redraws it

        `<~>`   changes lowercase to uppercase and vice versa

Repeating the Last Command

The . (period) repeats the last command to create, delete, or change text in the file. It is often used with the search command.

For example, suppose you forget to capitalize the S in United States. However, you do not want to capitalize the s in chemical states. One way to correct this problem is by searching for the word states. The first time you find it in the expression United States, you can change the s to S. Then continue your search. When you find another occurrence, you can simply type a period; **vi** will remember your last command and repeat the substitution of s for S.

Experiment with this command. For example, if you try to add a period at the end of a sentence while in command mode, the last text change will suddenly appear on the screen. Watch the screen to see how the text is affected.

Joining Two Lines

The <J> command joins lines. To enter this command, place the cursor on the current line, and press the <SHIFT> and **j** keys simultaneously. The current line is joined with the following line.

For example, suppose you have the following two lines of text:

```
Dear Mr.
Smith:
```

To join these two lines into one, place the cursor under any character in the first line and type

```
<J>
```

You will immediately see the following on your screen:

```
Dear Mr. Smith:
```

Notice that **vi** automatically places a space between the last word on the first line and the first word on the second line.

Clearing and Redrawing the Window

If another UNIX System user sends you a message using the write command while you are editing with **vi**, the message will appear in your current window, over part of the text you are editing. To restore your text after you have read the message, you must be in command mode. (If you are in text input mode, press the <ESC> key to return to command mode.) Then type <^l> (CTRL-l). **vi** will erase the message and redraw the window exactly as it appeared before the message arrived.

Changing Lowercase to Uppercase and Vice Versa

A quick way to change any lowercase letter to uppercase, or vice versa, is by putting the cursor on the letter to be changed and typing a <~> (tilde). For example, to change the letter a to A, press ~. You can change several letters by typing ~ several times, but you cannot precede the command with a number to change several letters with one command.

Figure 6-13 summarizes the special commands.

Command	Function
<.>	repeats the last command
<J>	joins the line below the current line with the current line
<^l>	clears and redraws the current window
<~>	changes lowercase to uppercase or vice versa

Figure 6-13: Summary of Special Commands

Using Line Editing Commands in vi

The **vi** editor has access to many of the commands provided by a line editor called **ex**. (For a complete list of **ex** commands see the *ex*(1) page in the *User's/System Administrator's Reference Manual*.) This section discusses some of the most commonly used commands.

The **ex** commands are very similar to the **ed** commands discussed in Chapter 5. If you are familiar with **ed**, you may want to experiment on a test file to see how many **ed** commands also work in **vi**.

Line editor commands begin with a **:** (colon). After the colon is typed, the cursor will drop to the bottom of the screen and display the colon. The remainder of the command will also appear at the bottom of the screen as you type it.

Temporarily Returning to the Shell: the :sh and :! Commands

When you enter **vi**, the contents of the buffer fill your screen, making it impossible to issue any shell commands. However, you may want to do so. For example, you may want to get information from another file to incorporate into your current text. You could get that information by running one of the shell commands that display the text of a file on your screen, such as the **cat** or **pg** command. However, quitting and re-entering the editor is time consuming and tedious. **vi** offers two methods of leaving the editor temporarily so that you can issue shell commands (and even edit other files) without having to write your buffer and quit: the **:!** command and the **:sh** command.

The **:!** command allows you to escape the editor and run a shell command on a single command line. From the command mode of **vi**, type **:!**. These characters will be printed at the bottom of your screen. Type a shell command immediately after the **!**. The shell will run your command, give you output, and print the message [Hit return to continue]. When you press the <RETURN> key, **vi** will refresh the screen and the cursor will reappear exactly where you left it.

The **ex** command **:sh** allows you to do the same thing but behaves differently on the screen. From the command mode of **vi**, type **:sh** and press the <RETURN> key. A shell command prompt will appear on the next line. Type your command(s) after the prompt as you would normally do while working in the shell. When you are ready to return to **vi**, type < ˆd> or **exit**; your screen will be refreshed with your buffer contents, and the cursor will appear where you left it.

Even changing directories while you are temporarily in the shell will not prevent you from returning to the **vi** buffer where you were editing your file when you type **exit** or < ˆd>.

Writing Text to a New File: the :w Command

The **:w** command (short for write) allows you to create a file by copying lines of text from the file you are currently editing into a file that you specify. To create your new file, you must specify a line or range of lines (with their line numbers) with the name of the new file on the command line. You can write as many lines as you like. The general format is

> :*line_number*[,*line_number*]**w** *filename*

For example, to write the third line of the buffer to a line named **three**, type

> **:3w three**<CR>

vi reports the successful creation of your new file with the following information:

> "three" [New file] 1 line, 20 characters

To write your current line to a file, you can use a . (period) as the line address:

> **:.w junk**<CR>

A new file called **junk** will be created. It will contain only the current line in the **vi** buffer.

You can also write a whole section of the buffer to a new file by specifying a range of lines. For example, to write lines 23 through 37 to a file, type the following:

> :**23,37w** *newfile*<**CR**>

Finding the Line Number

To determine the line number of a line, move the cursor to it and type : (colon). The colon will appear at the bottom of the screen. Type .= after it, and press the <RETURN> key:

```
If you want to know the number
of this line, type :.=<CR>



:.=
```

As soon as you press the <RETURN> key, your command line will disappear from the bottom line and be replaced by the number of your current line in the buffer:

```
If you want to know the number
of this line, type in :.=<CR>




34
```

You can move the cursor to any line in the buffer by typing **:** and the line number. The command line

:*n*<**CR**>

means to go to the *n*th line of the buffer.

Deleting the Rest of the Buffer

One of the easiest ways to delete all the lines between the current line and the end of the buffer is by using the line editor command **d** with the special symbols for the current and last lines:

:.,$d<**CR**>

The **.** represents the current line; the **$** sign, the last line.

Adding a File to the Buffer

To add text from a file below a specific line in the editing buffer, use the **:r** command (short for read.) For example, to put the contents of a file called **data** into your current file, place the cursor on the line above the location where you want it to appear. Type

:r data<**CR**>

You may also specify the line number instead of moving the cursor. For example, to insert the file **data** below line 56 of the buffer, type

> **:56r data<CR>**

Do not be afraid to experiment; you can use the **<u>** command to undo **ex** commands, too.

Making Global Changes

One of the most powerful commands in **ex** is the global command. The global command is described here to help those users who are familiar with the line editor. Even if you are not familiar with a line editor, you may want to try the command on a test file.

For example, say you have several pages of text about the DNA molecule in which you refer to its structure as a "helix." Now you want to change every occurrence of the word "helix" to "double helix." The **ex** editor's global command allows you to do this with one command line. First, you need to understand a series of commands:

:g/*pattern***/***command***<CR>**

> For each line containing *pattern*, **ex** executes *command*. For example, type **:g/helix<CR>**. The line editor will print all lines that contain the pattern helix.

:s/*pattern***/***new_words***/<CR>**

> For each line containing *pattern*, **ex** substitutes *new_words* for the first occurrence of *pattern*.

:s/*pattern***/***new_words***/g<CR>**

> If you add the letter g after the last delimiter of this command line, **ex** changes every occurrence of *pattern* on the current line to *new_words*. If you do not, **ex** changes only the first occurrence.

:g/*helix***/s//***double helix***/g<CR>**

> For each line containing *helix*, **ex** substitutes *double helix* for every occurrence of *helix*. The delimiters after the **s** do not need to have

helix typed in again. The command remembers the word from the delimiters after the global command **g**. This is a powerful command. For a more detailed explanation of global and substitution commands, see Chapter 5.

Figure 6-14 summarizes the line editor commands available in **vi**.

Command	Function
:	specifies that the commands that follow are line editor commands
:sh<CR>	temporarily returns you to the shell to perform shell commands
<^d>	escapes the temporary shell and returns you to the current window of **vi** to continue editing
:*n***<CR>**	goes to the *n*th line of the buffer
:*x,y***w** *data*<CR>	writes lines from the number *x* through the number *y* into a new file (*data*)
:$<CR>	goes to the last line of the buffer
:.,$d<CR>	deletes all the lines in the buffer from the current line to the last line
:r *shell.file*<CR>	inserts the contents of *shell.file* after the current line of the buffer
:s/*text/new_words/***<CR>**	replaces the first instance of the characters *text* on the current line with *new_words*
:s/*text/new_words/***g<CR>**	replaces every occurrence of *text* on the current line with *new_words*
:g/*text/***s//***new_words/***g<CR>**	replaces every occurrence of *text* in the file with *new_words*

Figure 6-14: Summary of Line Editor Commands

Quitting vi

There are five basic command sequences to quit the **vi** editor. Commands that are preceded by a colon (:) are line editor commands.

<ZZ> or **:wq<CR>**	Writes the contents of the **vi** buffer to the UNIX file currently being edited and quits **vi**.
:w *filename*<CR> **:q<CR>**	Writes the temporary buffer to a new file named *filename* and quits **vi**.
:w! *filename*<CR> **:q<CR>**	Overwrites an existing file called *filename* with the contents of the buffer and quits **vi**.
:q!<CR>	Quits **vi** without writing the buffer to a file and discards all changes made to the buffer.
:q<CR>	Quits **vi** without writing the buffer to a UNIX file. This works only if you have made no changes to the buffer; otherwise, **vi** will warn you that you must either save the buffer or use the **:q!<CR>** command to terminate.

The <ZZ> command and **:wq** command sequence both write the contents of the buffer to a file, quit **vi**, and return you to the shell. You have tried the <ZZ> command. Now try to exit **vi** with **:wq**. **vi** remembers the name of the file currently being edited, so you do not have to specify it when you want to write the buffer's contents back into the file. Type

   :wq<CR>

The system responds in the same way it does for the <ZZ> command. It tells you the name of the file and reports the number of lines and characters in the file.

What must you do to give the file a different name? For example, suppose you want to write to a new file called **junk**. Type

   :w junk<CR>

After you write to the new file, leave **vi**. Type

    :q<CR>

If you try to write to an existing file, you will receive a warning. For example, if you try to write to a file called **johnson**, the system will respond with

    `"johnson" File exists - use "w! johnson" to overwrite`

If you want to replace the contents of the existing file with the contents of the buffer, use the **:w!** command to overwrite **johnson**:

    :w! johnson<CR>

Your new file will overwrite the existing one.

If you edit a file called **memo**, make some changes to it, and then decide you don't want to keep the changes, or if you accidentally press a key that gives **vi** a command you cannot undo, leave **vi** without writing to the file. Type

    :q!<CR>

Figure 6-15 summarizes the quit commands.

Command	Function
<ZZ>	writes the file and quits **vi**
:wq<CR>	writes the file and quits **vi**
:w *filename*<CR> :q<CR>	writes the editing buffer to *filename* and quits **vi**
:w! *filename*<CR> :q<CR>	overwrites the existing file with the contents of the editing buffer and quits **vi**.
:q!<CR>	quits **vi** without writing the buffer to a file
:q<CR>	quits **vi** without writing the buffer to a file

Figure 6-15: Summary of the Quit Commands

Special Options For vi

The **vi** command has some special options. It allows you to

- recover a file lost by an interrupt to the UNIX System

- place several files in the editing buffer and edit each in sequence

- view a file at your own pace by using the **vi** cursor positioning commands

Recovering a File Lost by an Interrupt

If there is a system interrupt or disconnect, the system will exit the **vi** command without writing the text in the buffer back to its file. However, the UNIX System will store a copy of the buffer for you. When you log back in to the UNIX System, you will be able to restore the file with the **-r** option for the **vi** command. Type

   vi -r *filename*<**CR**>

The changes you made to *filename* before the interrupt occurred are now in the **vi** buffer. You can continue editing the file, or you can write the file and quit **vi**. The **vi** editor will remember the file name and write to that file.

Editing Multiple Files

If you want to edit more than one file in the same editing session, issue the **vi** command and specify each file name. Type

   vi *file1 file2*<**CR**>

vi responds by telling you how many files you are going to edit. For example:

   2 files to edit

After you have edited the first file, write your changes (in the buffer) to the file (*file1*). Type

:w<CR>

The system response to the **:w** <CR> command will be a message at the bottom of the screen giving the name of the file and the number of lines and characters in that file. Then you can bring the next file into the editing buffer by using the **:n** command. Type

:n<CR>

The system responds by printing a notice at the bottom of the screen, telling you the name of the next file to be edited and the number of characters and lines in that file.

Select two of the files in your current directory. Then enter **vi** and place the two files in the editing buffer at the same time. Notice the system responses to your commands at the bottom of the screen.

Viewing a File

It is often convenient to be able to inspect a file by using **vi**'s powerful search and scroll capabilities. However, you might want to protect yourself against accidentally changing a file during an editing session. The read-only option prevents you from writing in a file. To avoid accidental changes, you can set this option by invoking the editor as **view** rather than **vi**.

Figure 6-16 summarizes the special options for **vi**.

Option	Function
vi *file1 file2 file3*<**CR**>	enters *file1*, *file2*, and *file3* into the **vi** buffer to be edited
:w<**CR**> **:n**<**CR**>	writes the current file and calls the next file into the buffer
vi –r *file1*<CR>	restores the changes made to *file1*

Figure 6-16: Summary of Special Options for **vi**

Exercise 6

6-1.   Try to restore a file lost by an interrupt.

Enter **vi** and create some text in a file called **exer6**. Turn off your terminal without writing to a file or leaving **vi**. Turn your terminal back on and log in again. Then try to get back into **vi** and edit **exer6**.

6-2.   Place **exer1** and **exer2** in the **vi** buffer to be edited. Write **exer1** and call in the next file in the buffer, **exer2**.

Write **exer2** to a file called **junk**.

Quit **vi**.

6-3.   Try out the following command:

vi exer*<CR>

What happens? Try to quit all the files as quickly as possible.

6-4.   Look at **exer4** in read-only mode.

Scroll forward.

Scroll down.

Scroll backward.

Scroll up.

Quit and return to the shell.

Answers To Exercises

There is often more than one way to perform a task in **vi**. Any method that works is correct. The following are suggested ways of doing the exercises.

Exercise 1

1-1.   Ask your system administrator for your terminal's system name. Type

TERM=*terminal_name*<**CR**>

1-2.   Enter the **vi** command for a file called **exer1**:

vi exer1<**CR**>

Then use the append command (<**a**>) to enter the following text in your file:

```
This is an exercise!<CR>
Up, down<CR>
left, right,<CR>
build your terminal's<CR>
muscles bit by bit<ESC>
```

1-3.   Use the <**k**> and <**h**> commands.

1-4.   Use the <**x**> command.

1-5.   Use the <**j**> and <**l**> commands.

1-6. Enter **vi** and use the append command (<**a**>) to enter the following text:

> **and byte by byte**<ESC>

Then use <**j**> and <**l**> to move to the last line and character of the file. Use the <**a**> command again to add text. You can create a new line by pressing the <RETURN> key. To leave text input mode, press the <ESC> key.

1-7. Type

> <ZZ>

1-8. Type

> **vi exer1**<CR>

Notice the system response:

> "exer1" 7 lines, 102 characters

Exercise 2

2-1. Type
> **vi exer2**<CR>
> <**a**>**1**<CR>
> **2**<CR>
> **3**<CR>
> .
> .
> .
> **48**<CR>
> **49**<CR>
> **50**<ESC>

2-2.   Type

                <^f>
                <^b>
                <^u>
                <^d>

        Notice the line numbers as the screen changes.

2-3.   Type

                <G>
                <o>
                123456789 123456789<ESC>
                <**7h**>
                <**3l**>

        Typing <**7h**> puts the cursor
        on the 2 in the second set of numbers.
        Typing <**3l**> puts the cursor
        on the 5 in the
        second set of numbers.

2-4.   **$** = end of line
        0 = first character in the line

2-5.   Type

                <^>
                <**w**>
                <**b**>
                <**e**>

2-6.   Type

                <**1G**>
                <**M**>
                <**L**>
                <**H**>

2-7.   Type

                /8
                <**n**>
                /48

Exercise 3

3-1.   Type

      vi exer3<CR>

3-2.   Type

      <a> Append text <CR>
      Insert text<CR>
      a computer's <CR>
      job is boring.<ESC>

3-3.   Type

      <O>
      financial statement and<ESC>

3-4.   Type

      <3G>
      <i>Delete text<CR><ESC>

The text in your file now reads as follows:

```
Append text
Insert text
Delete text
a computer's
financial statement and
job is boring.
```

3-5.   The current line is a computer's. To create a line of text below that
line, use the **<o>** command.

3-6.   The current line is byte of the budget.
<G> puts you on the bottom line.
<A> lets you begin appending at the end of the line.
<CR> creates the new line.
Add the sentence: **But, it is an exciting machine.**
<ESC> leaves append mode.

3-7.   Type

        <1G>
        /text
        <i>some<space bar><ESC>

3-8.   **<ZZ>** will write the buffer to **exer3** and return you to the shell.

Exercise 4

4-1.   Type

        vi exer4<CR>
        <a> When in the course of human events<CR>
        there are many repetitive, boring<CR>
        chores, then one ought to get a<CR>
        robot to perform those chores.<ESC>

4-2.   Type

        <2G>
        <A> tedious and unsavory<BACKSPACE><CR>
        <ESC>

Press **<h>** until you get to the b in boring. Then type
<dw>. (You can also use **<6x>**.)

4-3.   You are at the second line. Type

        <2j>
        <I> congenial and computerized<ESC>
        <dd>

To delete the line and leave it blank, type

        <0> (zero moves the cursor to the beginning of the line)
        <D>

        <H>
        <3dd>

4-4.   Write and quit **vi**:

        <ZZ>

Remove the file:

rm exer4<CR>

Exercise 5

5-1. Type

vi exer2<CR>
<8G>
<cc> END OF FILE <ESC>

5-2. Type

<1G>
<8"zyy>
<G>
<"zp>

5-3. Type

<8G>
<cc> 8 is great<ESC>

5-4. Type

<G>
<2w>
<cw>
EXERCISE<ESC>
<2b>
<cw>
TO<ESC>

Exercise 6

6-1. Type

vi exer6<CR>
<a> (append several lines of text)
<ESC>

Turn off the terminal.

Turn on the terminal.
Log in on your UNIX System. Type
>**vi –r exer6<CR>**
>**:wq<CR>**

6-2. Type
>**vi exer1 exer2<CR>**
>**:w<CR>**
>**:n<CR>**
>
>**:w junk<CR>**
>**<ZZ>**

6-3. Type
>**vi exer*<CR>**
>
>Response:
>8 files to edit (**vi** calls all files with names that begin with **exer**.)
>
>**<ZZ>**
>**<ZZ>**

6-4. Type
>**view exer4<CR>**
>**<ˆf>**
>**<ˆd>**
>**<ˆb>**
>**<ˆu>**
>**:q<CR>**

7 Shell Tutorial

Command Language Exercises

Shell Programming

Modifying Your Login Environment

Shell Programming Exercises

Answers To Exercises

Introduction

This chapter describes how to use the UNIX System shell to do routine tasks. For example, it shows you how to use the shell to manage your files, to manipulate file contents, and to group commands together to make programs the shell can execute for you.

The chapter has two major sections. The first section, "Shell Command Language," covers in detail using the shell as a command interpreter. It tells you how to use shell commands and characters with special meanings to manage files, redirect standard input and output, and execute and terminate processes. The second section, "Shell Programming," covers in detail using the shell as a programming language. It tells you how to create, execute, and debug programs made up of commands, variables, and programming constructs like loops and case statements. Finally, it tells you how to modify your login environment.

The chapter offers many examples. You should log in to your UNIX System and recreate the examples as you read the text. As in the other examples in this guide, different type (**bold,** *italic,* and `constant width`) is used to distinguish your input from the UNIX System's output. See "Notational Conventions" in the Preface for details.

In addition to the examples, there are exercises at the end of both the "Shell Command Language" and "Shell Programming" sections. The exercises can help you better understand the topics discussed. The answers to the exercises are at the end of the chapter.

NOTE — Your UNIX System might not have all commands referenced in this chapter. If you cannot access a command, check with your system administrator.

If you want an overview of how the shell functions as both command interpreter and programming language, see Chapters 1 and 4 before reading this chapter. Also, refer to Appendix E, Summary of Shell Command Language.

Shell Command Language

This section introduces commands and, more importantly, some characters with special meanings that let you

- find and manipulate a group of files by using pattern matching

- run a command in the background or at a specified time

- run a group of commands sequentially

- redirect standard input and output from and to files and other commands

- terminate processes

It first covers the characters having special meanings to the shell and then covers the commands and notation for carrying out the tasks listed above. Figure 7-1 summarizes the characters with special meanings discussed in this chapter.

Character	Function
* ? [ ]	provide a shortcut for specifying file names by pattern matching
&	places commands in background mode, leaving your terminal free for other tasks
;	separates multiple commands on one command line
\	turns off the meaning of special characters, such as *, ?, [ ], &, ;, >, <, and ¦
'...'	turns off the delimiting meaning of a space and the special meaning of all special characters
"..."	turns off the delimiting meaning of a space and the special meaning of all special characters except $ and `
>	redirects output of a command into a file (replaces existing contents)
<	redirects input for a command to come from a file
>>	redirects output of a command to be added to the end of an existing file
¦	creates a pipe of the output of one command to the input of another command
`...`	allows the output of a command to be used directly as arguments on a command line
$	used with positional parameters and user-defined variables; also used as the default shell prompt symbol

Figure 7-1: Characters with Special Meanings in the Shell Language

Metacharacters

Metacharacters, a subset of the special characters, represent other characters. They are sometimes called wild cards because they are like the joker in a card game that can be used for any card. The metacharacters * (asterisk), ? (question mark), and [ ] (brackets) are discussed here.

These characters are used to match file names or parts of file names, thereby simplifying the task of specifying files or groups of files as command arguments. (The files whose names match the patterns formed from these metacharacters must already exist.) This is known as file name expansion. For example, you may want to refer to all file names containing the letter "a", all file names consisting of five letters, and so on.

The Metacharacter That Matches All Characters: the Asterisk (*)

The asterisk (*) matches any string of characters, including a null (empty) string. You can use the * to specify a full or partial file name. The * alone refers to all the file and directory names in the current directory. To see the effect of the *, try it as an argument to the **echo** command. Type

      echo *<CR>

The **echo** command displays its arguments on your screen. Notice that the system response to **echo *** is a listing of all the file names in your current directory. However, the file names are displayed horizontally rather than in vertical columns such as those produced by the **ls** command.

 The * is a powerful character. For example, if you type **rm *** you will erase all the files in your current directory. Be very careful how you use it!

For another example, say you have written several reports and have named them **report**, **report1**, **report1a**, **report1b.01**, **report25**, and **report316**. By typing **report1*** you can refer to all files that are part of report1, collectively. To find out how many reports you have written, you can use the **ls** command to list all files that begin with the string "report," as shown in the following example:

```
$ ls report*<CR>
report
report1
report1a
report1b.01
report25
report316
$
```

The * matches any characters after the string "report," including no letters at all. Notice that * matches the files in numerical and alphabetical order. A quick and easy way to print the contents of your report files in order on your screen is by typing the following command:

pr report*<CR>

Now try another exercise. Choose a character that all the file names in your current directory have in common, such as a lowercase "a". Then request a listing of those files by referring to that character. For example, if you choose a lowercase "a", type the following command line:

ls *a*<CR>

The system responds by printing the names of all the files in your current directory that contain a lowercase "a".

The * can represent characters in any part of the file name. For example, if you know that several files have their first and last letters in common, you can request a list of them on that basis. For such a request, your command line might look like this:

    ls F*E<CR>

The system response will be a list of file names that begin with F, end with E, and are in the following order:

    F123E
    FATE
    FE
    Fig3.4E

The order is determined by the ASCII sort sequence of numbers, uppercase letters, and lowercase letters.

The Metacharacter That Matches One Character: the Question Mark (?)

The question mark (**?**) matches any single character of a file name. Let's say you have written several chapters in a book that has twelve chapters, and you want a list of those you have finished through Chapter 9. Use the **ls** command with the **?** to list all chapters that begin with the string "chapter" and end with any single character, as shown below:

```
$ ls chapter?<CR>
chapter1
chapter2
chapter5
chapter9
$
```

The system responds by printing a list of all file names that match.

Although **?** matches any one character, you can use it more than once in a file name. To list chapters 10 through 12 of your book, type

   ls chapter??<CR>

Of course, if you want to list all the chapters in the current directory, use the *****:

   ls chapter*

Using the * or ? to Correct Typing Errors

Suppose you use the **mv** command to move a file, and you make an error and enter a character in the file name that is not printed on your screen. The system incorporates this non-printing character into the name of your file and subsequently requires it as part of the file name. If you do not include this character when you enter the file name on a command line, you get an error message. You can use ***** or **?** to match the file name with the non-printing character and rename it to the correct name.

Try the following example.

1.   Make a very short file called **trial**.

2.   Type

   mv trial trial<^g>1<CR>

   (Remember, to type <^**g**> you must hold down the <CTRL> key and press the g key.)

3.   Type

   ls trial1<CR>

   The system will respond with an error message:

   ```
   trial1: no such file or directory
   $
   ```

4.   Type

   ls trial?1<CR>

   The system will respond with the file name **trial1** (including the non-printing character), verifying that this file exists. Use the **?** again to correct the file name:

```
$ mv trial?1 trial1<CR>
$ ls trial1<CR>
trial1
$
```

The Metacharacters That Match One of a Set: Brackets ([ ])

Use brackets ([ ]) when you want the shell to match any one of several possible characters that may appear in one position in the file name. For example, if you include **[crf]** as part of a file name pattern, the shell will look for file names that have the letter "c", the letter "r", or the letter "f" in the specified position, as the following example shows:

```
$ ls [crf]at<CR>
cat
fat
rat
$
```

This command displays all file names that begin with the letter "c", "r", or "f" and end with the letters "at". Characters that can be grouped within brackets in this way are collectively called a "character class."

Brackets can also be used to specify a range of characters, whether numbers or letters. For example, if you specify

chapter[1-5]

the shell will match any files named **chapter1** through **chapter5**. This is an easy way to handle only a few chapters at a time.

Type the **pr** command with an argument in brackets:

    $ pr chapter[2-4]<CR>

This command will print the contents of **chapter2**, **chapter3**, and **chapter4**, in that order, on your terminal.

A character class may also specify a range of letters. If you specify **[A-Z]**, the shell will look only for uppercase letters; if **[a-z]**, only lowercase letters.

The uses of the metacharacters are summarized in Figure 7-2. Experiment with the metacharacters on the files in your current directory.

Character	Function
*	matches any string of characters, including an empty (null) string
?	matches any single character
[ ]	matches one of the sequence of characters specified within the brackets or one of the range of characters specified

Figure 7-2: Summary of Metacharacters

Special Characters

The shell language has other special characters that perform a variety of useful functions. Some of these additional special characters are discussed in this section; others are described in the next section, "Input and Output Redirection."

Running a Command in Background: the Ampersand (&)

Some shell commands take considerable time to execute. The ampersand (&) is used to execute commands in background mode, thus freeing your terminal for other tasks. The general format for running a command in background mode is

command **&**<CR>

NOTE   You should not run interactive shell commands, such as **read**, in the background.

In the example below, the shell is performing a long search in background mode. Specifically, the **grep** command is searching for the string "delinquent" in the file **accounts**.) Notice the **&** is the last character of the command line:

    $ grep delinquent accounts &<CR>
    21940
    $

When you run a command in the background, the UNIX System displays a process number; 21940 is the process number in the example. You can use this number to stop the execution of a background command. (Stopping the execution of processes is discussed in the "Executing and Terminating Processes" section.) The prompt on the last line means the terminal is free and waiting for your commands; **grep** has started running in background.

Running a command in background affects only the availability of your terminal; it does not affect the output of the command. Whether or not a command is run in background, it prints its output on your terminal screen, unless you redirect it to a file. (See "Redirecting Output to a File," later in this chapter, for details.)

If you want a command to continue running in background after you log off, you can submit it with the **nohup** command. (This command is discussed in "Using the **nohup** Command," later in this chapter.)

Executing Commands Sequentially: the Semicolon (;)

You can type two or more commands on one line as long as each pair is separated by a semicolon (;) as follows:

command1; *command2*; *command3*<**CR**>

The UNIX System executes the commands in the order that they appear in the line and prints all output on the screen. This process is called sequential execution.

Try this exercise to see how the ; works. Type

cd; pwd; ls<**CR**>

The shell executes these commands sequentially:

1. **cd** changes your location to your login directory

2. **pwd** prints the full path name of your current directory

3. **ls** lists the files in your current directory

If you do not want the system's responses to these commands to appear on your screen, refer to "Redirecting Output to a File" for instructions.

Turning Off Special Meanings: the Backslash (\)

The shell interprets the backslash (\) as an escape character that allows you to turn off any special meaning of the character immediately after it. To see how this works, try the following exercise. Create a two-line file called **trial** that contains the following text:

```
The all * game
was held in Summit.
```

Use the **grep** command to search for the asterisk in the file, as shown in the following example:

```
$ grep \* trial<CR>
The all * game
$
```

The **grep** command finds the * in the text and displays the line in which it appears. Without the \, the shell would interpret the * as a metacharacter and would match all file names in the current directory.

Turning Off Special Meanings: Quotes

Another way to escape the meaning of a special character is to use quotation marks. Single quotes ('...') turn off the special meaning of any character. Double quotes ("...") turn off the special meaning of all characters except **$** and ` (grave accent), which retain their special meanings within double quotes. An advantage of using quotes is that numerous special characters can be enclosed in the quotes; this can be more concise than using the backslash.

For example, if your file named **trial** also contained the line

```
He really wondered why? Why???
```

you could use the **grep** command to match the line with the three question marks as follows:

```
$ grep '???' trial<CR>
He really wondered why? Why???
$
```

If you had instead entered the command

```
grep ??? trial<CR>
```

the three question marks would have been used as shell metacharacters and matched all file names of length three.

Using Quotes to Turn Off the Meaning of a Space

A common use of quotes as escape characters is for turning off the special meaning of the blank space. The shell interprets a space on a command line as a delimiter between the arguments of a command. Both single and double quotes allow you to escape that meaning.

For example, to locate two or more words that appear together in text, make the words a single argument (to the **grep** command) by enclosing them in quotes. To find the two words "The all" in your file **trial**, enter the following command line:

```
$ grep 'The all' trial<CR>
The all * game
$
```

grep finds the string "The all" and prints the line that contains it. What would happen if you did not put quotes around that string?

The ability to escape the special meaning of a space is especially helpful when you are using the **banner** command. This command prints a message across a terminal screen in large, poster size letters.

To execute **banner**, specify a message consisting of one or more arguments (in this case usually words), separated on the command line by spaces. The **banner** command will use these spaces to delimit the arguments and print each argument on a separate line:

banner happy birthday to you<CR>

To print more than one argument on the same line, enclose the words you want to keep together in double quotes. For example, to send a birthday greeting to another user, type

banner happy birthday "to you"<CR>

Notice that the words "to" and "you" now appear on the same line. The space between them has lost its meaning as a delimiter.

Input and Output Redirection

In the UNIX System, some commands expect to receive their input from the keyboard (standard input), and most commands display their output at the terminal (standard output). However, the UNIX System lets you reassign the standard input and output to other files and programs. This is known as redirection. With redirection, you can tell the shell to

- take its input from a file rather than the keyboard

- send its output to file rather than the terminal

- use a program as the source of data for another program

The less than sign (<), the greater than sign (>), two greater than signs (>>), and the pipe (¦) redirect input and output.

Redirecting Input: the < Sign

To redirect input, specify a file name after a less than sign (<) on a command line:

command < *file*<**CR**>

For example, assume that you want use the **mail** command (described in Chapter 9) to send a message to another user with the login **colleague** and that you already have the message in a file named **report**. You can avoid retyping the message by specifying the file name as the source of input:

mail colleague < **report**<**CR**>

Redirecting Output to a File: the > Sign

To redirect output, specify a file name after the greater than sign (>) on a command line:

command > *file*<**CR**>

 If you redirect output to a file that already exists, the output of your command will overwrite the contents of the existing file.

Before redirecting the output of a command to a particular file, make sure that a file by that name does not already exist, unless you do not mind losing it. Because the shell does not allow you to have two files of the same name in a directory, it will overwrite the contents of the existing file with the output of your command if you redirect the output to a file with the existing file's name. The shell does not warn you about overwriting the original file.

To make sure there is no file with the name you plan to use, run the **ls** command, specifying your proposed file name as an argument. If a file with that name exists, **ls** will list it; if not, you will receive a message that the file was not found in the current directory. For example, checking for the existence of the files **temp** and **junk** would give you the following output:

```
$ ls temp<CR>
temp
$ ls junk<CR>
junk:   no such file or directory
$
```

This means you can name your new output file **junk**, but you cannot name it **temp** unless you no longer want the contents of the existing **temp** file.

Appending Output to an Existing File: the >> Symbol

To keep from destroying an existing file, you can also use the double redirection symbol (>>) as follows:

command >> *file*<**CR**>

This appends the output of a command to the end of the file *file*. If *file* does not exist, it is created when you use the >> symbol this way.

The following example shows how to append the output of the **cat** command to an existing file. First, the **cat** command is executed on both files without output redirection to show their respective contents. Then the contents of **trial2** is added after the last line of **trial1** by executing the **cat** command on **trial2** and redirecting the output to **trial1**:

```
$ cat trial1<CR>
This is the first line of trial1.
Hello.
This is the last line of trial1.
$
$ cat trial2<CR>
This is the beginning of trial2.
Hello.
This is the end of trial2.
$
$ cat trial2 >> trial1<CR>
$ cat trial1<CR>
This is the first line of trial1.
Hello.
This is the last line of trial1.
This is the beginning of trial2.
Hello.
This is the end of trial2.
$
```

Useful Applications of Output Redirection

Redirecting output is useful when you do not want it to appear on your screen immediately or when you want to save it. Output redirection is also especially useful when you run commands that perform clerical chores on text files. Two such commands are **spell** and **sort**.

The spell **Command**

The **spell** command compares every word in a file against its internal vocabulary list and prints a list of all potential misspellings on the screen. If **spell** does not have a listing for a word (such as a person's name), it will report that as a misspelling, too.

Running **spell** on a lengthy text file can take a long time and may produce a list of misspellings that is too long to fit on your screen. **spell** prints all its output at once; if it does not fit on the screen, the command scrolls it continuously off the top until it has all been displayed. A long list of misspellings will roll off your screen quickly and may be difficult to read.

You can avoid this problem by redirecting the output of **spell** to a file. In the following example, **spell** searches a file named **memo** and places a list of misspelled words in a file named **misspell**:

$ spell memo > misspell<CR>

Figure 7-3 summarizes the syntax and capabilities of the **spell** command.

Command Recap

command	options	arguments
spell	available*	*file*

Description:	**spell** collects words from a specified file or files and looks them up in a spelling list. Words that are not on the spelling list are displayed on your terminal.
Options:	**spell** has several options, including one for checking British spellings.
Remarks:	The list of misspelled words can be redirected to a file.

Table title: Command Recap — spell – finds spelling errors

*   See the *spell*(1) manual page in the *User's/System Administrator's Reference Manual* for all available options and an explanation of their capabilities.

Figure 7-3: Summary of the **spell** Command

The sort Command

The **sort** command arranges the lines of a specified file in alphabetical order (see Chapter 3 for details). Because users generally want to keep a file that has been alphabetized, output redirection greatly enhances the value of this command.

Be careful to choose a new name for the file that will receive the output of the **sort** command (the alphabetized list). When **sort** is executed, the shell first empties the file that will accept the redirected output. Then it performs the sort and places the output in the blank file. If you type

    sort list > list<CR>

the shell will empty **list** and then sort nothing into **list**.

Combining Background Mode and Output Redirection

Running a command in background does not affect the command's output; unless it is redirected, output is always printed on the terminal screen. If you are using your terminal to perform other tasks while a command runs in background, you will be interrupted when the command displays its output on your screen. However, if you redirect that output to a file, you can work undisturbed.

For example, in the "Special Characters" section you learned how to execute the **grep** command in background with **&**. Now suppose you want to find occurrences of the word test in a file named **schedule**. Run the **grep** command in background, and redirect its output to a file called **testfile**:

> **$ grep test schedule > testfile &<CR>**

You can then use your terminal for other work and examine **testfile** when you have finished it.

Redirecting Output to a Command: the Pipe (|)

The | character is called a pipe. Pipes are powerful tools that allow you to take the output of one command and use it as input for another command without creating temporary files. A multiple command line created in this way is called a pipeline.

The general format for a pipeline is

> *command1* | *command2* | *command3*...<**CR**>

The output of *command1* is used as the input of *command2*. The output of *command2* is then used as the input for *command3*.

To understand the efficiency and power of a pipeline, consider the contrast between two methods that achieve the same results:

- ■ To use the input/output redirection method, first run one command and redirect its output to a temporary file. Then, run a second command that takes the contents of the temporary file as its input. Finally, remove the temporary file after the second command has finished running.

- ■ To use the pipeline method, run one command and pipe its output directly into a second command.

For example, say you want to mail a happy birthday message in a banner to the owner of the login **david**. Doing this without a pipeline is a three-step procedure. You must perform the following steps:

1. Enter the **banner** command and redirect its output to a temporary file:

   banner happy birthday > message.tmp

2. Enter the **mail** command using **message.tmp** as its input:

   mail david < message.tmp

3. Remove the temporary file:

   rm message.tmp

However, by using a pipeline you can do this in one step:

banner happy birthday ¦ mail david<CR>

A Pipeline Using the cut and date Commands

The **cut** and **date** commands provide a good example of how pipelines can increase the versatility of individual commands. The **cut** command allows you to extract part of each line in a file. It looks for characters in a specified part of the line and prints them. To specify a position in a line, use the **-c** option and identify the part of the file you want by the numbers of the spaces it occupies on the line, counting from the left-hand margin.

For example, say you want to display only the dates from a file called **birthdays**. The file contains the following list:

```
Anne      12/26
Klaus     7/4
Mary      10/18
Peter     11/9
Nandy     4/23
Sam       8/12
```

The birthdays appear between the ninth and thirteenth spaces on each line.
To display them, type

cut –c9-13 birthdays<CR>

The output is shown below:

```
12/26
7/4
10/18
11/9
4/23
8/12
```

Figure 7-4 summarizes the syntax and capabilities of the **cut** command.

<table>
<tr><td colspan="3" align="center">**Command Recap**</td></tr>
<tr><td colspan="3" align="center">**cut** – cuts out selected fields from each line of a file</td></tr>
<tr><td align="center">*command*</td><td align="center">*options*</td><td align="center">*arguments*</td></tr>
<tr><td align="center">**cut**</td><td align="center">*–clist*
–flist [**-d**]</td><td align="center">*file*</td></tr>
</table>

Description:	**cut** extracts columns from a table or fields from each line of a file.
Options:	**–c** lists the number of character positions from the left. A range of numbers such as characters 1–9 can be specified by **–c1–9**.
	–f lists the field number from the left separated by a delimiter described by **–d**.
	-d gives the field delimiter for **–f**. The default is a space. If the delimiter is a colon, this would be specified by **–d :** .
Remarks:	If you find the **cut** command useful, you may also want to use the **paste** command and the **split** command.

Figure 7-4: Summary of the **cut** Command

The **cut** command is usually executed on a file. However, piping makes it possible to run this command on the output of other commands, too. This is useful if you want only part of the information generated by another command. For example, you may want to have the time printed. The **date** command prints the day of the week, date, and time as follows:

> $ **date**<CR>
> Sat Dec 27 13:12:32 EST 1986

Notice that the time is given between the twelfth and nineteenth spaces of the line. You can display the time (without the date) by piping the output of **date** into **cut**, specifying spaces **12–19** with the **–c** option. Your command line and its output will look like this:

> $ **date | cut –c12-19**<CR>
> 13:14:56

Figure 7-5 summarizes the syntax and capabilities of the **date** command.

Command Recap
date - displays the date and time

command	*options*	*arguments*
date	+%m%d%y* +%H%%M%S	available*

Description:	**date** displays the current date and time on your terminal.
Options:	+% followed by **m** (for month), **d** (for day), **y** (for year), **H** (for hour), **M** (for month), and **S** (for second) will echo these back to your terminal. You can add explanations such as:
	date '+%H:%M is the time'
Remarks:	If you are working on a small computer system of which you are both a user and the system administrator, you may be allowed to set the date and time using optional arguments to the **date** command. Check your reference manual for details. When working in a multiuser environment, the arguments are available only to the system administrator.

Figure 7-5: Summary of the **date** Command

---

* See the *date*(1) manual page in the *User's/System Administrator's Reference Manual* for all available options and an explanation of their capabilities.

Substituting Output for an Argument

The output of any command may be captured and used as arguments on a command line. This is done by enclosing the command in grave accents ('...') and placing it on the command line in the position where the output should be treated as arguments. This is known as command substitution.

For example, you can substitute the output of the **date** and **cut** pipeline command used previously for the argument in a **banner** printout by typing the following command line:

$ **banner** `date | cut –c12–19`<CR>

Notice the results: the system prints a banner with the current time.

The "Shell Programming" section in this chapter shows you how you can also use the output of a command line as the value of a variable.

Executing and Terminating Processes

This section discusses the following topics:

■ how to schedule commands to run at a later time by using the **batch** or **at** command

■ how to obtain the status of active processes

■ how to terminate active processes

■ how to keep background processes running after you have logged off

Running Commands at a Later Time With the batch and at Commands

The **batch** and **at** commands allow you to specify a command or sequence of commands to be run at a later time. With the **batch** command, the system determines when the commands run; with the **at** command, you determine when the commands run. Both commands expect input from standard input (the terminal); the list of commands entered as input from the terminal must be ended by pressing <ˆ**d**> (CTRL-d).

The **batch** command is useful if you are running a process or shell program that uses a large amount of system time. The **batch** command submits a batch job (containing the commands to be executed) to the system. The job is put in a queue and runs when the system load falls to an acceptable level. This frees the system to respond rapidly to other input and is a courtesy to other users.

The general format for **batch** is

>**batch**<**CR**>
>*first command*<**CR**>
>
>   .
>
>   .
>
>   .
>
>*last command*<**CR**>
><ˆ**d**>

If there is only one command to be run with **batch**, you can enter it as follows:

>**batch** *command_line*<**CR**>
><ˆ**d**>

The next example uses **batch** to execute the **grep** command at a convenient time. Here **grep** searches all files in the current directory for `dollar` and redirects the output to the file **dol.file**:

```
$ batch grep dollar * > dol-file<CR>
<ˆd>
job 155223141.b at Sun Dec 7 11:14:54 1986
$
```

After you submit a job with **batch**, the system responds with a job number, date, and time. This job number is not the same as the process number that the system generates when you run a command in the background.

Figure 7-6 summarizes the syntax and capabilities of the **batch** Command.

<table>
<tr><td colspan="3" align="center">Command Recap
batch – executes commands at a later time</td></tr>
<tr><td align="center">command</td><td align="center">options</td><td align="center">input</td></tr>
<tr><td align="center">batch</td><td align="center">none</td><td align="center">command_lines</td></tr>
<tr><td>Description:</td><td colspan="2">batch submits a batch job, which is placed in a queue and executed when the load on the system falls to an acceptable level.</td></tr>
<tr><td>Remarks:</td><td colspan="2">The list of commands must end with a <ˆd> (CTRL-d).</td></tr>
</table>

Figure 7-6: Summary of the **batch** Command

The **at** command allows you to specify an exact time to execute the commands. The general format for the **at** command is

> **at** *time*<**CR**>
> *first command*<**CR**>
> .
> .
> .
> *last command*<**CR**>
> <ˆ**d**>

The *time* argument consists of the time of day and, if the date is not today, the date.

The following example shows how to use the **at** command to mail a happy birthday banner to login **emily** on her birthday:

```
$ at 8:15am Feb 27<CR>
banner happy birthday ¦ mail emily<CR>
<ˆd>
job 453400603.a at Thurs Feb 27 08:15:00 1986
$
```

Notice that the **at** command, like the **batch** command, responds with the job number, date, and time.

If you decide you do not want to execute the commands currently waiting in a **batch** or **at** job queue, you can erase those jobs by using the **–r** option of the **at** command with the job number. The general format is

> **at –r** *jobnumber*<**CR**>

Try erasing the previous **at** job for the happy birthday banner. Type

> **at –r 453400603.a**<**CR**>

If you have forgotten the job number, the **at –l** command will give you a list of the current jobs in the **batch** or **at** queue, as the following screen shows:

```
$ at -l<CR>
user = mylogin 168302040.a at Sat Nov 29 13:00:00 1986
user = mylogin 453400603.a at Fri Feb 27 08:15:00 1987
$ "
```

Notice that the system displays the job number and the time the job will run.

Using the **at** command, mail yourself the file **memo** at noon to tell you it is lunch time. (You must redirect the file into **mail** unless you use the "here document," described in the "Shell Programming" section.) Then try the **at** command with the **-l** option:

```
$ at 12:00pm<CR>
mail mylogin < memo<CR>
<^d>
job 263131754.a at Jun 30 12:00:00 1986
$
$ at -l<CR>
user = mylogin 263131754.a at Jun 30 12:00:00 1986
$
```

Figure 7-7 summarizes the syntax and capabilities of the **at** command.

Command Recap

at – executes commands at a specified time

command	options	arguments
at	–r –l	*time (date)* *jobnumber*

Description: **at** executes commands at the time specified. You can use between one and four digits, and am or pm to show the time. To specify the date, give a month name followed by the number for the day. You do not need to enter a date if you want your job to run the same day. See the *at*(1) manual page in the *User's/System Administrator's Reference Manual* for other default times.

Options: The **–r** option with the job number removes previously scheduled jobs.

The **–l** option (no arguments) reports the job number and status of all scheduled **at** and **batch** jobs.

Remarks: Examples of how to specify times and dates with the **at** command are as follows:

at 08:15am Feb 27
at 5:14pm Sept 24

Figure 7-7: Summary of the **at** Command

Obtaining the Status of Running Processes

The **ps** command gives you the status of all the processes you are currently running. For example, you can use the **ps** command to show the status of all processes that you run in the background using **&** (described in the earlier section "Special Characters").

The next section, "Terminating Active Processes," discusses how you can use the PID (process identification) number to stop a command from executing. A PID number is a number from 1 to 30,000 that the UNIX System assigns to each active process.

In the following example, **grep** is run in the background, and then the **ps** command is issued. The system responds with the process identification (PID) and the terminal identification (TTY) numbers. It also gives the cumulative execution time for each process (TIME) and the name of the command that is being executed (COMMAND):

```
$ grep word * > temp &<CR>
28223
$
$ ps<CR>
PID             TTY   TIME COMMAND
28124           tty10 0:00   sh
28223           tty10 0:04   grep
28224           tty10 0:04   ps
$
```

Notice that the system reports a PID number for the **grep** command, as well as for the other processes that are running: the **ps** command itself and the **sh** (shell) command that runs while you are logged in. The shell program **sh** interprets the shell commands and is discussed in Chapters 1 and 4.

Figure 7-8 summarizes the syntax and capabilities of the **ps** command.

Command Recap		
ps – reports process status		
command	*options*	*arguments*
ps	several*	none
Description:	**ps** displays information about active processes.	
Options:	**ps** has several options. If none are specified, **ps** displays the status of all active processes you are running.	
Remarks:	**ps** gives you the PID (process identification). This is needed to stop the process from executing, or kill the process.	

*   See the *ps*(1) manual page in the *User's/System Administrator's Reference Manual* for all available options and an explanation of their capabilities.

Figure 7-8: Summary of the **ps** Command

Terminating Active Processes

The **kill** command is used to terminate active shell processes. The general format for the **kill** command is

    kill *PID*<**CR**>

You can use the **kill** command to terminate processes that are running in the background. Note that you cannot terminate background processes by pressing the <BREAK> or <DELETE> key.

The following example shows how you can terminate the **grep** command that you started executing in the background in the previous example:

> $ **kill 28223**<CR>
> 28223 Terminated
> $

Notice the system responds with a message and a $ prompt, showing that the process has been killed. If the system cannot find the PID number you specify, it responds with an error message:

> kill:28223:No such process

Figure 7-11 summarizes the syntax and capabilities of the **kill** command.

Command Recap		
kill – terminates a process		
command	*options*	*arguments*
kill	available*	*job number* or *PID*
Description:	**kill** terminates the process specified by the PID number.	

*   See the *kill*(1) manual page in the *User's/System Administrator's Reference Manual* for all
available options and an explanation of their capabilities.

Figure 7-9: Summary of the **kill** Command

Using the nohup **Command**

All processes are killed when you log off. If you want a background process to continue running after you log off, you must use the **nohup** command to submit that background command.

To execute the **nohup** command, follow this format:

    nohup *command* **&<CR>**

Notice that you place the **nohup** command before the command you intend to run as a background process.

For example, say you want the **grep** command to search all the files in the current directory for the string **word** and redirect the output to a file called **word.list**, and you wish to log off immediately afterward. Type the command line as follows:

    nohup grep word * > word.list & <CR>

You can terminate the **nohup** command by using the **kill** command.
Figure 7-10 summarizes the syntax and capabilities of the **nohup** command.

Command Recap
nohup – prevents interruption of command execution by hang ups

command	*options*	*arguments*
nohup	*none*	*command line*

Description:	**nohup** executes a command line, even if you hang up or quit the system.

Figure 7-10: Summary of the **nohup** Command

Now that you have mastered these basic shell commands and notations, use them in your shell programs! The exercises that follow will help you practice using shell command language. The answers to the exercises are at the end of the chapter.

Command Language Exercises

1-1. What happens if you use an * (asterisk) at the beginning of a file name? Try to list some of the files in a directory using the * with the last letter of one of your file names. What happens?

1-2. Try the following two commands; enter them as follows:

       cat[0-9]*<CR>
       echo *<CR>

1-3. Is it acceptable to use a **?** at the beginning or in the middle of a file name generation? Try it.

1-4. Do you have any files that begin with a number? Can you list them without listing the other files in your directory? Can you list only those files that begin with a lowercase letter between a and m? (Hint: use a range of numbers or letters in **[ ]**).

1-5. Is it acceptable to place a command in background mode on a line that is executing several other commands sequentially? Try it. What happens? (Hint: use **;** and **&**.) Can the command in background mode be placed in any position on the command line? Try placing it in various positions. Experiment with each new character that you learn to see the full power of the character.

1-6. Redirect the output of **pwd** and **ls** into a file by using the following command line:

       cd; pwd; ls; ed trial<CR>

Remember, if you want to redirect both commands to the same file, you have to use the >> (append) sign for the second redirection. If you do not, you will wipe out the information from the **pwd** command.

1-7. Instead of cutting the time out of the **date** response, try redirecting only the date, without the time, into **banner**. What is the only part you need to change in the time command line?

       banner 'date ¦ cut –c12-19'<CR>

Shell Programming

You can use the shell to create programs, or customize commands. Such programs are also called "shell procedures." This section tells you how to create and execute shell programs using commands, variables, positional parameters, return codes, and basic programming control structures.

The examples of shell programs in this section are shown two ways. First, the **cat** command is used in a screen to display the contents of a file containing a shell program:

```
$ cat testfile<CR>
first command
      .
      .
      .
last command
$
```

Second, the results of executing the shell program appear after a command line:

```
$ testfile<CR>
program_output
$
```

You should be familiar with an editor before you try to create shell programs. Refer to the tutorials in Chapter 5 (for the **ed** editor) and Chapter 6 (for the **vi** editor).

Shell Programs

Creating a Simple Shell Program

We will begin by creating a simple shell program that will do the following tasks, in order:

- print the current directory

- list the contents of that directory

- display this message on your terminal: "This is the end of the shell program."

Create a file called **dl** (short for directory list) using the editor of your choice, and enter the following:

> **pwd<CR>**
> **ls<CR>**
> **echo This is the end of the shell program.<CR>**

Now write and quit the file. You have just created a shell program! You can **cat** the file to display its contents, as the following screen shows:

```
$ cat dl<CR>
pwd
ls
echo This is the end of the shell program.
$
```

Executing a Shell Program

One way to execute a shell program is to use the **sh** command. Type

sh dl<CR>

The **dl** command is executed by **sh**, and the path name of the current directory is printed first, the list of files in the current directory is printed next, and the comment This is the end of the shell program is printed last. The **sh** command provides a good way to test your shell program to make sure it works.

If **dl** is a useful command, you can use the **chmod** command to make it an executable file; then you can type **dl** by itself to execute the command it contains. The following example shows how to use the **chmod** command to make a file executable and then run the **ls –l** command to verify the changes you have made in the permissions:

```
$ chmod u+x dl<CR>
$ ls -l<CR>
total 2
-rw-------          1  login  login    3661  Nov  2    10:28 mbox
-rwx------          1  login  login      48  Nov 15    10:50 dl
$
```

Notice that **chmod** turns on execute (**+x**) permission for the user (**u**). Now **dl** is an executable program. Try to execute it. Type

dl<CR>

You get the same results as before, when you entered **sh dl** to execute it. For further details about the **chmod** command, see Chapter 3.

Creating a bin **Directory for Executable Files**

To make your shell programs accessible from all your directories, you can make a **bin** directory from your login directory and move the shell files to **bin**.

You must also set your shell variable **PATH** to include your **bin** directory:

> PATH=$PATH:$HOME/bin

See "Variables" and "Using Shell Variables" in this chapter for more information about **PATH**.

The following example will remind you of which commands are necessary. In this example, **dl** is in the login directory. Type these command lines:

> cd<CR>
> mkdir bin<CR>
> mv dl bin/dl<CR>

Move to the **bin** directory and type the **ls –l** command. Does **dl** still have execute permission?

Now move to a directory other than the login directory, and type the following command:

> dl<CR>

What happened?

Figure 7-11 summarizes your new shell program, **dl**.

Shell Program Recap	
dl – displays the directory path and directory contents (user defined)	
command	*arguments*
dl	none
Description:	**dl** displays the output of the shell command **pwd** and **ls**.

Figure 7-11: Summary of the **dl** Shell Program

It is possible to give the **bin** directory another name; if you do so, you need to change your shell variable **PATH** again.

Warnings about Naming Shell Programs

You can give your shell program any appropriate file name. However, you should not give your program the same name as a system command. If you do, the system will execute your command instead of the system command. For example, if you had named your **dl** program **mv**, each time you tried to move a file, the system would have executed your directory list program instead of **mv**.

Another problem can occur if you name the **dl** file **ls**, and then try to execute the file. You would create an infinite loop, since your program executes the **ls** command. After some time, the system would give you the following error message:

```
Too many processes, cannot fork
```

What happened? You typed in your new command, **ls**. The shell read and executed the **pwd** command. Then it read the **ls** command in your program and tried to execute your **ls** command. This formed an infinite loop.

UNIX System designers wisely set a limit on how many times an infinite loop can execute. One way to keep this from happening is to give the path name for the system's **ls** command, **/bin/ls**, when you write your own shell program.

The following **ls** shell program would work:

```
$ cat ls<CR>
pwd
/bin/ls
echo This is the end of the shell program
```

If you name your command **ls**, then you can only execute the system **ls** command by using its full path name, **/bin/ls**.

Variables

Variables are the basic data objects shell programs manipulate, other than files. Here we discuss three types of variables and how you can use them:

- positional parameters
- special parameters
- named variables

Positional Parameters

A positional parameter is a variable within a shell program whose value is set from an argument specified on the command line invoking the program. Positional parameters are numbered and are referred to with a preceding **$**: **$1**, **$2**, **$3**, and so on.

A shell program may reference up to nine positional parameters. If a shell program is invoked on a command line that appears like this:

shell.prog pp1 pp2 pp3 pp4 pp5 pp6 pp7 pp8 pp9<CR>

then positional parameter **$1** within the program will be assigned the value **pp1**, positional parameter **$2** within the program will be assigned the value **pp2**, and so on, when the shell program is invoked.

Create a file called **pp** (short for positional parameters) to practice positional parameter substitution. Then enter the **echo** commands shown in the following screen. Enter the command lines so that running the **cat** command on your completed file will produce the following output:

```
$ cat pp<CR>
echo  The first positional parameter is: $1<CR>
echo  The second positional parameter is: $2<CR>
echo  The third positional parameter is: $3<CR>
echo  The fourth positional parameter is: $4<CR>
$
```

If you execute this shell program with the arguments **one**, **two**, **three**, and **four**, you will obtain the following results (first you must make the shell program **pp** executable using the **chmod** command):

```
$ chmod u+x pp<CR>
$
$ pp one two three four<CR>
The first positional parameter is: one
The second positional parameter is: two
The third positional parameter is: three
The fourth positional parameter is: four
$
```

The following screen shows the shell program **bbday**, which mails a greeting to the login entered in the command line:

```
$ cat bbday<CR>
banner happy birthday | mail $1
```

Try sending yourself a birthday greeting. If your login name is **sue**, your command line will be

bbday sue<CR>

Figure 7-12 summarizes the syntax and capabilities of the **bbday** shell program.

Shell Program Recap	
bbday – mails a banner birthday greeting (user defined)	
command	*arguments*
bbday	*login*
Description:	**bbday** mails the message happy birthday, in poster-sized letters, to the specified login.

Figure 7-12: Summary of the **bbday** Command

The **who** command lists all users currently logged in on the system. How can you make a simple shell program, called **whoson**, that will tell you if the owner of a particular login is currently working on the system?

Type the following command line into a file called **whoson**:

who | grep $1<CR>

The **who** command lists all current system users, and **grep** searches the output of the **who** command for a line containing the string contained as a value in the positional parameter $1.

Now try using your login as the argument for the new program **whoson**. For example, say your login is **sue**. When you issue the **whoson** command, the shell program substitutes **sue** for the parameter $1 in your program and executes as if it were

who | grep sue <CR>

The output is shown on the following screen:

```
$ whoson sue<CR>
sue     tty26       Jan 24 13:35
$
```

If the owner of the specified login is not currently working on the system, **grep** fails and **whoson** prints no output.

Figure 7-13 summarizes the syntax and capabilities of the **whoson** command.

Shell Program Recap		
whoson – displays login information if the user is logged in (user defined)		
command	*arguments*	
whoson	*login*	
Description:	If a user is on the system, **whoson** displays the user's login, the TTY number, and the time and date the user logged in.	

Figure 7-13: Summary of the **whoson** Command

The shell allows a command line to contains 128 arguments. However, a shell program is restricted to referencing nine positional parameters, **$1** through **$9**, at a given time. This restriction can be worked around using the **shift** command, described in the manual *Shell Commands and Programming*.

The special parameter **$***, described in the next section, can also be used to access the values of all command line arguments.

Special Parameters

$# This parameter, when referenced within a shell program, contains the number of arguments with which the shell program was invoked. Its value can be used anywhere within the shell program.

Enter the command line shown in the following screen in an executable shell program called **get.num**. Then run the **cat** command on the file:

```
$ cat get.num<CR>
echo The number of arguments is: $#
$
```

The program simply displays the number of arguments with which it is invoked. For example:

```
$ get.num test out this program<CR>
The number of arguments is: 4
$
```

Figure 7-14 summarizes the **get.num** shell program.

Shell Program Recap	
get.num – counts and displays the number of arguments (user defined)	
command	*arguments*
get.num	*(character_string)*
Description:	**get.num** counts the number of arguments given to the command and then displays the total.
Remarks:	This command demonstrates the special parameter **$#**.

Figure 7-14: Summary of the **get.num** Shell Program

$* This special parameter, when referenced within a shell program, contains a string with all the arguments with which the shell program was invoked, starting with the first. You are not restricted to nine parameters as with the positional parameters **$1** through **$9**..

You can write a simple shell program to demonstrate **$***. Create a shell program called **show.param** that will echo all the parameters. Use the command line shown in the following completed file:

```
$ cat show.param<CR>
echo The parameters for this command are: $*
$
```

show.param will echo all the arguments you give to the command. Make
show.param executable and try it out using these parameters:

Hello. How are you?

```
$ show.param Hello. How are you?<CR>
The parameters for this command are: Hello.  How are you?
$
```

Notice that **show.param** echoes Hello. How are you? Now try
show.param using more than nine arguments:

```
$ show.param one two 3 4 5 six 7 8 9 10 11<CR>
The parameters for this command are: one two 3 4 5 six 7 8 9 10 11
$
```

Once again, **show.param** echoes all the arguments you give. The **$*** parameter can be useful if you use file name expansion to specify arguments to the shell command.

Use the file name expansion feature with your **show.param** command. For example, say you have several files in your directory named for chapters of a book: **chap1**, **chap2**, and so on, through **chap7**. **show.param** will print a list of all those files:

```
$ show.param chap?<CR>
The parameters for this command are: chap1 chap2 chap3
chap4 chap5 chap6 chap7
$
```

Figure 7-15 summarizes the **show.param** shell program.

Shell Program Recap
show.param – displays all positional parameters (user defined)

command	*arguments*
show.param	(any positional parameters)

Description:	**show.param** displays all the parameters.
Remarks:	If the parameters are file name generations, the command will display each of those file names.

Figure 7-15: Summary of the **show.param** Shell Program

Named Variables

Another form of a variable that you can use within a shell program is a named variable. You assign values to named variables. The format for assigning a value to a named variable is

named_variable=value<**CR**>

Notice that there are no spaces on either side of the = sign.

In the following example, **var1** is a named variable, and **myname** is the value or character string assigned to that variable:

var1=myname<**CR**>

A **$** is used in front of a variable name in a shell program to reference the value of that variable. Using the example above, the reference **$var1** tells the shell to substitute the value **myname** (assigned to **var1**) for any occurrence of the character string **$var1**.

The first character of a variable name must be a letter or an underscore. The rest of the name can be composed of letters, underscores, and digits. As in shell program file names, it is not advisable to use a shell command name as a variable name. Also, the shell has reserved some variable names you should not use for your variables. A brief explanation of these reserved shell variable names follows:

- **CDPATH** defines the search path for the **cd** command.

- **HOME** is the default variable for the **cd** command (home directory).

- **IFS** defines the internal field separators (normally the space, the tab, and the carriage return).

- **LOGNAME** is your login name.

- **MAIL** names the file that contains your electronic mail.

- **PATH** determines the search path used by the shell to find commands.

- **PS1** defines the primary prompt (the default is **$**).

- **PS2** defines the secondary prompt (the default is >).

- **TERM** identifies your terminal type. It is important to set this variable if you are editing with **vi**.

- **TERMINFO** identifies the directory to be searched for information about your terminal, for example, its screen size.

- **TZ** defines the time zone (default is **EST5EDT**).

Many of these variables are explained in "Modifying Your Login Environment" later in this chapter. You can also read more about them on the **sh**(1) manual page in the *User's/System Administrator's Reference Manual*.

You can see the value of these variables in your shell in two ways. First, you can type

 echo $*variable_name*

The system displays the value of *variable_name*. Second, you can use the **env** command to print out the value of all defined variables in the shell. To do this, type **env** on a line by itself; the system displays a list of the variable names and values.

Assigning a Value to a Variable

If you edit with **vi**, you know you can set the **TERM** variable by entering the following command line:

    TERM=*terminal_name*<**CR**>

This is the simplest way to assign a value to a variable.

There are several other ways to do this:

- Use the **read** command to assign input to the variable.

- Redirect the output of a command into a variable by using command substitution with grave accents (' ... ').

- Assign a positional parameter to the variable.

The following sections discuss each of these methods in detail.

Using the read Command

The **read** command used within a shell program allows you to prompt the user of the program for the values of variables. The general format for the **read** command is

    read *variable*<**CR**>

The values assigned by **read** to *variable* will be substituted for $*variable* wherever it is used in the program. If a program executes the **echo** command just before the **read** command, the program can display directions such as Type in
.... The **read** command will wait until you type a character string, followed by a <RETURN> key, and then make that string the value of the variable.

The following example shows how to write a simple shell program called **num.please** to keep track of your telephone numbers. This program uses the following commands for the purposes specified:

echo	prompts you for a person's last name
read	assigns the input value to the variable **name**
grep	searches the file **list** for this variable

Your finished program should look like the one displayed here:

```
$ cat num.please<CR>
echo Type in the last name:
read name
grep $name list
$
```

Create a file called **list** that contains several last names and phone numbers. Then try running **num.please**.

The next example is a program called **mknum**, which creates a list. **mknum** includes the following commands for the purposes shown:

echo	prompts for a person's name
read	assigns the person's name to the variable **name**
grep	asks for the person's number
read	assigns the telephone number to the variable *num*
echo	adds the values of the variables *name* and *num* to the **list**

If you want the output of the **echo** command to be added to the end of **list**, you must use ≫ to redirect it. If you use >, **list** will contain only the last phone number you added.

Running the **cat** command on **mknum** displays the program's contents. When your program looks like this, you will be ready to make it executable with the **chmod** command:

```
$ cat mknum<CR>
echo Type in name
read name
echo Type in number
read num
echo $name $num >> list
$ chmod u+x mknum<CR>
$
```

Try out the new programs for your phone list. In the next example, **mknum** creates a new listing for Mr. Niceguy. Then **num.please** gives you Mr. Niceguy's phone number:

```
$ mknum<CR>
Type in the name
Mr. Niceguy<CR>
Type in the number
668-0007<CR>
$ num.please<CR>
Type in last name
Niceguy<CR>
Mr. Niceguy 668-0007
$
```

Notice that the variable **name** accepts both **Mr.** and **Niceguy** as the value.

Figures 7-16 and 7-17 summarize the **mknum** and **num.please** shell programs, respectively.

Shell Program Recap	
mknum – places a name and number in a phone list	
command	*arguments*
mknum	(interactive)
Description:	**mknum** asks you for the name and number of a person and adds that name and number to your phone list.
Remarks:	This is an interactive command.

Figure 7-16: Summary of the **mknum** Shell Program

Shell Program Recap	
num.please – displays a person's name and number	
command	*arguments*
num.please	(interactive)
Description:	**num.please** asks you for a person's last name and then displays the person's full name and telephone number.
Remarks:	This is an interactive command.

Figure 7-17: Summary of the **num.please** Shell Program

Substituting Command Output for the Value of a Variable

You can substitute a command's output for the value of a variable by using *command substitution*. This has the following format:

   variable = `command`<**CR**>

The output from *command* becomes the value of *variable*.

In one of the previous examples on piping, the **date** command was piped into the **cut** command to get the correct time. That command line was the following:

   date ¦ cut –c12-19<**CR**>

You can put this in a simple shell program called **t** that will give you the time.

```
$ cat t<CR>
time=`date | cut -c12-19`
echo The time is: $time
$
```

Remember there are no spaces on either side of the equal sign. Make the file executable, and you will have a program that gives you the time:

```
$ chmod u+x t<CR>
$ t<CR>
The time is: 10:36
$
```

Figure 7-18 summarizes your **t** program.

Shell Program Recap t – displays the correct time	
command	*arguments*
t	none
Description:	t gives you the correct time in hours and minutes.

Figure 7-18: Summary of the **t** Shell Program

Assigning Values with Positional Parameters

You can assign a positional parameter to a named parameter by using the following format:

   var1=$1<CR>

The next example is a simple program called **simp.p** that assigns a positional parameter to a variable. The following screen shows the commands in **simp.p**:

```
$ cat simp.p<CR>
var1=$1
echo $var1
$
```

Of course, you can also assign the output of a command that uses positional parameters to a variable, as follows:

person=`who ¦ grep $1`<CR>

In the next example, the program **log.time** keeps track of your **whoson** program results. The output of **whoson** is assigned to the variable **person** and added to the file **login.file** with the **echo** command. The last **echo** displays the value of **$person**, which is the same as the output from the **whoson** command:

```
$ cat log.time<CR>
person=`who | grep $1`
echo $person >> login.file
echo $person
$
```

The system response to **log.time** is shown in the following screen:

```
$ log.time maryann<CR>
maryann     tty61          Apr 11 10:26
$
```

Figure 7-19 summarizes the **log.time** shell program.

Shell Program Recap	
log.time – logs and displays a specified login (user defined)	
command	*arguments*
log.time	*login*
Description:	If the specified login is currently on the system, **log.time** places the line of information from the **who** command into the file **login.file** and then displays that line of information on your terminal.

Figure 7-19: Summary of the **log.time** Shell Program

Shell Programming Constructs

The shell programming language has several constructs that give added flexibility to your programs:

■ Comments allow you to document a program's function.

■ The "here document" allows you to include within the shell program itself lines to be redirected to be the input to some command in the shell program.

■ The **exit** command allows you to terminate a program at a point other than the end of the program and use return codes.

■ The looping constructs, **for** and **while**, allow a program to iterate through groups of commands in a loop.

■ The conditional control commands, **if** and **case**, execute a group of commands only if a particular set of conditions is met.

■ The **break** command allows a program to exit unconditionally from a loop.

Comments

You can place comments in a shell program in two ways. All text on a line following a # (pound) sign is ignored by the shell. The # sign can be at the beginning of a line, in which case the comment uses the entire line, or it can occur after a command, in which case the command is executed but the remainder of the line is ignored. The end of a line always ends a comment. The general format for a comment line is

   #*comment*<**CR**>

For example, a program that contains the following lines will ignore them when it is executed:

```
# This program sends a generic birthday greeting.<CR>
# This program needs a login as<CR>
# the positional parameter.<CR>
```

Comments are useful for documenting a program's function and should be included in any program you write.

The here Document

A "here document" allows you to place into a shell program lines that are redirected to be the input of a command in that program. It is a way to provide input to a command in a shell program without needing to use a separate file. The notation consists of the redirection symbol ≪ and a delimiter that specifies the beginning and end of the lines of input. The delimiter can be one character or a string of characters; the **!** is often used.

Figure 7-20 shows the general format for a here document.

```
command <<delimiter<CR>
...input lines...<CR>
delimiter<CR>
```

Figure 7-20: Format of a Here Document

In the next example, the program **gbday** uses a here document to send a generic birthday greeting by redirecting lines of input into the **mail** command:

```
$ cat gbday<CR>
mail $1 <<!
Best wishes to you on your birthday.
!
$
```

When you use this command, you must specify the recipient's login as the argument to the command. The input included with the use of the here document is

```
Best wishes to you on your birthday
```

For example, to send this greeting to the owner of login **mary**, type

```
$ gbday mary<CR>
```

Login **mary** will receive your greeting the next time she reads her mail messages:

```
$ mail<CR>
From mylogin Wed May 14 14:31 CDT 1986
Best wishes to you on your birthday
$
```

Figure 7-21 summarizes the format and capabilities of the **gbday** command.

Shell Program Recap	
gbday - sends a generic birthday greeting (user defined)	
command	*arguments*
gbday	*login*
Description:	**gbday** sends a generic birthday greeting to the owner of the login specified in the argument.

Figure 7-21: Summary of the **gbday** Command

Using ed **in a Shell Program**

The here document offers a convenient and useful way to use **ed** in a shell script. For example, suppose you want to make a shell program that will enter the **ed** editor, make a global substitution to a file, write the file, and then quit **ed**. The following screen shows the contents of a program called **ch.text** that does these tasks:

```
$ cat ch.text<CR>
echo Type in the file name.
read file1
echo Type in the exact text to be changed.
read old_text
echo Type in the exact new text to replace the above.
read new_text
ed - $file1 <<!
g/$old_text/s//$new_text/g
w
q
!
$
```

Notice the – (minus) option to the **ed** command. This option prevents the character count from being displayed on the screen. Also notice the format of the **ed** command for global substitution:

g/_old_text_**/s//**_new_text_**/g**<**CR**>

The program uses three variables: _file1_, _old_text_, and _new_text_. When the program is run, it uses the **read** command to obtain the values of these variables. The variables provide the following information:

file   the name of the file to be edited

_old_text_ the exact text to be changed

_new_text_ the new text

Once the variables are entered in the program, the here document redirects the global substitution, the write command, and the quit command into the **ed** command. Try the new **ch.text** command. The following screen shows sample responses to the program prompts:

```
$ ch.text<CR>
Type in the filename.
memo<CR>
Type in the exact text to be changed.
Dear John:<CR>
Type in the exact new text to replace the above.
To whom it may concern:<CR>
$ cat memo<CR>
To whom it may concern:
$
```

Notice that by running the **cat** command on the changed file, you could examine the results of the global substitution.

Figure 7-22 summarizes the format and capabilities of the **ch.text** command.

Shell Program Recap		
ch.text – changes text in a file		
command	*arguments*	
ch.text	(interactive)	
Description:	**ch.text** replaces text in a file with new text.	
Remarks:	This shell program is interactive. It will prompt you to type in the arguments.	

Figure 7-22: Summary of the **ch.text** Command

If you want to become more familiar with **ed**, see Chapter 5, "Line Editor Tutorial **(ed)**." The stream editor, **sed**, can also be used in shell programming.

Return Codes

Most shell commands issue return codes that indicate whether the command executed properly. By convention, if the value returned is 0 (zero), then the command executed properly; any other value indicates that it did not. The return code is not printed automatically but is available as the value of the shell special parameter **$?**.

Checking Return Codes

After executing a command interactively, you can see its return code by typing

>   **echo $?**

Consider the following example:

```
$ cat hi
This is file hi.
$ echo $?
0
$ cat hello
cat: cannot open hello
$ echo $?
2
$
```

In the first case, the file **hi** exists in your directory and has read permission for you. The **cat** command behaves as expected and displays the contents of the file. It exits with a return code of 0, which you can see using the parameter **$?**. In the second case, the file either does not exist or does not have read permission for you. The **cat** command prints a diagnostic message and exits with a return code of 2.

Using Return Codes With the exit **Command**

A shell program normally terminates when the last command in the file is executed. However, you can use the **exit** command to terminate a program at some other point. Perhaps more importantly, you can also use the **exit** command to issue return codes for a shell program. For more information about **exit**, see the *exit*(2) manual page in the *Programmer's Reference Manual.*

Looping

In the previous examples in this chapter, the commands in shell programs have been executed in sequence. The **for** and **while** looping constructs allow a program to execute a command or sequence of commands several times.

The for **Loop**

The **for** loop executes a sequence of commands once for each member of a list. Figure 7-23 shows its format.

```
for variable<CR>
        in a_list_of_values<CR>
do<CR>
        command 1<CR>
        command 2<CR>
             .
             .
             .
        last command<CR>
done<CR>
```

Figure 7-23: Format of the **for** Loop Construct

For each iteration of the loop, the next member of the list is assigned to the variable given in the **for** clause. References to that variable can be made anywhere in the commands within the **do** clause.

It is easier to read a shell program if the looping constructs are visually clear. Since the shell ignores spaces at the beginning of lines, each section of commands can be indented as it was in the above format. Also, if you indent each command section, you can easily check to make sure each **do** has a corresponding **done** at the end of the loop.

The variable can be any name you choose. For example, if you call it **var**, then the values given in the list after the keyword **in** will be assigned in turn to **var**; references within the command list to **$var** will make the value available. If the **in** clause is omitted, the values for **var** will be the complete set of arguments given to the command and available in the special parameter **$***. The command list between the keywords **do** and **done** will be executed once for each value.

When the commands have been executed for the last value in the list, the program will execute the next line below **done**. If there is no line, the program will end.

The easiest way to understand a shell programming construct is to try an example. Create a program that will move files to another directory Include the following commands for the purposes shown:

echo	Prompts the user for a path name to the new directory.
read	Assigns the path name to the variable **path**.
for *variable*	Calls the variable **file**; it can be referenced as **$file** in the command sequence.
in *list_of_values*	Supplies a list of values. If the **in** clause is omitted, the list of values is assumed to be **$*** (all the arguments entered on the command line).
do *command_sequence*	Provides a command sequence. The construct for this program will be:

```
do
    mv $file $path/$file<CR>
done
```

The following screen shows the text for the shell program **mv.file**:

```
$ cat mv.file<CR>
echo Please type in the directory path
read path
for file
    in memo1 memo2 memo3
do
    mv $file $path/$file
done
$
```

In this program, the values for the variable **file** are already in the program. To change the files each time the program is invoked, assign the values using positional parameters or the **read** command. When positional parameters are used, the **in** keyword is not needed, as the next screen shows:

```
$ cat mv.file<CR>
echo type in the directory path
read path
for file
do
    mv $file $path/$file
done
$
```

You can move several files at once with this command by specifying a list of file names as arguments to the command. (This can be done most easily using the file name expansion mechanism described earlier).

Figure 7-24 summarizes the **mv.file** shell program.

Shell Program Recap	
mv.file – moves files to another directory (user defined)	
command	*arguments*
mv.file	*filenames* (interactive)
Description:	**mv.file** moves files to a new directory.
Remarks:	This program requires file names to be given as arguments. The program prompts for the path to the new directory.

Figure 7-24: Summary of **mv.file** Shell Program

The while **Loop**

Another loop construct, the **while** loop, uses two groups of commands. It will continue executing the sequence of commands in the second group, the **do...done** list, as long as the final command in the first group, the **while** list, returns a status of true (meaning the command can be executed).

The general format of the **while** loop is shown in Figure 7-25.

```
while<CR>
     command 1<CR>
          .
          .
          .
     last command<CR>
do<CR>
     command 1<CR>
          .
          .
          .
     last command<CR>
done<CR>
```

Figure 7-25: Format of the **while** Loop Construct

For example, a program called **enter.name** uses a **while** loop to enter a list of names into a file. The program consists of the following command lines:

```
$ cat enter.name<CR>
while
    read x
do
    echo $x>>xfile
done
$
```

With some added refinements, the program becomes

```
$ cat enter.name<CR>
echo Please type in each person's name and then a <CR>
echo Please end the list of names with a <^d>
while read x
do
    echo $x>>xfile
done
echo xfile contains the following names:
cat xfile
$
```

Notice that after the loop is completed, the program executes the commands below the **done**.

You used special characters in the first two **echo** command lines, so you must use quotes to turn off the special meaning. The next screen shows the results of **enter.name**:

```
$ enter.name<CR>
Please type in each person's name and then a <CR>
Please end the list of names with a <^d>
Mary Lou<CR>
Janice<CR>
<^d>
xfile contains the following names:
Mary Lou
Janice
$
```

Notice that after the loop completes, the program prints all the names contained in **xfile**.

The Shell's Garbage Can: /dev/null

The file system has a file called **/dev/null**, where you can have the shell deposit any unwanted output.

Try out **/dev/null** by destroying the results of the **who** command. First, type in the **who** command. The response tells you who is on the system. Now, try the **who** command, but redirect the output into **/dev/null**:

who > /dev/null<CR>

Notice that the system responded with a prompt. The output from the **who** command was placed in **/dev/null** and was effectively discarded.

Conditional Constructs

if...then

The **if** command tells the shell program to execute the **then** sequence of commands only if the final command in the **if** command list is successful. The **if** construct ends with the keyword **fi**.

The general format for the **if** construct is shown in Figure 7-26.

```
    if<CR>
          command1<CR>
                  .
                  .
                  .
          last command<CR>
     then<CR>
          command1<CR>
                  .
                  .
                  .
          last command<CR>
    fi<CR>
```

Figure 7-26: Format of the **if...then** Conditional Construct

For example, a shell program called **search** demonstrates the use of the **if...then** construct. **search** uses the **grep** command to search for a word in a file. If **grep** is successful, the program will echo that the word is found in the file. Copy the **search** program (shown on the following screen) and try it yourself:

```
$ cat search<CR>
echo Type in the word and the file name.
read word file
if grep $word $file
   then echo $word is in $file
fi
$
```

Notice that the **read** command assigns values to two variables. The first characters you type, up until a space, are assigned to **word**. The rest of the characters, including embedded spaces, are assigned to **file**.

A problem with this program is the unwanted display of output from the **grep** command. If you want to dispose of the system response to the **grep** command in your program, use the file **/dev/null**, changing the **if** command line to the following:

> **if grep $**word** $**file** > /dev/null<CR>**

Now execute your **search** program. It should respond only with the message specified after the **echo** command.

if...then...else

The **if...then** construction can also issue an alternate set of commands with **else** when the **if** command sequence is false. It has the format shown in Figure 7-27.

```
if<CR>
      command1<CR>
               .
               .
               .
      last command<CR>
then<CR>
      command1<CR>
               .
               .
               .
      last command<CR>
else<CR>
      command1<CR>
               .
               .
               .
      last command<CR>
fi<CR>
```

Figure 7-27: Format of the **if...then...else** Conditional Construct

You can now improve your **search** command so that it will tell you when it cannot find a word, as well as when it can. The following screen shows how your improved program will look:

```
$ cat search<CR>
echo Type in the word and the file name.
read word file
if
   grep $word $file >/dev/null
then
   echo $word is in $file
else
   echo $word is NOT in $file
fi
$
```

Figure 7-28 summarizes your enhanced **search** program.

Shell Program Recap	
search - tells you if a word is in a file (user defined)	
command	*arguments*
search	interactive
Description:	**search** reports whether a word is in a file.
Remarks:	The command prompts you for the arguments (the word and the file).

Figure 7-28: Summary of the **search** Shell Program

The test **Command for Loops**

The **test** command, which checks to see if certain conditions are true, is a useful command for conditional constructs. If the condition is true, the loop will continue. If the condition is false, the loop will end, and the next command will be executed. Some of the useful options for the **test** command are

test –r *file*<**CR**>	true if the file exists and is readable
test –w *file*<**CR**>	true if the file exists and has write permission
test –x *file*<**CR**>	true if the file exists and is executable
test –s *file*<**CR**>	true if the file exists and has at least one character
test *var1* **–eq** *var2*<**CR**>	true if *var1* equals *var2*
test *var1* **–ne** *var2*<**CR**>	true if *var1* does not equal *var2*

You may want to create a shell program to move all the executable files in the current directory to your **bin** directory. You can use the **test –x** command to select the executable files. Review the example of the **for** construct that occurs in the **mv.file** program, shown in the following screen:

```
$ cat mv.file<CR>
echo type in the directory path
read path
for file
do
  mv $file $path/$file
done
$
```

Create a program called **mv.ex** that includes an **if test –x** statement in the **do...done** loop to move executable files only. Your program will be as follows:

```
$ cat mv.ex<CR>
echo type in the directory path
read path
for file
  do
    if test -x $file
       then
          mv $file $path/$file
    fi
  done
$
```

The directory path will be the path from the current directory to the **bin** directory. However, if you use the value for the shell variable **HOME**, you will not need to type in the path each time. **$HOME** gives the path to the login directory. **$HOME/bin** gives the path to your **bin**.

In the following example, **mv.ex** does not prompt you to type in the directory name, and therefore, does not read the **path** variable:

```
$ cat mv.ex<CR>
for file
  do
    if test -x $file
       then
          mv $file $HOME/bin/$file
    fi
  done
$
```

Test the command by using all the files in the current directory and specifying the ***** metacharacter as the command argument. The command lines shown in the following example execute the command from the current directory, and then change to **bin** and list the files in that directory. All executable files should be there:

```
$ mv.ex *<CR>
$ cd; cd bin; ls<CR>
list_of_executable_files
$
```

Figure 7-29 summarizes the format and capabilities of the **mv.ex** shell program.

Shell Program Recap	
mv.ex – moves all executable files in the current directory to the **bin** directory	
command	*arguments*
mv.ex	* (all file names)
Description:	**mv.ex** moves all files in the current directory with execute permission to the **bin** directory.
Remarks:	All executable files in the **bin** directory (or any directory shown by the **PATH** variable) can be executed from any directory.

Figure 7-29: Summary of the **mv.ex** Shell Program

───

case..esac

The **case...esac** construction has a multiple choice format that allows you to choose one of several patterns and then execute a list of commands for that pattern. The pattern statements must begin with the keyword **in**, and a **)** must be placed after the last character of each pattern. The command sequence for each pattern is ended with **;;**. The **case** construction must end with **esac** (the letters of the word case reversed).

The general format for the **case** construction is shown in Figure 7-30.

```
case  word<CR>
in<CR>
    pattern1)<CR>
        command  line  1<CR>
                .
                .
                .
        last  command  line<CR>
    ;;<CR>
    pattern2)<CR>
        command  line  1<CR>
                .
                .
                .
        last  command  line<CR>
    ;;<CR>
    pattern3)<CR>
        command  line  1<CR>
                .
                .
                .
        last  command  line<CR>
    ;;<CR>
    *)<CR>
        command  1<CR>
                .
                .
                .
        last  command<CR>
    ;;<CR>
esac<CR>
```

Figure 7-30: The **case...esac** Conditional Construct

The **case** construction tries to match *word* following the word **case** with *pattern* in the first pattern section. If there is a match, the program executes the command lines after the first pattern and up to the corresponding *;;* .

If the first pattern is not matched, the program proceeds to the second pattern. Once a pattern is matched, the program does not try to match any more of the patterns but goes to the command following **esac**.

The * used as a pattern matches *word*, allowing you to give a set of commands to be executed if no other pattern matches. To do this, it must be placed as the last possible pattern in the **case** construct so that the other patterns are checked first. This provides a useful way to detect erroneous or unexpected input.

The patterns that can be specified in the *pattern* part of each section may use the metacharacters *, ?, and [ ] as described earlier in this chapter for the shell's file name expansion capability. This provides useful flexibility.

The **set.term** program contains a good example of the **case...esac** construction. This program sets the shell variable TERM according to the type of terminal you are using. It uses the following command line:

TERM=*terminal_name*<**CR**>

(For an explanation of the commands used, see the **vi** tutorial in Chapter 6.) In the following example, the terminal is a Teletype 4420, Teletype 5410, or Teletype 5420.

set.term first checks to see whether the value of **term** is 4420. If it is, the program makes T4 the value of **TERM** and terminates. If it the value of **term** is not 4420, the program checks for other values: 5410 and 5420. It executes the commands under the first pattern that it finds and then goes to the first command after the **esac** command.

The pattern * , meaning everything else, is included at the end of the terminal patterns. It will warn that you do not have a pattern for the terminal specified and will allow you to exit the **case** construct:

```
$ cat set.term<CR>
echo If you have a TTY 4420 type in 4420
echo If you have a TTY 5410 type in 5410
echo If you have a TTY 5420 type in 5420
read term
case $term
        in
            4420)
                TERM=T4
            ;;
            5410)
                TERM=T5
            ;;
            5420)
                TERM=T7
            ;;
            *)
            echo not a correct terminal type
            ;;
esac
export TERM
echo end of program
$
```

Notice the use of the **export** command. You use **export** to make a variable available within your environment and to other shell procedures. What would happen if you placed the * pattern first? The **set.term** program would never assign a value to TERM since it would always match the first pattern *, which means everything.

Figure 7-31 summarizes the format and capabilities of the **set.term** shell program.

Shell Program Recap
set.term - assigns a value to TERM (user defined)

command	*arguments*
set.term	interactive

Description:	**set.term** assigns a value to the shell variable TERM and then exports that value to other shell procedures.
Remarks:	This command asks for a specific terminal code to be used as a pattern for the **case** construction.

Figure 7-31: Summary of the **set.term** Shell Program

Unconditional Control Statements: the break and continue Commands

The **break** command unconditionally stops the execution of any loop in which it is encountered and goes to the next command after the **done, fi**, or **esac** statement. If there are no commands after that statement, the program ends.

In the example for **set.term**, you could have used the **break** command instead of **echo** to leave the program, as the next example shows:

```
$ cat set.term<CR>
echo If you have a TTY 4420 type in 4420
echo If you have a TTY 5410 type in 5410
echo If you have a TTY 5420 type in 5420
read term
case $term
        in
            4420)
            TERM=T4
        ;;
        5410)
            TERM=T5
        ;;
        5420)
            TERM=T7
        ;;
        *)
            break
        ;;
esac
export TERM
echo end of program
$
```

The **continue** command causes the program to go immediately to the next iteration of a **do** or **for** loop without executing the remaining commands in the loop.

Debugging Programs

At times you may need to debug a program. Debugging is the process of finding and correcting errors. The **sh** command has two options (listed below) that can help you debug a program:

sh –v *shellprogramname*   prints the shell input lines as they are read by the system

sh –x *shellprogramname*   prints commands and their arguments as they are executed

To try out these two options, create a shell program that has an error in it. For example, create a file called **bug** that contains the following list of commands:

```
$ cat bug<CR>
today=`date`
echo enter person
read person
mail $1
$person
When you log off come into my office please.
$today.
MLH
$
```

Notice that **today** equals the output of the **date** command, which must be enclosed in grave accents for command substitution to occur.

The mail message sent to Tom ($1) at login **tommy** ($2) should read as the following screen shows:

```
$ mail<CR>
From mlh  Thu  Apr 10  11:36  CST  1984
Tom
When you log off come into my office please.
Thu  Apr 10  11:36:32  CST  1986
MLH
?
```

If you try to execute **bug**, you will have to press the <BREAK> or <DELETE> key to end the program.

To debug this program, try executing **bug** using **sh –v**. This will print the lines of the file as they are read by the system, as shown below:

```
$ sh –v bug tom<CR>
today=`date`
echo enter person
enter person
read person
tommy
mail $1
```

Notice that the output stops on the **mail** command since there is a problem with **mail**. You must use the here document to redirect input into **mail**.

Before you fix the **bug** program, try executing it with **sh –x**, which prints the commands and their arguments as they are read by the system:

```
$ sh -x bug tom tommy<CR>
+date
today=Thu Apr 10 11:07:23 CST 1986
+ echo enter person
enter person
+ read person
tommy
+ mail tom
$
```

Once again, the program stops at the **mail** command. Notice that the substitutions for the variables have been made and are displayed.

The corrected **bug** program is as follows:

```
$ cat bug<CR>
today=`date`
echo enter person
read person
mail $1 <<!
$person
When you log off come into my office please.
$today
MLH
!
$
```

The **tee** command is a helpful command for debugging pipelines. While simply passing its standard input to its standard output, it also saves a copy of its input into the file whose name is given as an argument.

The general format of the **tee** command is

command1 ¦ **tee** *saverfile* ¦ *command2*<**CR**

saverfile is the file that saves the output of *command1* for you to study.

For example, say you want to check on the output of the **grep** command in the following command line:

who ¦ grep $1 ¦ cut –c1-9<CR>

You can use **tee** to copy the output of **grep** into a file called *check* without disturbing the rest of the pipeline:

who ¦ grep $1 ¦ tee check ¦ cut –c1-9<CR>

The file **check** contains a copy of the **grep** output, as shown in the following screen:

```
$ who ¦ grep mlhmo ¦ tee check ¦ cut –c1-9<CR>
mlhmo
$ cat check<CR>
mlhmo    tty61    Apr  10    11:30
$
```

Modifying Your Login Environment

The UNIX System lets you modify your login environment in several ways. One modification that users commonly want to make is to change the default values of the erase (#) and line kill (@) characters.

When you log in, the shell first examines a file in your login directory named **.profile** (pronounced "dot profile"). This file contains commands that control your shell environment.

Because **.profile** is a file, it can be edited and changed to suit your needs. On some systems you can edit this file yourself, while on others, the system administrator does this for you. To see whether you have a **.profile** in your home directory, type

ls –al $HOME

If you can edit the file yourself, you may want to be cautious the first few times. Before making any changes to your **.profile**, make a copy of it in another file called **safe.profile**. Type

cp .profile safe.profile<CR>

You can add commands to your **.profile** just as you add commands to any other shell program. You can also set some terminal options with the **stty** command and set some shell variables.

Adding Commands to Your .profile

Practice adding commands to your **.profile**. Edit the file and add the following **echo** command to the last line of the file:

echo Good Morning! I am ready to work for you.

Write and quit the editor.

Whenever you make changes to your **.profile** and you want to initiate them in the current work session, you can execute the commands in **.profile** directly using the **.** (dot) shell command. The shell will re-initialize your environment by reading the commands in your **.profile**. Try this now. Type

. .profile<CR>

The system should respond with the following:

```
Good Morning! I am ready to work for you.
$
```

Setting Terminal Options

The **stty** command can make your shell environment more convenient. There are three options you can use with **stty**: **–tabs**, **erase** < **ˆh**>, and **echoe**. The following list describes these options:

stty –tabs   This option preserves tabs when you are printing. It expands the tab setting to eight spaces, which is the default. The number of spaces for each tab can be changed. (See *stty*(1) in the *User's/System Administrator's Reference Manual* for details.)

stty erase < **ˆh**> This option allows you to use the erase key on your keyboard to erase a letter, instead of the default character #. Usually the <BACKSPACE> key is the erase key.

stty echoe   If you have a terminal with a screen, this option erases characters from the screen as you erase them with the <BACKSPACE> key.

If you want to use these options for the **stty** command, you can create those command lines in your **.profile** just as you would create them in a shell program. If you use the **tail** command, which displays the last few lines of a file, you can see the results of adding those four command lines to your **.profile**:

```
$ tail -4 .profile<CR>
echo Good Morning! I am ready to work for you
stty -tabs
stty erase <^h>
stty echoe
$
```

Figure 7-32 summarizes the format and capabilities of the **tail** command.

Command Recap
tail – displays the last portion of a file

command	options	arguments
tail	*-n*	*filename*

Description: **tail** displays the last lines of a file.

Options: Use *-n* to specify the number of lines *n* (the default is ten lines). You can specify a number of blocks (*-n***b**) or characters (*-n***c**) instead of lines.

Figure 7-32: Summary of the **tail** Command

Creating an rje **Directory**

We have often talked about sharing useful programs with other users in this chapter. Similarly, these users may have programs or other files that they want to share with you. So that these users can send you the files easily, you should create an **rje** (remote job entry) directory:

> **mkdir rje**
> **chmod go+w rje**

Notice that you have to change the permissions of the directory using **chmod**. When you have an **rje** directory with the correct permissions, other users can send you files using the **uucp** command. See the *uucp*(1) manual page in the *User's/System Administrator's Reference Manual* for details.

Using Shell Variables

Several of the variables reserved by the shell are used in your **.profile**. You can display the current value for any shell variable by entering the following command:

> **echo $***variable_name*

Four of the most basic shell variables are discussed next.

> **HOME**
>
> > This variable gives the path name of your login directory. Use the **cd** command to go to your login directory and type
>
> > **pwd<CR>**

What was the system response? Now type

> **echo $HOME<CR>**

Was the system response the same as the response to **pwd**?

$HOME is the default argument for the **cd** command. If you do not specify a directory, **cd** will move you to **$HOME**.

PATH

This variable gives the search path for finding and executing commands. To see the current values for your **PATH** variable type

echo $PATH<CR>

The system will respond with your current PATH value:

```
$ echo $PATH<CR>
:/mylogin/bin:/bin:/usr/bin:/usr/lib
$
```

The colon (:) is a delimiter between path names in the string assigned to the $PATH variable. When nothing is specified before a : , then the current directory is understood. Notice how, in the last example, the system looks for commands in the current directory first, then in **/mylogin/bin/**, then in **/bin**, then in **/usr/bin**, and finally in **/usr/lib**.

If you are working on a project with several other people, you may want to set up a group **bin**, a directory of special shell programs used only by your project members. The path might be named **/project1/bin**. Edit your **.profile**, and add **:/project1/bin** to the end of your **PATH**, as in the next example:

PATH=":/mylogin/bin:/bin:/usr/lib:/project1/bin"<CR>

TERM

This variable tells the shell what kind of terminal you are using. To assign a value to it, you must execute the following three commands in this order:

TERM=*terminal_name*<**CR**>
export TERM<**CR**>
tput init

The first two lines, used together, are necessary to tell the computer what type of terminal you are using. The last line, containing the **tput** command, tells the terminal that the computer is expecting to communicate with the type of terminal specified in the TERM variable. Therefore, this command must always be entered after the variable has been exported.

If you do not want to specify the **TERM** variable each time you log in, add these three command lines to your **.profile**; they will be executed automatically whenever you log in. To determine what terminal name to assign to the TERM variable, see the instructions in Appendix F, "Setting Up the Terminal." This appendix also contains details about the **tput** command.

If you log in on more than one type of terminal, it would also be useful to have your **set.term** command in your **.profile**.

PS1

This variable sets the primary shell prompt string (the default is the $ sign). You can change your prompt by changing the **PS1** variable in your **.profile**.

Try the following example. Note that to use a multi-word prompt, you must enclose the phrase in quotes. Type the following variable assignment in your **.profile**:

PS1="Your command is my wish"<CR>

Now execute your **.profile** (with the . command) and watch for your new prompt sign:

$ . .profile<CR>
Your command is my wish

The mundane $ sign is gone forever, or at least until you delete the **PS1** variable from your **.profile**.

Shell Programming Exercises

2-1.   Create a shell program called **time** from the following command line:

   banner `date | cut -c12-19`<CR>

2-2.   Write a shell program that will give only the date in a banner display. Be careful not to give your program the same name as a UNIX System command.

2-3.   Write a shell program that will send a note to several people on your system.

2-4.   Redirect the **date** command without the time into a file.

2-5.   Echo the phrase "Dear colleague" in the same file that contains the date command without erasing the date.

2-6.   Using the above exercises, write a shell program that will send a memo to the same people you sent a note to in Exercise 2-3. Include the following in your memo:

   the current date and the words "Dear colleague" at the top of the memo

   the body of the memo (stored in an existing file)

   the closing statement

2-7.   How can you read variables into the **mv.file** program?

2-8.   Use a **for** loop to move a list of files in the current directory to another directory. How can you move all your files to another directory?

2-9.   How can you change the program **search** so that it searches through
        several files?

        Hint:

        **for file
        in $***

2-10.   Set the **stty** options for your environment.

2-11.   Change your prompt to the word Hello.

2-12.   Check the settings of the variables **$HOME**, **$TERM**, and **$PATH** in
        your environment.

Answers To Exercises

Command Language Exercises

1-1.   The * at the beginning of a file name refers to all files that end in that file name, including that file name.

```
$ ls *t<CR>
cat
123t
new.t
t
$
```

1-2.   The command **cat [0-9]*** will produce the following output:

```
1memo
100data
9
05name
```

The command **echo *** will produce a list of all the files in the current directory.

1-3.   You can place **?** in any position in a file name.

1-4.   The command **ls [0-9]*** will list only those files that start with a number.

The command **ls [a-m]*** will list only those files that start with the letters "a" through "m".

1-5. If you placed the sequential command line in the background mode, the immediate system response was the PID number for the job.

No, the **&** (ampersand) must be placed at the end of the command line.

1-6. The command line would be

cd; pwd > junk; ls >> junk; ed trial<CR>

1-7. Change the **-c** option of the command line to read

banner `date | cut -c1-10`<CR>

Shell Programming Exercises

2-1.

```
$ cat time<CR>
banner `date | cut -c12-19`
$
$ chmod u+x time<CR>
$ time<CR>
(banner display of the time 10:26)
$
```

2-2.

```
$ cat mydate<CR>
banner `date | cut -c1-10`
$
```

2-3.

```
$ cat tofriends<CR>
echo Type in the name of the file containing the note.
read note
mail janice marylou bryan < $note
$
```

Or, if you used parameters for the logins, instead of the logins themselves, your program may have looked like this:

```
$ cat tofriends<CR>
echo Type in the name of the file containing the note.
read note
mail $* < $note
$
```

2-4.   date | cut -c1-10 > file1<CR>

2-5.   echo Dear colleague >> file1<CR>

2-6.

```
$ cat send.memo<CR>
date | cut -c1-10 > memo1
echo Dear colleague >> memo1
cat memo >> memo1
echo A memo from M. L. Kelly >> memo1
mail janice marylou bryan < memo1
$
```

2-7.

```
$ cat mv.file<CR>
echo type in the directory path
read path
echo type in file names, end with <^d>
  while
  read file
    do
      mv $file $path/$file
    done
echo all done
$
```

2-8.

```
$ cat mv.file<CR>
echo Please type in directory path
read path
for file in $*
  do
    mv $file $path/$file
  done
$
```

The command line for moving all files in the current directory is

$ **mv.file *<CR>**

2-9.   See hint given with exercise 2-9.

```
$ cat search<CR>
for file
  in $*
  do
    if grep $word $file >/dev/null
    then echo $word is in $file
    else echo $word is NOT in $file
    fi
  done
$
```

2-10.   Add the following lines to your **.profile**:

stty –tabs<CR>
stty erase <^h><CR>
stty echoe<CR>

2-11.   Add the following command lines to your **.profile**:

PS1=Hello<CR>
export PS1

2-12.   To check the values of these variables in your home environment, type

☐   **$ echo $HOME<CR>**

☐   **$ echo $TERM<CR>**

☐   **$ echo $PATH<CR>**

8 C-shell Tutorial

Introduction

The C-shell program, **csh**, is a command language interpreter for UNIX System users. The C-shell, like the standard UNIX shell, **sh**, is an interface between you and the UNIX commands and programs. It translates command lines typed at a terminal into corresponding system actions; gives you access to information, such as your login name, home directory, and mailbox; and lets you construct shell procedures for automating system tasks.

This chapter explains how to use the C-shell. It also explains the syntax and function of C-shell commands and features, and shows you how to use these features to create shell procedures. For a complete description of the C-shell and its capabilities, see *csh*(1) in the *User's/System Administrator's Reference Manual.*

Starting the C-shell

You can invoke the C-shell from another shell by typing the following command:

csh

You can also tell the system to start the C-shell for you when you log in. If you have given the C-shell as your login shell in your **/etc/passwd** file entry, the system automatically starts the C-shell each time you log in.

After the system starts the C-shell, the shell searches your home directory for two command files, **.cshrc** and **.login**. The **.cshrc** file contains the commands you wish to execute each time you start a C-shell, and the **.login** file contains the commands you wish to execute after logging in to the system. The following example shows the contents of a typical **.login** file:

```
set ignoreeof
set mail=(/usr/spool/mail/bill)
set time=15
set history=10
mail
```

Once the shell finds these two files, it executes the commands contained in them and then displays the C-shell prompt.

When the C-shell finishes processing the **.login** file, it prompts you with the system default prompt:

%

You can now enter commands. To log out, type the following command:

logout

The C-shell then executes commands from the **.logout** file if it exists in your home directory. After that, the C-shell terminates and UNIX logs you out of the system. If there is no **.logout** file in your home directory, the C-shell logs you off the system. For more information about the **.logout** file, see *csh*(1) in the *User's/System Administrator's Reference Manual*.

Setting C-Shell Variables

The C-shell maintains a set of variables for customizing your working environment. You can type the **set** command with no arguments to display the values of all variables currently defined in the C-shell.

One of the most important variables is *path*. This variable contains a list of directory names. When you type a command name at your terminal, the C-shell examines each named directory in turn until it finds an executable file whose name corresponds to the name you typed.

You can use the **set** command to assign values to these variables. The **set** command has several forms, the most useful of which is

set name = value

The following example shows some shell variables and their typical default values:

> **home** **/usr/bill**
> **path**   **(. /bin /usr/bin)**

In this example, the *path* variable sets the command search path to begin with the current directory, indicated by period (.), then **/bin**, and finally **/usr/bin**. Standard UNIX commands reside in **/bin** and **/usr/bin**. For this reason, it is convenient to place these directories in your search path. To do this, add the following line to your **.cshrc** file:

set path=(. /bin /usr/bin)

Sometimes a number of locally developed programs reside in the directory **/usr/local** . If you want all C-shells that you invoke to have access to these new programs, add the new directory to the *path* variable in your **.cshrc** file, as shown in the following example:

    set path=(. /bin /usr/bin /usr/local)

After you change one of the variables in your **.cshrc** file, you must log out and log in again. This causes the C-shell to read the **.cshrc** file again. When you log in, the C-shell examines each directory that you insert into your path and determines which commands are contained there, except for the current directory which the C-shell treats specially. This means that if commands are added to a directory in your search path after you have started the C-shell, they will not necessarily be found. If you wish to use a command that has been added after you have logged in, you can give the following command to the C-shell:

    rehash

The **rehash** command causes the shell to recompute its internal table of command locations so that it will find the newly added command. Since the C-shell has to look in the current directory for each command anyway, placing it at the end of the path specification usually works best and reduces overhead.

Other useful built-in C-shell variables are *home*, which shows your home directory, and *ignoreeof*, which can be set in your **.login** file to tell the C-shell not to exit when it receives an end-of-file (CTRL-D) from a terminal. The *ignoreeof* variable is one of several "toggle" shell variables. You do not need to specify exact values for these variables; you need only specify whether the variable is "on" or "off." For example, to set *ignoreeof*, type the following command line:

    set ignoreeof

To turn **ignoreeof** off, type the following command line:

    unset ignoreeof

Another useful built-in C-shell variable is *noclobber*. Use this variable to prevent inadvertently overwriting the contents of an existing file. The arrow symbols, < and >, redirect the standard output of a command, just as they do in the regular shell and overwrite the previous contents of the named file. This means you could accidentally overwrite a valuable file if you try to redirect output to an existing file. To tell the C-shell not to automatically overwrite files when instructed to with the arrow symbol, place the following command in your **.login** file:

> **set noclobber**

Suppose you have a file called **now** in your current directory. Because you have set the *noclobber* option, typing the following command will give you an error message stating that the file already exists:

> **date > now**

If you really want to overwrite the contents of **now**, you can type the following command:

> **date >! now**

The ">!" is a special syntax that indicates overwriting or "clobbering" the file is okay. The space between the exclamation point (!) and the word "now" is critical here, since "!now" would be an invocation of the history feature and would have a totally different effect. The C-shell history feature is described in more detail in the following section.

Using the C-shell History List

The C-shell can be instructed to maintain a history list containing the text of previous commands. The **history** feature can be used to repeat previous commands or to correct minor typing mistakes in commands. You can use metacharacter notations that represent previously used shell commands, or words from commands, to form new commands.

This section teaches you how to use the **history** list. In this tutorial, you will use the **history** feature to create a sample file, compile the file, execute the file, and perform various other commands on the file.

To learn how to use the **history** feature, follow these steps:

1. Create a file named **bug.c** using a text editor. Type the following five lines into the file:

    main()

    {

          printf("hello);

    }

    This file is a very simple C program that has a few intentional bugs in it.

2. Display the **bug.c** file you just created by typing the following command line:

    cat bug.c

3. Compile the **bug.c** file by typing the following:

    cc !$

    This command line makes use of the **history** feature invoked by the exclamation mark (!). The dollar sign ($) means to use the last argument to the previous command as the argument to this command. Your terminal displays

    ```
    cc bug.c
    bug.c
    bug.c(4) : warning : newline in string constant
    bug.c(5) : syntax error: '}'
    ```

    The C-shell echoes the command as if it had been typed without the use of the **history** feature and then executes the command. The compilation yields error diagnostics, so now you must edit the **bug.c** file.

4. Using an editor, edit line 4 of the **bug.c** file to look like the following line:

    ```
    printf("hello");
    ```

5. Recompile the **bug.c** file by typing

    !c

    This command line invokes the **history** feature and repeats the last executed command that started with a "c". Your terminal displays

    ```
    cc bug.c
    bug.c
    ```

    If other commands beginning with the letter "c" executed recently, you could have typed "!c:p" as the command line. This command line would print the last command starting with "c" without executing it, so that you can check to see whether you really want to execute the implied command.

6. Run the default output file **a.out** that resulted from compiling the **bug.c** file. To do this, type

    a.out

    The system displays the following message:

    ```
    hello%
    ```

    Note that the C-shell prompt (%) appears on the same line as the output of **a.out**. Suppose this is a bug that you must correct.

7. Edit line 4 of the **bug.c** file to look like

    printf("hello\n");

    This will cause the C-shell prompt to be placed on a new line when the output file is run again.

8. Recompile the **bug.c** file by typing

    !c –o bug

    This command line invokes the **history** feature, executes the last command beginning with "c", and uses the **–o** option to tell the compiler to name the output file **bug** rather than the default **a.out**. The system displays the following message:

    ```
    cc bug.c —o bug
    bug.c
    ```

9. Compare the sizes of the binary program images of the **a.out** and **bug** files by typing the following:

    size a.out bug

    The output of this command will be similar to the following example:

    ```
    a.out: 4226 + 490 + 1064 = 5780 = 0x1694
    bug: 4226 + 492 + 1064 = 5782 = 0x1696
    ```

10. List the output files **a.out** and **bug** in long format by typing

    ls –l !*

    This command line invokes the **ls** command, invokes the **history** feature, and uses all the arguments specified in the previous command as arguments to this command. The output of this command line will be similar to the following:

    ```
    ls —l a.out bug
    -rwxr-xr-x    1 bill  group   3932    Dec 19 09:41   a.out
    -rwxr-xr-x    1 bill  group   3932    Dec 19 09:41   bug
    ```

11. Run the output file **bug** to verify that its output is correct. To do this, type

    bug

    The system displays the following message:

    ```
    hello
    ```

12. Print a program listing of the file **bug.c** by typing

    pr bug.c ¦ lpt

    This command line invokes the **pr** command and pipes its output to a lineprinter (**lpt**). The lineprinter notation **lpt** should really be **lpr**. We introduced an intentional spelling error in this command line so you could learn about more helpful **history** features. The system displays the following message:

    ```
    lpt: Command not found.
    ```

13. Correct the spelling error in the **pr** command line and request a printout of the program listing again. To do this, type

    ˆlptˆlpr

    This command line replaces the string after the first caret with the string after the second caret in the previous command and repeats the previous command with the new string. Your terminal displays

    ```
    pr bug.c | lpr
    ```

There are also other features available for repeating commands. The **history** command prints out a numbered list of previous commands. You can then refer to these commands by number. You can also refer to a previous command by searching for a string that appeared in it. For a complete description of these features, see *csh*(**1**) in the *User's/System Administrator's Reference Manual*.

Using Aliases

The C-shell has an **alias** command that transforms commands immediately after they are input. You can use this feature to simplify the commands you type, to supply default arguments to commands, or to perform transformations to commands and their arguments. The **alias** command is similar to a macro facility. You can assign a short abbreviation (an alias) to represent a longer command. You can define an alias for your current login session, or you can set it up to be valid for each login session.

For example, if it is inconvenient to type "history" each time you wish to see the last several commands the system executed, you can create an alias for the **history** command. To set up an alias that will be in effect for every subsequent login session, place the following C-shell command in your **.cshrc** file:

alias h history

After you have placed this command in your **.cshrc** file, tell the C-shell to read the **.cshrc** file again. You can do this either by logging out and logging in again, or by using the C-shell **source** command. From now on, you can view the contents of your history list by typing the following command alias:

h

To set up the "h" alias for your current login session only, type the following line at the shell prompt:

alias h history

To view the list of your current aliases, use the **alias** command with no arguments.

Suppose you want the **ls** command to always show file sizes so that you do not have to remember to use the **-s** option. To set up this shortcut for this login session only, type the following **alias** command line at the prompt:

alias ls ls –s

Or, if you wish to preserve the original function of the **ls** command (long listing without file sizes), you can create a new "command," **dir**, that performs the same function as the **ls -s** command. To do this, type the following line at the prompt:

> **alias dir ls –s**

After you have created the **dir** command, the following commands would give identical results during this login session:

> **dir ˜/accounts**
> **ls –s ˜/accounts**

Note that the tilde (˜) is a special C-shell symbol that represents the user's home directory. For example, the path of billc's **.login** file can be expressed as **/usr/billc/.login**, or **˜/.login**.

You can also define aliases with multiple commands or pipelines, showing where the arguments to the original command are to be substituted using the **history** feature. For example, if you want to invoke the **ls** command automatically whenever you invoke the **cd** command, type the following command line:

> **alias cd 'cd \!* ; ls '**

Single quotation marks enclose the entire alias definition to prevent most substitutions from occurring and to prevent the semicolon (;) from being recognized as a metacharacter. The exclamation mark (!) is escaped with a backslash (\) to prevent it from using its standard interpretation when the **alias** command is used. The "\!*" substitutes the entire argument list to the **cd** command; no error is given if there are no arguments. The semicolon, which separates commands, indicates that the commands are to be done in sequence. For example, you can create a command that looks up its first argument in the password file with the following command line:

> **alias whois 'grep \!ˆ /etc/passwd'**

Because the C-shell reads the **.cshrc** file each time it starts up, the C-shell will start slowly if you place a large number of aliases there. Try to limit your aliases to a reasonable number (10 to 15). Too many aliases can also cause delays and make the system seem sluggish when you execute commands from within an editor or from within other programs.

Redirecting Input and Output

Commands have a diagnostic output (error or status messages) in addition to their standard output. This diagnostic output is normally directed to the terminal even if the standard output is redirected to a file or a pipe. Occasionally, it is useful to direct the diagnostic output (along with the standard output) to a file. For instance, if you want to redirect the output of a long running command into a file and wish to have a record of any diagnostic error messages it produces, you can use a command line with the following form:

> **command > & file**

The > & tells the C-shell to route the diagnostic output and the standard output into **file**. If **file** already exists and cannot be overwritten (**noclobber** is set), you can also use a command line of the following form:

> **command >&!**
> **file**

Similarly, you can tell the shell to route standard and diagnostic output through the pipe to the lineprinter. To do this, type the following command line:

> **command !& lpr**

To append output to the end of an existing file, you can use a command line of the following form:

> **command >> file**

Note that you can use the double arrows to append data to an existing file even if **noclobber** is set. This is because appending to a file does not overwrite the original contents of that file. If **noclobber** is set, an error results if **file** does not exist; otherwise, the C-shell creates **file**. To append a file that does not exist with **noclobber** set, you can use a command line of the following form:

> **command >>!**
> **file**

Creating Background and Foreground Jobs

When you type one or more commands together as a pipeline or as a sequence of commands separated by semicolons, the C-shell creates a single job consisting of these commands taken as a unit. Single commands without pipes or semicolons create the simplest jobs. Usually, every line that you type to the C-shell creates a job. For example, each of the following lines creates a job:

> **sort < data**
> **ls –s ¦ sort –n ¦ head –5**
> **mail harold**

If you type the ampersand (&) metacharacter at the end of the command line, you start the job as a background job. In this case, the C-shell does not wait for the job to finish but immediately prompts for another command. The job runs in the background at the same time that normal (foreground) jobs continue to be read and executed by the C-shell. For example, you can run the **du** program in the background while performing other tasks by typing

> **du > usage &**

The **du** command reports on the disk usage of your working directory and puts the output into the file **usage**. The ampersand causes the C-shell to return immediately with a prompt for the next command without waiting for **du** to finish. The **du** program continues executing in the background until it finishes, even though you can type and execute more commands in the meantime. Background jobs are unaffected by signals from the keyboard, such as the INTERRUPT or QUIT signals.

The **kill** command terminates a background job immediately. Normally, you do this by specifying the process number of the job you want killed. You can list the process numbers by using the **ps** command. For more information on the **ps** command and its output, see *ps*(1) in the *User's/System Administrator's Reference Manual*.

Using Built-in Commands

Built-in C-shell commands are executed within the shell. This section briefly describes how to use some of the built-in C-shell commands. For complete descriptions of these commands, as well as a complete list of built-in C-shell commands, see *csh*(1) in the *User's/System Administrator's Reference Manual*.

The following list describes some of the commonly used built-in commands:

Command   **Description**

alias   Assigns new aliases and displays existing aliases. With no arguments, **alias** prints the list of current aliases. You can also check the current meaning of an alias by typing it as the argument to the **alias** command. For example, to print the current alias for the character "h", type the following command line:

    alias h

Suppose you assigned "h" as an alias for the **history** command earlier, the shell will display the following line:

    history

If you did not assign an alias for the **history** command earlier, the shell will display only the shell prompt.

The **unalias** command removes an alias from the C-shell. For example, if you used the **alias** command earlier to assign the alias "h" for the **history** command, you could remove that alias by typing the following command line:

    unalias h

env   Prints out the current environment settings. The output for this command might look like the following example:

```
HOME=/usr/bill
SHELL=/bin/csh
PATH=:/usr/ucb:/bin:/usr/bin:/usr/local
TERM=ansi
USER=bill
```

history   Displays the contents of the history list.

logout   Terminates a C-shell login.

rehash   Causes the C-shell to recompute a table of command locations. This recomputation is necessary if you add a command to a directory in the current C-shell's search path and expect the C-shell to find it. Otherwise, the hashing algorithm may tell the C-shell that the command was not in that directory when the hash table was computed.

repeat   Repeats a command several times. For example, to make five copies of the file **one** in the file **five**, you can type

     repeat 5 cat one >> five

setenv   Sets variables in the environment. For example, if you are working from an ANSI-type terminal, you can set the value of the TERM environment variable to "ANSI" by typing

     setenv TERM ansi

source   Instructs the current C-shell to read commands from a file. Therefore, if you wish to have a change that you have made to the **.cshrc** file take effect before the next time you log in, you could use the following command:

     source .cshrc

time   Times a command, no matter how much CPU time it takes. For
example, to time a **who** command, type the following command
line:

time who

The output of this command might look like the following example:

```
maryw tty03 Jan 11 13:09
billc tty02 Jan 11 13:19
tomd console Jan 11 11:07

0.0u 0.0s 0:01 15%
```

According to this sample output, the **who** command used 0.0
seconds of user time (0.0u) and 0.0 seconds of system time (0.0s)
in less than a second (0.01) of elapsed time. The percentage,
"15%", indicates that over the period when it was active the
who command used an average of 13 percent of the available
CPU cycles of the machine.

unset   Removes variable definitions from the C-shell.

Creating Command Scripts

In UNIX System V, you can place commands in files and invoke C-shells to read and execute commands from these files. These command files are called *C-shell scripts*. This section describes the C-shell features that are useful when creating C-shell scripts. Before you begin writing C-shell scripts, you must be familiar with the UNIX concepts presented earlier in this *Guide*.

Using the argv Variable

A C-shell *command script* is like a "mini" program run by the shell. The script is an executable file that contains one or more C-shell commands. To interpret a **csh** command script, type a command of the following form:

   csh *script argument*

where

script is the name of the file containing a group of C-shell commands.

argument is a sequence of command arguments.

The C-shell places these arguments in the **argv** variable, a special variable that is set by the C-shell, and then begins to read commands from *script*. These parameters are accessed just as any other C-shell variables.

You can make the *script* file executable by typing either of the following command lines:

   chmod 755 script

   chmod +x script

If you want the **/bin/csh** file to be invoked automatically when you execute your **script** file, you must place a C-shell comment character (#) at the beginning of the file. If the file does not begin with a number sign (#), the standard shell, **/bin/sh**, is used to execute it. After your **script** file is complete, you can execute it by typing the following command:

   script

Substituting Shell Variables

After each input line is broken into words and history substitutions are performed on it, the input line is parsed into distinct commands. Then, before each command is executed, the C-shell performs variable substitution on these distinct commands. Keyed by the dollar sign ($), this substitution replaces the names of variables with their values. To echo the current value of the **argv** variable into the output of a C-shell script, place the following command line in the script:

echo $argv

If **argv** has not been defined, the C-shell script will respond to this command line by displaying an error message.

There are a number of notations for accessing components and attributes of variables. You can use notations to check whether a shell variable has been set with the **set** command. For example, the following notation expands to 1 if *variable* is set or to 0 if *variable* is not set:

$?*variable*

This notation is the fundamental tool for checking whether particular variables have been assigned values. All other references to undefined variables cause errors.

The following notation expands to the number of elements in *variable* :

$#*variable*

To understand how to use shell variables, try the following steps, which let you practice defining, checking, accessing, and undefining C-shell variables:

1. Set the values of **argv** by typing the following command line at the C-shell prompt:

   set argv=(a b c)

2. Determine whether any shell variables have been assigned during this session by typing

   echo $?argv

   The system displays "1", indicating that the **argv** variable has been set.

3. Determine the number of elements in the named variable **argv** by typing

    echo $#argv

    The system displays "3", indicating that there are three elements in the **argv** variable.

4. However, if you remove the current definition of the **argv** variable from the C-shell, the system will display "0" since there are no longer any elements in the **argv** variable. To check this, first remove the current definition of the **argv** variable by typing the following command line:

    unset argv

5. Then verify that the **argv** variable is no longer defined by typing

    echo $?argv

    Now that you have undefined the **argv** variable, there are no elements in it. Thus, the notation expands to 0, and the system displays this digit. Because there are no elements in the variable, you can tell that the variable is not set.

6. Determine the current value of the **argv** variable by typing

    echo $argv

    The system displays the following message, confirming that **argv** is not set:

    `Undefined variable: argv.`

7. Reset the value of the **argv** variable to the same value as when you began this session by typing the following command line at the C-shell prompt:

    set argv=(a b c)

8. Determine the first element of the variable **argv** by typing

    $argv[1]

    The system displays the first element in the group of elements you assigned to **argv** in step 7:

    `a`

You can determine the first and second elements of the **argv** variable by typing

$argv[1-2]

The system displays

a b

In addition to providing specific element numbers, you can put a range of numbers inside the brackets. To do this, use the following form:

$argv[$n$-$m$]

where n is the low end of the range and m is the high end of the range. You do not have to know how many elements are present; if m exceeds the number of elements in **argv**, the shell returns an empty vector and no error results if n is within the actual range of elements present. You can also give a subrange of the form "n-". If there are less than n elements in the given variable, no words are substituted. This form will not produce any errors, even if n is not within the range of actual elements present.

In addition, the following two commands can be used interchangeably where n is an integer which represents the nth element of **argv**:

$$n$
$argv[n]

One minor difference between "$n" and "**$argv**[n]" should be noted here. The form "**$argv**[$n$]" yields an error if n is not in the range 1–$#**argv**, while "$n" never yields an out-of-range subscript error. This difference is necessary for compatibility with the way previous shells handle parameters.

Another important point is that it is never an error to give a subrange of the form "n–"; if there are less than "n" components of the given variable, no words are substituted. A range of the form, m–n, also returns an empty vector without giving an error when m exceeds the number of elements of the given variable. An empty vector without an error returns only if the subscript n is in range.

9. Determine the last element of the variable **argv** by typing

    $argv[$#argv]

    The system displays

    c

    This is a convenient expansion because you do not need to know how many elements are in the **argv** variable to determine the value of the last element. You can let the shell determine the number of elements, then you can tell the shell to use that number in another notation, as this example illustrates. In this example, the shell processes the contents of the brackets first, determining that there are three elements in the **argv** variable.

    Then, the shell substitutes a "3" for the contents of the brackets. At this point, the shell finishes processing the notation as if you had typed the following command line:

    $argv[3]

    The system displays the current value of the third **argv** element:

    c

The following two commands can also be used interchangeably; the first form is a shorthand version of the second:

$*
$argv

The following notation expands to the process number of the current C-shell:

$$

Since this process number is unique in the system, you can use it in the generation of unique temporary file names.

Using Expressions

To construct useful C-shell scripts, the C-shell evaluates expressions that are based on the values of variables. In fact, all the arithmetic operations of the C language are available in the C-shell with the same precedence that they have in C. In particular, the "= =" and "!=" operators compare strings, and the "&&" and "¦¦" operators implement the logical AND and OR operations. The "=~" and "!~" special operators are similar to "= =" and "!=" except that the right-hand string can have pattern-matching characters (*, ?, or [and]). These operators test whether the string on the left matches the pattern on the right.

For the full list of expression components, see *test*(1) in the *User's/System Administrator's Reference Manual*.

Using Control Structures

A *control structure* is a set of steps that systematically analyzes similar "pieces" of data. C-shell scripts often contain control structures, since scripts are written to perform identical operations repeatedly on large sets of data. The C-shell recognizes several command structures, including the following structures:

> **foreach** *variable expression*
> **end**

> **if** (*expression*) **then**
> *command*
> **endif**

This structure can also be written in the following two forms:

> **if** (*expression*) (*command*)

or

> **if** (*expression*) \
> *command*

The second form requires that the final backslash (\) immediately precedes the end-of-line. The command must not involve the following and must not be another control command:

> ¦ & ;

More general **if** statements also admit a sequence of **else–if** pairs followed by a single **else** and an **endif** , as shown in the following example:

> **if** (*expression*) **then**
> > *commands*
>
> **else if** (*expression*) **then**
> > *commands*
>
> **...**
>
> **else**
> > *commands*
>
> **endif**

The other control construct is a statement with the following form:

> **if** (*expression*) **then**
> > *command*
> >
> > **...**
>
> **endif**

The placement of the keywords in this statement is inflexible due to the current implementation of the C-shell. The following two formats are not acceptable to the C-shell:

> **if** (*expression*) **# Won't work!**
> **then**
> > *command*
> >
> > **...**
>
> **endif**

and

> **if** (*expression*) **then** *command* **endif # Won't work**

The C-shell does have another form of the **if** statement:

> **if** (*expression*) *command*

This statement can also be written as follows:

> **if** (*expression*) \
> > *command*

The C-shell also has the control structures, **while** and **switch**, which are similar to those control structures of C. These take the following forms:

> **while** (*expression*)
>> *commands*
>
> **end**

and

> **switch** (*word*)
>
> **case str1:**
>> *commands*
>>
>> **breaksw**
>
> ...
>
> **case strn:**
>> *commands*
>>
>> **breaksw**
>
> **default:**
>> *commands*
>>
>> **breaksw**
>
> **endsw**

For more information about control structures, see *csh*(1) in the *User's/System Administrator's Reference Manual*. C programmers should note that **breaksw** exits from a **switch**, whereas **break** exits a **while** or **foreach** loop. The two commands are often confused.

Finally, the C-shell recognizes a **goto** statement with labels that resemble C labels, as shown in the following example:

> **loop:**
>> *commands*
>>
>> **goto loop**

The following sample C-shell script uses the expression feature of the C-shell, as well as some of its control structures:

```
#
# Copyc copies those C programs in the specified list
# to the directory ~/backup if they differ from the files
# already in ~/backup
#
set noglob
foreach i ($argv)

        if ($i !~ *.c) continue  # not a .c file so do nothing

        if (! -r ~/backup/$i:t) then
             echo $i:t not in backup...not cp\'ed
             continue
        endif

        cmp -s $i ~/backup/$i:t # to set $status

        if ($status != 0) then
             echo new backup of $i
             cp $i ~/backup/$i:t
        endif
    end
```

This script uses the **foreach** command, which iteratively executes the group of commands between the **foreach** and **end** statements for each valid value of the variable *i*. If you want to look more closely at what happens during execution of a **foreach** loop, you can use the debug command **break** to stop execution at any point. To resume execution, use the debug command **continue**. The value of the iteration variable (*i* in this case) will stay at whatever it was when the last **foreach** loop was completed.

In this sample script, the **noglob** variable is set to prevent file name expansion of the members of **argv**. Set **noglob** if the arguments to a C-shell script are file names that have already been expanded or if the arguments contain metacharacters for file name expansion.

Also note that the C-shell will not execute C-shell scripts that do not begin with the number sign character (#). In other words, you cannot execute C-shell scripts that do not begin with comments.

Another important feature in C-shell scripts is the colon (:) modifier. You can use the **:r** modifier to extract the root of a file name, or you can use **:e** to extract the extension. Suppose the *i* variable has the value "/mnt/foo.bar". Type the following command line:

echo $i $i:r

The system displays

    /mnt/foo.bar /mnt/foo

This example shows how the **:r** modifier strips off the trailing ".**bar**". Other modifiers take off the last component of a path name leaving the **:h** head or all but the last component of a path name leaving the tail, **:t**. These modifiers are fully described in *csh*(1) in the *User's/System Administrator's Reference Manual*. You can also use the command substitution feature to modify strings. Since each usage of this feature involves the creation of a new process, it is more time consuming than the colon (:) modification feature. Also, note that the current implementation of the C-shell limits the number of colon modifiers on a $ substitution to 1. Therefore, if you type a command of the form

% echo $i $i:h:t

your display will be similar to the following:

    /a/b/c /a/b:t

Finally, note that the number sign character (#) lexically introduces a C-shell comment in C-shell scripts (but not from the terminal). All subsequent characters on the input line after a # are discarded by the C-shell. You can put this # character in single quotation marks, using the acute accent symbol (') or backslash (\) to place it in an argument word.

Supplying Input to Commands

Commands that are run from C-shell scripts receive, by default, the standard input of the C-shell that is running the script. The standard input lets C-shell scripts fully participate in pipelines but requires extra notation for commands that are to take inline data.

Therefore, you need a metacharacter notation for supplying inline data to commands in C-shell scripts. For example, consider the following script, which uses the editor to delete leading blanks from the lines in each specified argument file:

```
# deblank -- remove leading blanks
foreach i ($argv)
ed - $i << ' EOF'
1,$s/^[ ]*//
w
q
' EOF'
end
```

The following notation means that the standard input for the **ed** command is to come from the text in the C-shell script file up to the next line consisting of exactly EOF:

```
<< ' EOF'
```

Because the EOF is enclosed in single quotation marks, the C-shell will not perform variable substitution on the intervening lines. In this case, since the "1,$" form was used in the editor script, you need to ensure that this dollar sign is not a variable substitution. To prevent the C-shell from performing variable substitution on the dollar sign ($), type a backslash (\) before the dollar sign, as shown in the following example:

```
1,\$s/^[ ]*//
```

By enclosing the EOF terminator in single quotation marks, you can also prevent the $ from undergoing variable substitution.

Another quotation feature is the double quotation mark ("), which lets only some expansion features occur on the quoted string. This feature also makes this string into a single word as the single quotation mark (') does. For more information about using quotation marks with the C-shell, see *csh*(1) in the *User's/System Administrator's Reference Manual*.

Catching Interrupts

If your C-shell script creates temporary files, you may want to catch interruptions of the C-shell script so that you can clean up these files. You can start this process by issuing a command line of the following form, where *label* is a label in your program:

> **onintr** *label*

If the C-shell receives an interrupt, it performs a "goto label" that lets you remove the temporary files. The C-shell then executes an **exit** command to exit from the C-shell script. If you wish to exit with nonzero status, you can type the following command to exit with status 1:

> **exit (1)**

Starting a Loop at a Terminal

You can also use the **foreach** control structure at the terminal to perform a number of similar commands. For instance, if there are three shells in use on a particular system, **/bin/sh**, **/bin/nsh**, and **/bin/csh**, you can count the number of persons using each shell by typing the following commands:

> grep –c csh$ /etc/passwd
> grep –c nsh$ /etc/passwd
> grep –c –v sh$ /etc/passwd

Since these commands are similar, you can use the **foreach** command to simplify them, as shown in the following example:

> $ foreach i ('sh$' 'csh$' '–v sh$')
> ?
> grep –c $i /etc/passwd
> ?
> end

Note that the C-shell prompts for input with a question mark (?) when reading the body of the loop. This prompting occurs only when you enter the **foreach** command interactively.

You can also perform loops with variables containing lists of file names or other words. To understand the basic looping concepts, try the following steps. Suppose there are two files in your current directory called **csh.n** and **csh.rm**:

1. Set the value of variable *a* to the list of all the file names in the current directory by typing

    set a=(` ls`)

2. Display the current value of variable *a* by typing

    echo $a

    The system displays

    ```
    csh.n csh.rm
    ```

3. List all the file names in the current directory by typing

    ls

    The system displays

    ```
    csh.n
    csh.rm
    ```

4. Determine the number of file names in the current directory by typing

    echo $#a

    The system displays

    ```
    2
    ```

The C-shell converts the output of a command within grave accent (`) marks to a list of words, as shown in the above terminal session. You can also place the quoted string within double quotation marks (" ") to take each (nonempty) line as a component of the variable. This prevents the lines from being split into words at spaces and tabs. An **:x** modifier exists that you can use later to expand each component of the original variable into another variable by splitting it into separate words at embedded spaces and tabs.

Using Substitution to Expand Strings

In the C-shell, you can use substitution techniques to expand groups of strings, such as groups of file names, that have common parts. One form of file name expansion uses the bracket characters, { and }. These characters specify that the enclosed strings, separated by commas (,), will be consecutively substituted into the containing characters, with the results expanded from left to right. Therefore, a command line of the form

A{str1,str2,...strn}B

will expand to the following:

Astr1B Astr2B ...
AstrnB

By using brackets, you cause this expansion to occur before the other file name expansions, and it may be applied recursively. The results of each expanded string are sorted separately, preserving left-to-right order. The resulting file names are not required if no other expansion features are used. This means you can use this feature to generate arguments that are not file names but which have common parts.

For example, to create the subdirectories **hdrs**, **retrofit**, and **csh** in your home directory, type the following command line:

mkdir ~/{hdrs,retrofit,csh}

This expansion feature is useful when the common prefix is long, as shown in the following example:

chown root /usr/demo/{file1,file2}

Substituting Commands

Before the shell expands file names, it replaces any command enclosed in grave accent marks (` `) with the output from that command. For example, you can use the following command line to save the current directory in the *pwd* variable:

set pwd=`pwd`

You can type the following command to run the **vi** editor, supplying as arguments those files that end in .**c** and have the "TRACE" string in them.

vi `grep –l TRACE *.c`

Command expansion also occurs to input that is redirected with << and within double quotation marks (" "). For more information about the hierarchy of C-shell expansions and substitutions, see *csh*(1) in the *User's/System Administrator's Reference Manual*.

Special Characters

The following table lists the special characters used by **csh** and the UNIX System. A number of these characters also have special meaning in expressions. For a more complete list, see *csh*(1) in the *User's/System Administrator's Reference Manual*.

Syntactic Metacharacters

;   separates commands to be executed sequentially

!   separates commands in a pipeline

( )   brackets expressions and variable values

&   follows commands to be executed without waiting for completion

File Name Metacharacters

/   separates components of a file's path name

.   separates root parts of a file name from extensions

?   expansion character that matches any single character

*   expansion character that matches any sequence of characters

[ ]   expansion sequence that matches any single character from a set of characters

~   used at the beginning of a file name to indicate home directories

{ }   specifies groups of arguments with common parts

Quotation Metacharacters

\   prevents meta-meaning of the following single character

'   prevents meta-meaning of a group of characters

"   same as ' but allows variable and command expansion

Input/Output Metacharacters

<   indicates redirected input

>   indicates redirected output

Expansion/Substitution Metacharacters

$ indicates variable substitution

!   indicates history substitution

:   precedes substitution modifiers

^   used in special forms of history substitution

`   indicates command substitution

Other Metacharacters

begins scratch file names; indicates C-shell comments

–   prefixes option (flag) arguments to commands

9 Communication Tutorial

Introduction

The UNIX System offers a choice of commands that enables you to communicate with other UNIX System users. Specifically, the commands allow you to send and receive messages from other users (on either your system or another UNIX System), exchange files, and form networks with other UNIX Systems. Through networking, a user on one system can exchange messages and files between computers, and execute commands on remote computers.

To help you take advantage of these capabilities, this chapter will teach you how to use the following commands:

For exchanging messages:	**mail**, **mailx**, **uname**, and **uuname**
For transferring files:	**uucp**, **uuto**, **uupick**, and **uustat**
For networking:	**ct**, **cu**, and **uux**

Exchanging Messages

To send messages, you can use either the **mail** or **mailx** command. These commands deliver your message to a file belonging to the recipient. When the recipient logs in (or while already logged in), he or she receives a message that says you have mail. The recipient can use either the **mail** or **mailx** command to read your message and reply at his or her leisure.

The main difference between **mail** and **mailx** is that only **mailx** offers the following features:

■ a choice of text editors (**ed** or **vi**) for handling incoming and outgoing messages

■ a list of waiting messages that allows the user to decide which messages to handle and in what order

■ several options for saving files

■ commands for replying to messages and sending copies (of both incoming and outgoing messages) to other users

You can also use **mail** or **mailx** to send short files containing memos, reports, and so on. However, if you want to send someone a file that is over a page long, use one of the commands designed for transferring files: **uuto** or **uucp**. (See "Sending Large Files" later in this chapter for descriptions of these commands.)

mail

This section presents the **mail** command. It discusses the basics of sending mail to one or more people simultaneously, whether they are working on the local system (the same system as you) or on a remote system. It also covers receiving and handling incoming mail.

Sending Messages

The basic command line format for sending mail is

> **mail** *login*<**CR**>

where *login* is the recipient's login name on a UNIX System. This login name can be either of the following:

- a login name if the recipient is on your system (for example, **bob**)

- a system name and login name if the recipient is on another UNIX System that can communicate with yours (for example, **sys2!bob**)

For the moment, assume that the recipient is on the local system. (We will deal with sending mail to users on remote systems later.) Type the **mail** command at the system prompt, press the <RETURN> key, and start typing the text of your message on the next line. There is no limit to the length of your message. When you have finished typing it, send the message by typing a period (.) or a < ^**d**> (control-d) at the beginning of a new line.

The following example shows how this procedure will appear on your screen:

```
$ mail phyllis<CR>
My meeting with Smith's<CR>
group tomorrow has been moved<CR>
up to 3:00 so I won't be able to<CR>
see you then.  Could we meet<CR>
in the morning instead?<CR>
.<CR>
$
```

The prompt on the last line means that your message has been queued (placed in a waiting line of messages) and will be sent.

Undeliverable Mail

If you make an error when typing the recipient's login, the **mail** command will not be able to deliver your mail. Instead, it will print two messages telling you that it has failed and that it is returning your mail. Then it will return your mail in a message that includes the system name and login name of both the sender and intended recipient, and an error message stating the reason for the failure.

For example, say you (owner of the login **kol**) want to send a message to a user with the login **chris** on a system called **marmaduk**. Your message says The meeting has been changed to 2:00. Failing to notice that you have incorrectly typed the login as **cris**, you try to send your message:

```
$ mail cris<CR>
The meeting has been changed to 2:00.
.<CR>
mail: Can't send to cris
mail: Return to kol
you have mail in /usr/mail/kol
$
```

The mail that is waiting for you in **/usr/mail** will be useful if you do not know why the **mail** command has failed or if you want to retrieve your mail so that you can resend it without typing it in again. It contains the following:

```
$ mail<CR>
From kol Sat Jan 18 17:33 EST 1986
>From kol Sat Jan 18 17:33 EST 1986 forwarded by kol
***** UNDELIVERABLE MAIL sent to cris, being returned by marmaduk!kol *****
mail: ERROR # 8 'Invalid recipient' encountered on system marmaduk

The meeting has been changed to 2:00.

?
```

To learn how to display and handle this message, see "Managing Incoming Mail" later in this chapter.

Sending Mail to One Person

The following screen shows a typical message:

```
$ mail tommy<CR>
Tom,<CR>
There's a meeting of the review committee<CR>
at 3:00 this afternoon.  D.F. wants your<CR>
comments and an idea of how long you think<CR>
the project will take to complete.<CR>
B.K.<CR>
.<CR>
$
```

When Tom logs in at his terminal (or while he is already logged in), he receives a message that tells him he has mail waiting:

```
$ you have mail
```

To find out how he can read his mail, see the section "Managing Incoming Mail" in this chapter.

You can practice using the **mail** command by sending mail to yourself. Type in the **mail** command and your login ID, and then write a short message to yourself. When you type the final period or <ˆd>, the mail will be sent to a file named after your login ID in the **/usr/mail** directory, and you will receive a notice that you have mail.

Sending mail to yourself can also serve as a handy reminder system. For example, suppose you (login ID **bob**) want to call someone the next morning. Send yourself a reminder in a mail message:

```
$ mail bob<CR>
Call Accounting and find out<CR>
why they haven't returned my 1985 figures!<CR>
.<CR>
$
```

When you log in the next day, a notice will appear on your screen informing you that you have mail waiting to be read.

Sending Mail to Several People Simultaneously

You can send a message to a number of people by including their login names on the **mail** command line. For example:

```
$ mail tommy jane wombat dave<CR>
Diamond cutters,<CR>
The game is on for tonight at diamond three.<CR>
Don't forget your gloves!<CR>
Your Manager<CR>
.<CR>
$
```

Figure 9-1 summarizes the syntax and capabilities of the **mail** command.

Command Recap		
mail – sends a message to another user's login		
command	*options*	*arguments*
mail	none	[*system_name!*]*login*

Description:	Typing **mail** followed by one or more login names sends the message typed on the lines following the command line to the specified login(s).
Remarks:	Typing a period or a $<\hat{\ }d>$ (followed by the <RETURN> key) at the beginning of a new line sends the message.

Figure 9-1: Summary of Sending Messages with the **mail** Command

Sending Mail to Remote Systems: the uname and uuname Commands

Until now, we have assumed that you are sending messages to users on the local UNIX System. However, your company may have three separate computer systems, each in a different part of a building, or you may have offices in several locations, each with its own system.

You can send mail to users on other systems simply by adding the name of the recipient's system before the login ID on the command line:

mail sys2!bob<CR>

Notice that the system name and the recipient's login ID are separated by an exclamation point.

Before you can run this command, however, you need to know the following three things:

- whether or not your system and the remote system communicate
- the name of the remote system
- the recipient's login name

The **uname** and **uuname** commands allow you to find this information.

If you can, get the name of the remote system and the recipient's login name from the recipient. If the recipient does not know the system name, have him or her issue the following command on the remote system:

uname –n<CR>

The command will respond with the name of the system. For example:

$ uname –n<CR>
dumbo
$

Once you know the remote system name, the **uuname** command can help you verify that your system can communicate with the remote system. At the prompt, type

uuname<CR>

This generates a list of remote systems with which your system can communicate. If the recipient's system is on that list, you can send messages to it by **mail**.

You can simplify this step by using the **grep** command to search through the **uuname** output. At the prompt, type

uuname ¦ grep *system*<CR>

(Here *system* is the recipient's system name.) If **grep** finds the specified system name, it prints it on the screen. For example:

$ uuname ¦ grep dumbo<CR>
dumbo
$

This means that **dumbo** can communicate with your system. If **dumbo** does not communicate with your system, **uuname** returns a prompt:

$ uuname ¦ grep dumbo<CR>
$

To summarize our discussion of **uname** and **uuname**, consider an example. Suppose you want to send a message to login **sarah** on the remote system **dumbo**. Verify that **dumbo** can communicate with your system and send your message. The following screen shows both steps:

```
$ uuname ¦ grep dumbo<CR>
dumbo
$ mail dumbo!sarah<CR>
Sarah,<CR>
The final counts for the writing seminar<CR>
are as follows:<CR>
<CR>
Our department - 18<CR>
Your department - 20<CR>
<CR>
Tom<CR>
.<CR>
$
```

Figures 9-2 and 9-3 summarize the syntax and capabilities of the **uname** and **uuname** commands, respectively.

Command Recap		
uname – displays the system name		
command	*options*	*arguments*
uname	**–n** and others*	none
Description:	**uname –n** displays the name of the system on which your login resides.	

* See the *uname*(1) manual page in the *User's/System Administrator's Reference Manual* for all available options and an explanation of their capabilities.

Figure 9-2: Summary of the **uname** Command

Command Recap		
uuname – displays a list of networked systems		
command	*options*	*arguments*
uuname	none	none
Description:	**uuname** displays a list of remote systems that can communicate with your system.	

Figure 9-3: Summary of the **uuname** Command

Managing Incoming Mail

As stated earlier, the **mail** command also allows you to display messages sent to you by other users on your screen so you can read them. If you are logged in when someone sends you mail, the following message is printed on your screen:

you have mail

This means that one or more messages are being held for you in a file called **/usr/mail/**_your_login_, usually referred to as your mailbox. To display these messages on your screen, type the **mail** command without any arguments:

mail<CR>

The messages will be displayed one at a time, beginning with the one most recently received. A typical **mail** message display looks like this:

```
$ mail
From tommy Wed May 21 15:33 CST 1986
Bob,
Looks like the meeting has been cancelled.
Do you still want the material for the technical review?
Tom

?
```

The first line, called the header, provides information about the message: the login name of the sender and the date and time the message was sent. The lines after the header (up to the line containing the ?) comprise the text of the message.

If a long message is being displayed on your terminal screen, you may not be able to read it all at once. You can interrupt the printing by typing < ^s> (control-s). This will freeze the screen, giving you a chance to read. When you are ready to continue, type < ^q> and the printing will resume.

After displaying each message, the **mail** command prints a ? prompt and waits for a response. You have many options: for example, you can leave the current message in your mailbox while you read the next message, you can delete the current message, or you can save the current message for future reference. For a list of **mail**'s available options, type a **?** in response to **mail**'s ? prompt.

To display the next message without deleting the current message, press the <RETURN> key after the question mark:

    ?<CR>

The current message remains in your mailbox, and the next message is displayed. If you have read all the messages in your mailbox, a prompt appears.

To delete a message, type a **d** after the question mark:

    ? d<CR>

The message is deleted from your mailbox. If there is another message waiting, it is then displayed. If not, a prompt appears as a signal that you have finished reading your messages.

To save a message for later reference, type an **s** after the question mark:

    ? s<CR>

This saves the message, by default, in a file called **mbox** in your home directory. To save the message in another file, type the name of that file after the **s** command.

For example, to save a message in a file called **mailsave** (in your current directory), enter the response shown after the question mark:

    ? s mailsave<CR>

If **mailsave** is an existing file, the **mail** command appends the message to it. If there is no file by that name, the **mail** command creates one and stores your message in it. You can later verify the existence of the new file by using the **ls** command, which lists the contents of your current directory.

You can also save the message in a file in a different directory by specifying a path name. For example:

> **? s project1/memo<CR>**

This is a relative path name that identifies a file called **memo** (where your message will be saved) in a subdirectory called **project1** of your current directory. You can use either relative or full path names when saving mail messages. (For instructions on using path names, see Chapter 3.)

To quit reading messages, enter the response shown after the question mark:

> **? q<CR>**

Any messages that you have not read are kept in your mailbox until the next time you use the **mail** command.

To stop the printing of a message entirely, press the <BREAK> key. The **mail** command will stop the display, print a ? prompt, and wait for a response from you.

Figure 9-4 summarizes the syntax and capabilities of the **mail** command for reading messages.

Command Recap		
mail – reads messages sent to your login		
command	*options*	*arguments*
mail	available*	none

Description:	When issued without options, the **mail** command displays any messages waiting in your mailbox (the system file **/usr/mail/***your_login*).
Remarks:	A question mark (**?**) at the end of a message means that a response is expected. A full list of possible responses is given in the *User's/System Administrator's Reference Manual*.

* See the *mail*(1) manual page in the *User's/System Administrator's Reference Manual* for all available options and an explanation of their capabilities.

Figure 9-4: Summary of Reading Messages with the **mail** Command

mailx

This section introduces the **mailx** facility. It explains how to set up your **mailx** environment, send messages with the **mailx** command, and handle messages that have been sent to you. The material is presented in four parts:

■ **mailx** Overview

■ How to Send Messages

■ How to Manage Incoming Mail

■ The **.mailrc** File

mailx **Overview**

The **mailx** command is an enhanced version of the **mail** command. There are many options to **mailx** that are not available in **mail** for sending and reading mail. For example, you can define an alias for a single login or for a group. This allows you to send **mail** to an individual using a name or word other than their login ID and to send **mail** to a whole group of people using a single name or word. When you use **mailx** to read incoming mail, you can save it in various files, edit it, forward it to someone else, respond to the person who originated the message, and so forth. By using **mailx** environment variables, you can develop an environment to suit your individual tastes.

If you type the **mailx** command with one or more logins as arguments, **mailx** decides you are sending mail to the named users, prompts you for a summary of the subject, and then waits for you to type in your message or issue a command. The section "How to Send Messages" describes features that are available to you for editing, incorporating other files, adding names to copy lists, and more.

If you enter the **mailx** command with no arguments, **mailx** checks incoming mail for you in a file named **/usr/mail/***your_login*. If there is mail for you in that file, you are shown a list of the items and given the opportunity to read, store, remove or transfer each one to another file. The section entitled "How to Manage Incoming Mail" provides some examples and describes the options available.

If you choose to customize **mailx**, you should create a start-up file in your home directory called **.mailrc**. The section "The **.mailrc** File" describes variables you can include in your start-up file.

mailx has two modes of functioning: input mode and command mode. You must be in input mode to create and send messages. Command mode is used to read incoming mail. You can use any of the following methods to control the way **mailx** works for you:

- Entering options on the command line. (See the *mailx*(1) manual page in the *User's/System Administrator's Reference Manual*.)

- Issuing commands when you are in input mode, for example, creating a message to send. These commands are always preceded by a ˜ (tilde) and are referred to as tilde escapes. (See the *mailx*(1) manual page in the *User's/System Administrator's Reference Manual*.)

■ Issuing commands when you are in command mode, for example, reading incoming mail.

■ Storing commands and environment variables in a start-up file in your home directory called **$HOME/.mailrc**.

Tilde escapes are discussed in "How to Send Messages," command mode commands in "How to Manage Incoming Mail," and the **.mailrc** file in "The **.mailrc** File."

Command Line Options

In this section, we will look at command line options.

The syntax for the **mailx** command is

    mailx [*options*] [*name...*]

The *options* are flags that control the action of the command, and *name...* represents the intended recipients.

Anything on the command line other than an option preceded by a hyphen is read by **mailx** as a *name*; that is, the login or alias of a person to whom you are sending a message.

Two of the command line options deserve special mention:

■ **–f** [*filename*]: Allows you to read messages from *filename* instead of your mailbox.

    Because **mailx** lets you store messages in any file you name, you need the **–f** option to review these stored options. The default storage file is **$HOME/mbox**, so the command

        mailx –f

    is used to review messages stored there.

■ **–n**: Do not initialize from the system default **mailx.rc** file.

    If you have your own **.mailrc** file (see "The **.mailrc** File"), **mailx** will not look through the system default file for specifications when you use the **–n** option but will go directly to your **.mailrc** file. This results in faster initialization, substantially faster when the system is busy.

How to Send Messages: the Tilde Escapes

To send a message to another UNIX System user, enter the following command:

$ mailx daves<CR>

The specified login name belongs to the person who is to receive the message. The system puts you into input mode and prompts you for the subject of the message. (You may have to wait a few seconds for the Subject: prompt if the system is very busy.) This is the simplest way to use the **mailx** command; it differs very little from the way you use the **mail** command.

The following examples show how you can edit messages you are sending, incorporate existing text into your messages, change the header information, and perform other tasks that take advantage of the **mailx** command's capabilities. Each example is followed by an explanation of the key points illustrated in the example.

```
$ mailx daves<CR>
Subject:
```

Whether to include a subject or not is optional. If you elect not to, press the <RETURN> key. The cursor moves to the next line, and the program waits for you to enter the text of the message:

```
$ mailx daves<CR>
Subject: meeting<CR>
We're having a meeting for novice mailx users in<CR>
the auditorium at 9:00 tomorrow.<CR>
Would you be willing to give a demonstration?<CR>
Bob<CR>
˜. <CR>
cc:<CR>
$
```

There are two important things to notice about the above example:

■ You break up the lines of your message by pressing the <RETURN> key at the end of each line. This makes it easier for the recipient to read the message and prevents you from overflowing the line buffer.

■ You end the text and send the message by entering a tilde and a period together (˜.) at the beginning of a line. The system responds with an end-of-text notice (EOT) and a prompt.

There are several commands available to you when you are in input mode (as we were in the example). Each of them consists of a tilde (˜), followed by an alphabetic character, entered at the beginning of a line. Together they are known as tilde escapes. (See the *mailx*(1) manual page in the *User's/System Administrator's Reference Manual*.) Most of them are used in the examples in this section.

You can include the subject of your message on the command line by using the **–s** option. For example, the command line

```
$ mailx –s "meeting" daves<CR>
```

is equivalent to

```
$ mailx daves<CR>
Subject: meeting<CR>
```

The subject line will look the same to the recipient of the message. Notice that when putting the subject on the command line, you must enclose a subject that has more than one word in quotation marks.

Editing the Message

When you are in the input mode of **mailx**, you can invoke an editor by entering the ˜**e** (tilde e) escape at the beginning of a line. The following example shows how to use a tilde:

```
$ mailx daves<CR>
Subject: Testing my tilde<CR>
When entering the text of a message<CR>
that has somehow gotten grabled<CR>
you may invoke your favorite editor<CR>
by means of a ˜e (tilde e).
                            .
                            .
                            .
```

Notice that you have misspelled a word in your message. To correct the error, use ˜**e** to invoke the editor, in this case, the default editor, **ed**:

```
                         .
                         .
                         .
~e<CR>
12
/grabled/p
that has somehow gotten grabled
s/gra/gar/p
that has somehow gotten garbled
w
132
q
(continue)
What more can I tell you?
                         .
                         .
                         .
```

In this example the **ed** editor was used. Your **.profile** or a **.mailrc** file controls which editor will be invoked when you issue a ~e escape command. The ~v (tilde v) escape invokes an alternate editor (most commonly, **vi**).

When you exited from **ed** (by typing **q**), the **mailx** command returned you to input mode and prompted you to continue your message. At this point, you may want to preview your corrected message by entering a ~p (tilde p) escape. The ~p escape prints out the entire message up to the point where the ~p was entered. Thus, at any time during text entry, you can review the current contents of your message:

```
˜p
Message contains:
To: daves
Subject: Testing my tilde

When entering the text of a message
that has somehow gotten garbled
you may invoke your favorite editor
by means of a tilde e (˜e).
What more can I tell you?
(continue)
˜.
EOT
$
```

Incorporating Existing Text into Your Message

mailx provides four ways to incorporate material from another source into the message you are creating. You can

- read a file into your message

- read a message you have received into a reply

- incorporate the value of a named environment variable into a message

- execute a shell command and incorporate the output of the command into a message

The following examples show the first two of these functions, which are the most commonly used of these four functions. For information about the other two, see the *mailx*(1) manual page of the *User's/System Administrator's Reference Manual*.

Reading a File into a Message

The following example illustrates how to read a file into a message:

```
$ mailx daves<CR>
Subject: Work Schedule<CR>
As you can see from the following<CR>
~r letters/file1
"letters/file1"    10/725
we have our work cut out for us.
Please give me your thoughts on this.
- Bob
~.
EOT
$
```

As the example shows, the ~r (tilde r) escape is followed by the name of the file you want to include. The system displays the file name and the number of lines and characters it contains. You are still in input mode and can continue with the rest of the message. When the recipient gets the message, the text of **letters/file1** is included. (You can, of course, use the ~p (tilde p) escape to preview the contents before sending your message.)

Incorporating a Message from Your Mailbox into a Reply

The following example illustrates how to incorporate a mail message into a reply:

```
$ mailx<CR>
mailx version 2.14  2/9/85  Type ? for help.
"usr/mail/roberts": 2 messages 1 new
>N   1 abc       Tue May 1  08:09  8/155  Meeting Notice
     2 hqtrs     Mon Apr 30 16:57  4/127  Schedule
? m jones<CR>
Subject: Hq Schedule<CR>
Here is a copy of the schedule from headquarters...<CR>
~f 2<CR>
Interpolating: 2
(continue)
As you can see, the boss will be visiting our district on<CR>
the 14th and 15th.<CR>
- Robert
~.
EOT
?
```

There are several important points illustrated in this example:

■ The sequence begins in command mode, where you read and respond to your incoming mail. Then you switch into input mode by issuing the command **m jones** (meaning send a message to jones).

■ The ~**f** escape is used in input mode to call in one of the messages in your mailbox and make it part of the outgoing message. The number **2** after the ~**f** means message 2 is to be interpolated (read in).

■ **mailx** tells you that message 2 is being interpolated and then tells you to continue.

■ When you finish creating and sending the message, you are back in command mode, as shown by the ? prompt. You may now do something else in command mode or exit **mailx** by typing **q**.

An alternate command, the ˜**m** (tilde m) escape, works the way that ˜**f** does except the read-in message is indented one tab stop. Both the ˜**m** and ˜**f** commands work only if you start out in command mode and then enter a command that puts you into input mode. Other commands that work this way will be covered in the section "How to Manage Incoming Mail."

Changing Parts of the Message Header

The header of a **mailx** message has four components:

■ subject

■ recipient(s)

■ carbon copy list

■ blind carbon copy list (a list of intended recipients that is not shown on the copies sent to other recipients)

When you enter the **mailx** command followed by a login or an alias, you are put into input mode and prompted for the subject of your message. Once you end the subject line by pressing the <RETURN> key, **mailx** expects you to type the text of the message. If, at any point in input mode, you want to change or supplement some of the header information, there are four tilde escapes that you can use: ˜**h**, ˜**t**, ˜**c**, and ˜**b**.

˜**h**   Displays all the header fields: subject, recipient, carbon copy list, and blind copy list. You can change a current value, add to it, or, by pressing the <RETURN> key, accept it.

˜**t**   Lets you add names to the list of recipients. Names can be either login names or aliases.

˜**c**   Lets you create or add to a carbon copy list for the message. Enter either login names or aliases of those to whom a copy of the message should be sent.

˜b   Lets you create or add to a blind carbon copy list for the message.

All tilde escapes must be in the first position on a line. For the ˜t, ˜c or ˜b, any additional material on the line is taken to be input for the list in question. Any additional material on a line that begins with a ˜h is ignored.

Adding Your Signature

If you want, you can establish two different signatures with the **sign** and **Sign** environment variables. These can be invoked with the ˜a (tilde a) or ˜A (tilde A) escape, respectively. Assume you have set the value Supreme Commander to be called by the ˜A escape. Here's how it would work:

```
$ mailx –s orders all<CR>
Be ready to move out at 0400 hours.<CR>
˜A<CR>
Supreme Commander
˜.<CR>
EOT
$
```

Having both escapes (˜a and ˜A) allows you to set up two forms for your signature. However, because the sender's login automatically appears in the message header when the message is read, no signature is required to identify you.

Keeping a Record of Messages You Send

The **mailx** command offers several ways to keep copies of outgoing messages. Two that you can use without setting any special environment variables are the ˜w (tilde w) escape and the –F option on the command line.

The ˜**w** followed by a file name causes the message to be written to the named file:

```
$ mailx bdr<CR>
Subject: Saving Copies<CR>
When you want to save a copy of<CR>
the text of a message, use the tilde w.<CR>
˜w savemail
"savemail" 2/71
˜
.
EOT
$
```

If you now display the contents of **savemail**, you will see this:

```
$ cat savemail<CR>
When you want to save a copy of
the text of a message, use the tilde w.
$
```

The drawback to this method, as you can see, is that none of the header information is saved.

Using the **–F** option on the command line preserves the header information. It works as follows:

```
$ mailx –F –s Savings bdr<CR>
This method appends this message to a
file in my current directory named bdr.
~.
EOT
$
```

We can check the results by looking at the file **bdr**:

```
$ cat bdr<CR>
From: kol  Fri May 2  11:14:45  1986
To: bdr
Subject: Savings

This method appends this message to a
file in my current directory named bdr.
$
```

The **–F** option appends the text of the message to a file named after the
first recipient. If you have used an alias for the recipient(s), the alias is first
converted into the appropriate login(s), and the first login is used as the file
name. As noted above, if you have a file by that name in your current directory, the text of the message is appended to it.

Exiting from mailx

When you have finished composing your message, you can leave **mailx** by typing any of the following three commands:

˜. Tilde period (˜.) is the standard way of leaving input mode. It also sends the message. If you entered input mode from the command mode of **mailx**, you now return to the command mode (as shown by the ? prompt you receive after typing this command). If you started out in input mode, you now return to the shell (as shown by the shell prompt).

˜q Tilde q (˜q) simulates an interrupt. It lets you exit the input mode of **mailx**. If you have entered text for a message, it will be saved in a file called **dead.letter** in your home directory.

˜x Tilde x (˜x) simulates an interrupt. It lets you exit the input mode of **mailx** without saving anything.

Summary

In the preceding paragraphs we have described and shown examples of some of the tilde escape commands available when sending messages via the **mailx** command. (See the *mailx*(1) manual page in the *User's/System Administrator's Reference Manual*.)

How to Manage Incoming Mail

mailx has over fifty commands which help you manage your incoming mail. See the *mailx*(1) manual page in the *User's/System Administrator's Reference Manual* for an alphabetical list of all of them (and their synonyms). The most commonly used commands and arguments are described in the following subsections:

■ the *msglist* argument

■ commands for reading and deleting mail

■ commands for saving mail

■ commands for replying to mail

■ commands for getting out of **mailx**

The msglist **Argument**

Many commands in **mailx** take a form of the *msglist* argument. This argument provides the command with a list of messages on which to operate. If a command expects a *msglist* argument and you do not provide one, the command is performed on the current message. Any of the following formats can be used for *msglist*:

n	message number *n*
ˆ	the first undeleted message
$	the last message
*	all messages
n-m	an inclusive range of message numbers
user	all messages from *user*
/*string*	All messages with *string* in the subject line (case is ignored)
:*c*	all messages of type *c* where *c* is

> **d** - deleted messages
> **n** - new messages
> **o** - old messages
> **r** - read messages
> **u** - unread messages

The context of the command determines whether this type of specification makes sense.

Here are two examples (the ? is the command mode prompt):

```
? d 1-3        [ Delete messages 1, 2 and 3 ]
? s bdr bdr    [ Save all messages from user bdr in a
               file named bdr. ]

?
```

Additional examples may be found throughout the next three subsections.

Commands for Reading and Deleting Mail

When a message arrives in your mailbox, the following notice appears on your screen:

```
you have mail
```

The notice appears when you log in or when you return to the shell from another procedure.

Reading Mail

To read your mail, enter the **mailx** command with or without arguments. Execution of the command places you in the command mode of **mailx**. The next thing that appears on your screen is a display that looks something like this:

```
mailx version 2.14   10/19/86      Type ? for help
"/usr/mail/bdr":   3 messages   3 new
 > N 1 rbt          Thur Apr 30 14:20   8/190   Review Session
   N 2 admin        Thur Apr 30 15:56   5/84    New printer
   N 3 daves        Fri  May  1 08:39  64/1574 Reorganization
 ?
```

The first line identifies the version of **mailx** used on your system, displays the date, and reminds you that help is available by typing a question mark (**?**). The second line shows the path name of the file used as input to the display (the file name is normally the same as your login name) together with a count of the total number of messages and their status. The rest of the display is header information from the incoming messages. The messages are numbered in sequence with the last one received at the bottom of the list. To the left of the numbers there may be a status indicator: N for new and U for unread. A greater than sign (>) points to the current message. Other fields in the header line show the login of the originator of the message; the day, date and time it was delivered; the number of lines and characters in the message; and the message subject. The last field may be blank.

When the header information is displayed on your screen, you can print messages either by pressing the <RETURN> key or entering a command followed by a *msglist* argument. If you enter a command with no *msglist* argument, the command acts on the message pointed at by the > sign. Pressing the <RETURN> key is the equivalent of a typing the **p** (for print) command without a *msglist* argument; the message displayed is the one pointed at by the > sign. To read some other message (or several others in succession), enter a **p** (for print) or **t** (for type) followed by the message number(s). Here are some examples:

> ? <CR>   [*Print the current message.*]
> ? **p 2**<CR>[*Print message number 2.*   ]
> ? **p daves**<CR> [*Print all messages from user daves.*]

The command **t** (for type) is a synonym of **p** (for print).

Scanning Your Mailbox

The **mailx** command lets you look through the messages in your mailbox while you decide which ones need your immediate attention.

When you first enter the **mailx** command mode, the banner tells you how many messages you have and displays the header line for twenty messages. (If you are dialed into the computer system, only the header lines for ten messages are displayed.) If the total number of messages exceeds one screenful, you can display the next screen by entering the **z** command. Typing **z**– causes a previous screen (if there is one) to be displayed. If you want to see the header information for a specific group of messages, enter the **f** (for from) command followed by the *msglist* argument.

Here are examples of those commands:

> ? **z**   [*Scroll forward one screenful of header lines.*]
> ? **z**–   [*Scroll backward one screenful.*]
> ? **f daves** [*Display headers of all messages from user daves.*]

Switching to Other Mail Files

When you enter **mailx** by issuing the command

   $ **mailx**<CR>

you are looking at the file **/usr/mail/***your_login*.

mailx lets you switch to other mail files and use any of the **mailx** commands
on their contents. (You can even switch to a non-mail file, but if you try to
use **mailx** commands, you are told No applicable messages.) The switch to
another file is done with the **fi** or **fold** command (they are synonyms) followed by the *filename*. The following special characters work in place of the
filename argument:

%   the current mailbox

%*login* the mailbox of the owner of *login* (if you have the required per-
         missions)

the previous file

&   the current mbox

Here is an example of how this might look on your screen:

```
$ mailx<CR>

mailx version 2.14 10/19/86  Type ? for help.
"usr/mail/daves":  3 messages 2 new 3 unread
   U 1 jaf        Sat May 9 07:55   7/137    test25
 > N 2 todd       Sat May 9 08:59   9/377    UNITS requirements
   N 3 has        Sat May 9 11:08  29/1214   access to bailey

? fi &    [ Enter this command to transfer to your mbox. ]

Held 3 messages in /usr/mail/daves
"/fs1/daves/mbox":  74 messages 10 unread
   .
   .
   .
? q<CR>
$
```

Deleting Mail

To delete a message, enter a **d** followed by a *msglist* argument. If the *msglist* argument is omitted, the current message is deleted. The messages are not deleted until you leave the mailbox file you are processing. Prior to that, the **u** (for undelete) gives you the opportunity to change your mind. Once you have issued the quit command (**q**) or switched to another file, however, the deleted messages are gone.

mailx permits you to combine the delete and print command and enter a **dp**. This is like saying, "Delete the message I just read and show me the next one." Here are some examples of the delete command:

```
? d *     [ Delete all my messages. ]
? d r     [ Delete all messages that have been read. ]
? dp      [ Delete the current message and print the next one. ]
? d 2-5   [ Delete messages 2 through 5. ]
```

Commands for Saving Mail

All messages not specifically deleted are saved when you quit **mailx**. Messages that have been read are saved in a file in your home directory called **mbox**. Messages that have not been read are held in your mailbox (**/usr/mail/**_your_login_).

The command to save messages comes in two forms: with an uppercase **s** or a lowercase **s**. The syntax for the uppercase version is

> **S** [_msglist_]

Messages specified by the _msglist_ argument are saved in a file in the current directory named for the author of the first message in the list.

The syntax for the lowercase version is

> **s** [_msglist_] [_filename_]

Messages specified by the _msglist_ argument are saved in the file named in the _filename_ argument. If you omit the _msglist_ argument, the current message is saved. If you are using logins for file names, this can lead to some ambiguity. If **mailx** is puzzled, you will get an error message.

Commands for Replying to Mail

The command for replying to mail comes in two forms: with an upper-case **r** or a lowercase **r**. The principal difference between the two forms is that the uppercase form (**R**) causes your response to be sent only to the originator of the message, while the lowercase form (**r**) causes your response to be sent not only to the originator but also to all other recipients. (There are other differences between these two forms. For details, see the *mailx*(1) manual page in the *User's/System Administrator's Reference Manual*.)

When you reply to a message, the original subject line is picked up and used as the subject of your reply. Here's an example of the way it looks:

```
$ mailx<CR>

mailx version 2.14 10/19/83  Type ? for help.
"usr/mail/daves":  3 messages 2 new 3 unread
   U 1 jaf          Wed May 9 07:55   7/137    test25
 > N 2 todd         Wed May 9 08:59   9/377    UNITS requirements
   N 3 has          Wed May 9 11:08  29/1214   access to bailey

? R 2
To: todd
Subject: Re: UNITS requirements
```

Assuming the message about UNITS requirements had been sent to some additional people and the lowercase **r** had been used, the header might have appeared like this:

```
? r 2
To: todd eg has jcb bdr
Subject: Re: UNITS requirements
```

Commands for Getting Out of mailx

There are two standard ways of leaving **mailx**: with a **q** or with an **x**. If you leave **mailx** with a **q**, you see messages that summarize what you did with your mail. They look like this:

```
? q<CR>
Saved 1 message in /fs1/bdr/mbox
Held 1 message in /usr/mail/bdr
$
```

From the example, we can surmise that user **bdr** had at least two messages and read one then either left the other unread or issued a command asking that it be held in **/usr/mail/bdr**. If there were more than two messages, the others were deleted or saved in other files. **mailx** does not issue a message about those.

If you leave **mailx** with an **x**, it is almost as if you had never entered. Mail read and messages deleted are retained in your mailbox. However, if you have saved messages in other files, that action has already taken place and is not undone by the **x**.

mailx **Command Summary**

In the preceding subsections we have described some of the most frequently used **mailx** commands. (See the *mailx*(1) manual page in the *User's/System Administrator's Reference Manual* for a complete list.) If you need help while you are in the command mode of **mailx**, type either a **?** or **help** after the **?** prompt. A list of **mailx** commands and what they do will be displayed on your terminal screen.

The .mailrc File

The **.mailrc** file contains commands to be executed when you invoke **mailx**.

There may be a system-wide start-up file (**/usr/lib/mailx/mailx.rc**) on your system. If it exists, it is used by the system administrator to set common variables. Variables set in your **.mailrc** file take precedence over those in **mailx.rc**.

Most **mailx** commands are legal in the **.mailrc** file. However, the following commands are NOT legal entries:

! (or) **shell**	escapes to the shell
Copy	saves messages in *msglist* in a file whose name is chosen by the author
edit	invokes the editor
visual	invokes vi
followup	responds to a message
Followup	responds to a message, sending a copy to *msglist*
mail	switches into input mode
reply	responds to a message
Reply	responds to the author of each message in *msglist*

You can create your own **.mailrc** with any editor or copy a friend's. Figure 9-5 shows a sample **.mailrc** file.

```
if r
                    cd $HOME/mail
endif
set allnet append asksub askcc autoprint dot
set metoo quiet save showto header hold keep keepsave
set outfolder
set folder='mail'
set record='outbox'
set crt=24
set EDITOR='/bin/ed'
set sign='Roberts'
set Sign='Jackson Roberts, Supervisor'
set toplines=10
alias fred          fjs
alias bob           rcm
alias alice         ap
alias mark          mct
alias donna         dr
alias pat           pat
group robertsgrp    fred bob alice pat mark
group accounts      robertsgrp donna
```

Figure 9-5: Sample **.mailrc** File

The example in Figure 9-5 includes the commands you are most likely to find useful: the **set** command and the **alias** or **group** command.

The **set** command is used to establish values for environment variables. The command syntax is

> **set**
> **set** *name*
> **set** *name* = *string*
> **set** *name* = *number*

When you issue the **set** command without any arguments, **set** produces a list of all defined variables and their values. The argument *name* refers to an environmental variable. More than one *name* can be entered after the **set** command. Some variables take a string or numeric value. String values are enclosed in single quotes.

When you put a value in an environment variable by making an assignment such as **HOME**=*my_login*, you are telling the shell how to interpret that variable. However, this type of assignment in the shell does not make the value of the variable accessible to other UNIX System programs that need to reference environment variables. To make it accessible, you must export the variable. If you set the **TERM** variable in your environment when doing the exercises in Chapter 6 or Chapter 7, you will remember using the **export** command, as shown in the following example:

> $ **TERM**=5425
> $ **export TERM**

When you export variables from the shell in this way, programs that reference environment variables are said to import them. Some of these variables (such as **EDITOR** and **VISUAL**) are not peculiar to **mailx** but may be specified as general environment variables and imported from your execution environment. If a value is set in **.mailrc** for an imported variable, it overrides the imported value. There is an **unset** command, but it works only against variables set in **.mailrc**; it has no effect on imported variables.

There are forty-one environment variables that can be defined in your **.mailrc**, too many to be fully described in this document. For complete information, consult the *mailx*(1) manual page in the *User's/System Administrator's Reference Manual*.

Three variables used in the example in Figure 9-5 deserve special attention because they demonstrate how to organize the filing of messages. These variables are **folder**, **record**, and **outfolder**. All three are interrelated and control the directories and files in which copies of messages are kept.

To put a value into the **folder** variable, use the following format:

> set **folder**=*directory*

This specifies the directory in which you want to save standard mail files. If the directory name specified does not begin with a **/** (slash), it is presumed to be relative to **$HOME**. If **folder** is an exported shell variable, you can specify file names (in commands that call for a *filename* argument) with a **/** before the name; the name will be expanded so that the file is put into the **folder** directory.

To put a value in the **record** variable, use the following format:

    set record=*filename*

This directs **mailx** to save a copy of all outgoing messages in the specified file. The header information is saved along with the text of the message. By default, this variable is disabled.

The **outfolder** variable causes the file in which you store copies of outgoing messages (enabled by the variable **record**=) to be located in the **folder** directory. It is established by being named in a **set** command. The default is **nooutfolder**.

The **alias** and **group** commands are synonyms. In Figure 9-5, the **alias** command is used to associate a name with a single login; the **group** command is used to specify multiple names that can be called in with one pseudonym. This is a nice way to distinguish between single and group aliases, but if you want, you can treat the commands as exact equivalents. Notice, too, that aliases can be nested.

In the **mailrc** file shown in Figure 9-5, the alias **robertsgroup** represents five users; three of them are specified by previously defined aliases and one is specified by a login. The fifth user, **pat**, is specified by both a login and an alias. The next group command in the example, **accounts**, uses the alias **robertsgroup** plus the alias **donna**. It expands to twelve logins.

The **.mailrc** file in Figure 8-5 includes an **if-endif** command. The full syntax of that command is

    if s⌐r *mail_commands*

    else *mail_commands*

    endif

The **s** and **r** stand for send and receive, so you can cause some initializing commands to be executed according to whether **mailx** is entered in input mode (send) or command mode (receive). In the preceding example, the command is issued to change directory to **$HOME/mail** if reading mail. The user in this case had elected to set up a subdirectory for handling incoming mail.

The environment variables shown in this section are those most commonly included in the **.mailrc** file. You can, however, specify any of them for one session only whenever you are in command mode. For a complete list of the environment variables you can set in **mailx** see the *mailx*(1) manual page in the *User's/System Administrator's Reference Manual*.

Transferring Files

This section describes the commands available for transferring files: the **mail** command for small files (a page or less) and the **uucp** and **uuto** commands for long files. The **mail** command can be used for transferring a file either within a local system or to a remote system. The **uucp** and **uuto** commands transfer files from one system to another.

Sending Small Files: the mail Command

To send a file in a **mail** message, you must redirect the input to that file on the command line. Use the < (less than) redirection symbol as follows:

> **mail** *login* < *filename*<**CR**>

(For further information on input redirection, see Chapter 7.) Here *login* is the recipient's login ID, and *filename* is the name of the file you want to send. For example, to send a copy of a file called **agenda** to the owner of login **sarah** (on your system) type the following command line:

> $ **mail sarah** < **agenda**<**CR**>
> $

The prompt that appears on the second line means the contents of **agenda** have been sent. When **sarah** issues the **mail** command to read her messages, she will receive **agenda**.

To send the same file to more than one user on your system, use the same command line format with one difference: in place of one login ID, type several separated by spaces. For example:

> $ **mail sarah tommy dingo wombat** < **agenda**<**CR**>
> $

Again, the prompt returned by the system in response to your command is a signal that your message has been sent.

The same command line format with one addition can also be used to send a file to a user on a remote system that can communicate with yours. In this case, you must specify the name of the remote system before the user's login name. Separate the system name and the login name with an **!** (exclamation point):

> **mail** *system!login* < *filename*<**CR**>

For example:

> **$ mail dumbo!wombat** < **agenda**<**CR**>
> **$**

The system prompt on the second line means that your message (containing the file) has been queued for sending.

If you are using **mailx**, you cannot use the **mail** command line syntax to send a file. Instead, use the ˜**r** option as follows:

```
$ mailx phyllis
Subject: Memo
˜r memo
$
```

Sending Large Files

The **uucp** and **uuto** commands allow you to transfer files to a remote computer. **uucp** allows you to send files to the directory of your choice on the destination system. If you are transferring a file to a directory that you own, you will have permission to put the file in that directory. (See Chapter 3 for information on directory and file permissions.) However, if you are transferring the file to another user's directory, you must be sure, in advance, that the user has given you permission to write a file to his or her directory. In addition, because you must specify path names that are often long and require accuracy, **uucp** command lines may be cumbersome and lead to error.

The **uuto** command is an enhanced version of **uucp**. It automatically sends files to a public directory on the recipient's system called **/usr/spool/uucppublic**. This means you cannot choose a destination file. However, it also means that you can transfer a file at any time without having to request write permission from the owner of the destination directory. Finally, the **uuto** command line is shorter and less complicated than the **uucp** command line. When you type a **uuto** command line, the likelihood of making an error is greatly reduced.

Getting Ready: Do You Have Permission?

Before you actually send a file with the **uucp** or **uuto** command, you need to find out whether or not the file is transferrable. To do that, you must check the file's permissions. If you own the files and they are not correct, you must use the **chmod** command to change them. (Permissions and the **chmod** command are covered in Chapter 3.)

There are two permission criteria that must be met before a file can be transferred using **uucp** or **uuto**:

■ The file to be transferred must have read permission (**r**) for others.

■ The directory that contains the file must have read (**r**) and execute (**x**) permission for others.

For example, assume that you have a file named **chicken** under a directory named **soup** (in your home directory). You want to send a copy of the **chicken** file to another user with the **uuto** command. First, check the permissions on **soup**:

```
$ ls -l<CR>
total 4
drwxr-xr-x      2   reader   group1     45    Feb 9    10:43    soup
$
```

The response of the **ls** command shows that **soup** has read (**r**) and execute (**x**) permissions for all three groups; no changes have to be made. Now use the **cd** command to move from your home directory to **soup**, and check the permissions on the file **chicken**:

```
$ ls -l chicken<CR>
total 4
-rw-------        1    reader   group1   3101    Mar 1   18:22    chicken
$
```

The command's output means that you (the user) have permission to read the file **chicken**, but no one else does. To add read permissions for your group (**g**) and others (**o**), use the **chmod** command:

$ **chmod go+r chicken**<CR>

Now check the permissions again with the **ls -l** command:

```
$ ls -l chicken<CR>
total 4
-rw-r--r--        1    reader   group1   3101    Mar01   18:22    chicken
$
```

This confirms that the file is now transferable; you can send it with the **uucp** or **uuto** command. After you send copies of the file, you can reverse the procedure and replace the previous permissions.

The uucp **Command**

The **uucp** command (short for UNIX-to-UNIX System copy) allows you to copy a file directly to the home directory of a user on another computer, or to any other directory you specify and for which you have write permission.

uucp is not an interactive command. It performs its work silently, invisible to the user. Once you issue this command, you may run other processes.

Transferring a file between computers is a multiple-step procedure. First, a work file that contains instructions for the file transfer must be created. When requested, a data file (a copy of the file being sent) is also made. Then, the file is ready to be sent. When you issue the **uucp** command, it performs the preliminary steps described above (creating the necessary files in a dedicated directory called a **spool** directory) and then calls the **uucico** daemon that actually transfers the file. (Daemons are system processes that run in background.) The file is placed in a queue, and **uucico** sends it at the first available time.

Thus, the **uucp** command allows you to transfer files to a remote computer without knowing anything except the name of the remote computer and, possibly, the login ID of the remote user(s) to whom the file is being sent.

Command Line Syntax

uucp allows you to send

■ one file to a file or a directory

■ multiple files to a directory

To deliver your file(s), **uucp** must know the full path name of both the *source-file* and the *destination-file*. However, this does not mean you must type out the full path name of both files every time you use the **uucp** command. There are several abbreviations you can use once you become familiar with their formats; **uucp** will expand them to full path names.

To choose the appropriate designations for your *source-file* and *destination-file*, begin by identifying the *source-file*'s location relative to your own current location in the file system. (We'll assume, for the moment, that the *source-file* is in your local system.) If the *source-file* is in your current directory, you can specify it by its name alone (without a path). If the *source-file* is not in your current directory, you must specify its full path name.

How do you specify the *destination-file*? Because it is on a remote system, the *destination-file* must always be specified with a path name that begins with the name of the remote system. After that, however, **uucp** gives you a choice: you can specify the full path or use either of two forms of abbreviation. Your *destination-file* should have one of the following three formats:

- *system_name!full_path*

- *system_name!~login_name[/directory_name/filename]*

- *systemname!~/login_name[/directory_name/filename]*

The login name, in this case, belongs to the recipient of the file.

Until now, we have described what to do when you want to send a file from your local system to a remote system. However, it is also possible to use **uucp** to send a file from a remote system to your local system. In either case, you can use the formats described above to specify either *source-files* or *destination-files*. The important distinction in choosing one of these formats is not whether a file is a *source-file* or a *destination-file*, but where you are currently located in the file system relative to the files you are specifying. Therefore, in the formats shown above, the *login_name* could refer to the login of the owner or the recipient of either a *source-file* or a *destination-file*.

For example, let's say you are login **kol** on a system called **mickey**. Your home directory is **/usr/kol** and you want to send a file called **chap1** (in a directory called **text** in your home directory) to login **wsm** on a system called **minnie**. You are currently working in **/usr/kol/text**, so you can specify the *source-file* with its relative path name, **chap1**. Specify the *destination-file* in any of the ways shown in the following command lines:

■ Specify the *destination-file* with its full path name:

uucp chap1 minnie!/usr/wsm/receive/chap1

■ Specify the *destination-file* with ˜*login_name* (which expands to the name of the recipient's home directory) and a name for the new file:

uucp chap1 minnie!˜wsm/receive/chap1

(The file will go to **minnie!/usr/wsm/receive/chap1**.)

■ Specify the *destination-file* with ˜*login_name* (which expands to the recipient's home directory) but without a name for the new file; **uucp** will give the new file the same name as the *source-file*:

uucp chap1 minnie!˜wsm/receive

(The file will go to **minnie!/usr/wsm/receive/chap1**.)

■ Specify the *destination-file* with ˜/*login_name*. This expands to the recipient's subdirectory in the public directory on the remote system:

uucp chap1 minnie!˜/wsm

(The file will go to **minnie!/usr/usr/spool/uucppublic/wsm**.)

Sample Usage of Options with the uucp Command

Suppose you want to send a file called **minutes** to a remote computer named **eagle**. Enter the command line shown in the following screen:

```
$ uucp –m –s status –j minutes eagle!/usr/gws/minutes<CR>
eagleN3f45
$
```

This sends the file **minutes** (located in your current directory on your local computer) to the remote computer **eagle** and places it under the path name **/usr/gws** in a file named **minutes**. When the transfer is complete, the user **gws** on the remote computer is notified by mail.

The **–m** option ensures that you (the sender) are also notified by mail as to whether or not the transfer has succeeded. The **–s** option followed by the name of the file (**status**) asks the program to put a status report of the file transfer in the specified file (**status**).

 Be sure to include a file name after the **–s** option. If you do not, you will get this message: `uucp failed completely`.

The job ID (`eagleN3f45`) is displayed in response to the **–j** option.

Even if **uucp** does not notify you of a successful transfer soon after you send a file, do not assume that the transfer has failed. Not all systems equipped with networking software have the hardware needed to call other systems. Files being transferred from these so called passive systems must be collected periodically by active systems equipped with the required hardware (see "How the **uucp** Command Works" for details). Therefore, if you are transferring files from a passive system, you may experience some delay. Check with your system administrator to find out whether your system is active or passive.

The previous example uses a full path name to specify the *destination-file*. There are two other ways the *destination-file* can be specified:

■ The login directory of **gws** specified through use of the ~ (tilde):

   eagle!~gws/minutes

is interpreted as

   eagle!/usr/gws/minutes

■ The **uucppublic** area is referenced by a similar use of the tilde prefix to the path name. For example:

eagle!~/gws/minutes

is interpreted as

/usr/spool/uucppublic/gws/minutes

How the uucp **Command Works**

This section is an overview of what happens when you issue the **uucp** command. An understanding of the processes involved may help you to be aware of the command's limitations and requirements: why it can perform some tasks and not others, why it performs tasks when it does, and why you may or may not be able to use it for tasks that **uucp** performs. For further details see the *Operations/System Administration Guide* and the *User's/System Administrator's Reference Manual*.

When you enter a **uucp** command, the **uucp** program creates a work file and usually a data file for the requested transfer. (**uucp** does not create a data file when you use the **–c** option.) The work file contains information required for transferring the file(s). The data file is simply a copy of the specified source file. After these files are created in the spool directory, the **uucico** daemon is started.

The **uucico** daemon attempts to establish a connection to the remote computer that is to receive the file(s). It first gathers the information required for establishing a link to the remote computer from the **Systems** file. This is how **uucico** knows what type of device to use in establishing the link. Then **uucico** searches the **Devices** file looking for the devices that match the requirements listed in the **Systems** file. After **uucico** finds an available device, it attempts to establish the link and log in on the remote computer.

When **uucico** logs in on the remote computer, it starts the **uucico** daemon on the remote computer. The two **uucico** daemons then negotiate the line protocol to be used in the file transfer(s). The local **uucico** daemon transfers the file(s) that you are sending to the remote computer; the remote **uucico** places the file in the specified path name(s) on the remote computer. After your local computer completes the transfer(s), the remote computer may send files that are queued for your local computer. The remote computer can be denied permission to transfer these files with an entry in the **Permissions** file. If this is done, the remote computer must establish a link to your local computer to perform the transfers.

If the remote computer or the device selected to make the connection to the remote computer is unavailable, the request remains queued in the spool directory. Each hour (default), **uudemon.hour** is started by **cron**, which in turn starts the **uusched** daemon. When the **uusched** daemon starts, it searches the spool directory for the remaining work files, generates the random order in which these requests are to be processed, and then starts the transfer process (**uucico**) described in the previous paragraphs.

The transfer process described generally applies to an active computer. An active computer (one with calling hardware and networking software) can be set up to poll a passive computer. Because it has networking software, a passive computer can queue file transfers. However, it cannot call the remote computer because it does not have the required hardware. The **Poll** file (**/usr/lib/uucp/Poll**) contains a list of computers that are to be polled in this manner.

Figure 9-6 summarizes the syntax and capabilities of the **uucp** command.

Command Recap
uucp – copies a file from one computer to another

command	*options*	*arguments*
uucp	**–j1**, **–m**, **–s** and others*	*source-file*

Description:	**uucp** performs preliminary tasks required to copy a file from one computer to another and calls **uucico**, the daemon (background process) that transfers the file. The user need only issue the **uucp** command for a file to be copied.
Remarks:	By default, the only directory to which you can write files is **/usr/spool/uucppublic**. To write to directories belonging to another user, you must receive write permission from that user. Although there are several ways of representing path names as arguments, it is recommended that you type full path names to avoid confusion.

* See the *uucp*(1) manual page in the *User's/System Administrator's Reference Manual* for all available options and an explanation of their capabilities.

Figure 9-6: Summary of the **uucp** Command

The uuto **Command**

The **uuto** command allows you to transfer files to the public directory of another system. The basic format for the **uuto** command is

  uuto *filename system!login*<**CR**>

where *filename* is the name of the file to be sent, *system* is the recipient's system, and *login* is the recipient's login name.

If you send a file to someone on your local system, you may omit the system name and use the following format:

  uuto *filename login*<**CR**>

Sending a File: the –m **Option and** uustat **Command**

Now that you know how to determine if a file is transferable, let's take an example and see how the whole thing works.

The process of sending a file by **uuto** is referred to as a job. When you issue a **uuto** command, your job is not sent immediately. First, the file is stored in a queue (a waiting line of jobs) and assigned a job number. When the job's number comes up, the file is transmitted to the remote system and placed in a public directory there. The recipient is notified by a **mail** message and must use the **uupick** command (discussed later in the chapter) to retrieve the file.

For the following discussions, assume this information:

wombat	your login name
sys1	your system name
marie	recipient's login name
sys2	recipient's system name
money	file to be sent

Also assume that the two systems can communicate with each other.

To send the file **money** to login **marie** on system **sys2**, enter the following:

```
$ uuto money sys2!marie<CR>
$
```

The prompt on the second line is a signal that the file has been sent to a job queue. The job is now out of your hands; all you can do is wait for confirmation that the job reached its destination.

How do you know when the job has been sent? The easiest method is to alter the **uuto** command line by adding a **–m** option, as follows:

```
$ uuto –m money sys2!marie<CR>
$
```

This option sends a **mail** message back to you when the job has reached the recipient's system. The message may look something like this:

```
$ mail<CR>
From uucp Thur Apr3 09:45 EST 1986
file /sys1/wombat/money, system sys1
copy succeeded
?
```

If you would like to check if the job has left your system, you can use the **uustat** command. This command keeps track of all the **uucp** and **uuto** jobs you submit and reports the status of each on demand. For example:

```
$ uustat<CR>
1145 wombat sys2 10/05-09:31 10/05-09:33 JOB IS QUEUED
$
```

The elements of this sample status message are as follows:

- ■ 1145 is the job number assigned to the job of sending the file **money** to **marie** on **sys2**.

- ■ **wombat** is the login name of the person requesting the job.

- ■ sys2 is the recipient's system.

- ■ 10/05-09:31 is the date and time the job was queued.

- ■ 10/05-09:33 is the date and time this **uustat** message was sent.

- ■ The final part is a status report on the job. Here the report shows that the job has been queued but has not yet been sent.

To receive a status report on only one **uuto** job, use the **-j** option and specify the job number on the command line:

   uustat -j*jobnumber*<CR>

For example, to get a report on the job described in the previous example, specify 1145 (the job number) after the **–j** option:

```
$ uustat -j1145<CR>
1145 wombat sys2 10/05-09:31 10/05-09:37 COPY FINISHED,JOB DELETED
$
```

This status report shows that the job was sent and deleted from the job queue; it is now in the public directory of the recipient's system. Other status messages and options for the **uustat** command are described in the *User's/System Administrator's Reference Manual*.

That is all there is to sending files. To practice, try sending a file to yourself.

Figures 9-7 and 9-8 summarize the syntax and capabilities of the **uuto** and **uustat** commands, respectively.

Command Recap

uuto – sends files to another login

command	*options*	*arguments*
uuto	**–m** and others*	*file system!***login**

Description:	**uuto** sends a specified file to the public directory of a specified system and notifies the intended recipient (by mail addressed to his or her login) that the file has arrived there.
Remarks:	Files to be sent must have read permission for others; the file's parent directory must have read and execute permissions for others.
	The **–m** option notifies the sender by mail when the file has arrived at its destination.

*   See the *uuto*(1) manual page in the *User's/System Administrator's Reference Manual* for all available options and an explanation of their capabilities.

Figure 9-7: Summary of the **uuto** Command

Command Recap
uustat – checks job status of a **uucp** or **uuto** job

command	*options*	*arguments*
uustat	**–j** and others*	none

Description:	**uustat** reports the status of all **uucp** and **uuto** jobs you have requested.
Remarks:	The **–j** option followed by a job number allows you to request a status report on only the specified job.

* See the *uustat*(1) manual page in the *User's/System Administrator's Reference Manual* for all available options and an explanation of their capabilities.

Figure 9-8: Summary of the **uustat** Command

Receiving Files Sent with uuto: the uupick Command

When a file sent by **uuto** reaches the public directory on your UNIX System, you receive a **mail** message. To continue the previous example, the owner of login **marie** receives the following mail message when the file **money** has arrived in her system's public directory:

```
$ mail
From uucp Wed May 14 09:22 EST 1986
/usr/spool/uucppublic/receive/marie/sys1//money from sys1!wombat arrived
$
```

The message contains the following pieces of information:

■ The first line tells you when the file arrived at its destination.

■ The second line, up to the two slashes (//), gives the path name to the part of the public directory where the file has been stored.

■ The rest of the line after the two slashes gives the name of the file and the sender.

Once you have disposed of the **mail** message, you can use the **uupick** command to store the file where you want it. Type the following command after the system prompt:

uupick<CR>

The command searches the public directory for any files sent to you. If it finds any, it reports the filename(s). It then prints a ? prompt as a request for further instructions from you.

For example, say the owner of login **marie** issues the **uupick** command to retrieve the **money** file. The command will respond as follows:

$ uupick<CR>
from system sys1: file money
?

There are several available responses; we will look at the most common responses and what they do.

The first thing you should do is move the file from the public directory and place it in your login directory. To do so, type an **m** after the question mark:

> ?
> **m**<**CR**>
> $

This response moves the file into your current directory. If you want to put it in some other directory instead, follow the **m** response with the directory name:

> ?
> **m** *other_directory*<**CR**>

If there are other files waiting to be moved, the next one is displayed, followed by the question mark. If not, **uucpick** returns a prompt.

If you do not want to do anything to that file now, press the <RETURN> key after the question mark:

> ?
> <**CR**>

The current file remains in the public directory until the next time you use the **uupick** command. If there are no more messages, the system returns a prompt.

If you already know that you do not want to save the file, you can delete it by typing **d** after the question mark:

> ?
> **d**<**CR**>

This response deletes the current file from the public directory and displays the next message (if there is one). If there are no additional messages about waiting files, the system returns a prompt.

Finally, to stop the **uupick** command, type a **q** after the question mark:

> ?
> **q**<**CR**>

Any unmoved or undeleted files will wait in the public directory until the next time you use the **uupick** command.

Other available responses are listed in the *User's/System Administrator's Reference Manual.*

Figure 9-9 summarizes the syntax and capabilities of the **uupick** command.

Command Recap		
uupick – searches for files sent by **uuto** or **uucp**		
command	*options*	*arguments*
uupick	**–s**	*system name*
Description:	**uupick** searches the public directory of your system for files sent by **uuto** or **uucp**. If any are found, the command displays information about the file and prompts you for a response.	
Remarks:	The question mark (?) at the end of the message shows that a response is expected. A complete list of responses is given in the *User's/System Administrator's Reference Manual.*	

Figure 9-9: Summary of the **uupick** Command

Networking

Networking is the process of linking computers and terminals so that users may be able to

 log in on a remote computer as well as a local one

■ log in and work on two computers in one work session (without alternately logging off one and logging in on the other)

■ exchange data between computers

The commands presented in this section make it possible for you to perform these tasks. The **ct** command allows you to connect your computer to a remote terminal that is equipped with a modem. The **cu** command enables you to connect your computer to a remote computer, and the **uux** command lets you run commands on a remote system without being logged in on it.

> NOTE
>
> On some small computers, the presence of these commands may depend on whether or not networking software is installed. If it is not installed on your system, you will receive a message such as the following when you type a networking command:
>
> cu: not found
>
> Check with your system administrator to verify the availability of networking commands on your UNIX System.

Connecting to a Remote Terminal: the ct Command

The **ct** command connects your computer to a remote terminal equipped with a modem and allows a user on that terminal to log in. To do this, the command dials the phone number of the modem. The modem must be able to answer the call automatically. When **ct** detects that the call has been answered, it issues a **getty** (login) process for the remote terminal and allows a user on it to log in on the computer.

This command can be useful when issued from the opposite end, that is, from the remote terminal itself. If you are using a remote terminal that is far from your computer and want to avoid long distance charges, you can use **ct** to have the computer place a call to your terminal. Simply call the computer, log in, and issue the **ct** command. The computer will hang up the current line and call your remote terminal back.

If **ct** cannot find an available dialer, it tells you that all dialers are busy and asks if it should wait until one becomes available. If you answer yes, it asks how long (in minutes) it should wait for one.

Command Line Format

To execute the **ct** command, follow this format:

   ct [*options*] *telno*<**CR**>

The argument *telno* is the telephone number of the remote terminal.

Sample Command Usage

Suppose you are logged in on a computer through a local terminal and you want to connect a remote terminal to your computer. The phone number of the modem on the remote terminal is 932-3497. Enter this command line:

   ct –h –w5 –s1200 9=9323497<**CR**>

 NOTE The equal sign (=) represents a secondary dial tone, and dashes (–) following the phone number represent delays (the dashes are useful following a long distance number).

ct will call the modem, using a dialer operating at a speed of 1200 baud. If a dialer is not available, the **–w5** option will cause **ct** to wait for a dialer for five minutes before quitting. The **–h** option tells **ct** not to disconnect the local terminal (the terminal on which the command was issued) from the computer.

Now imagine that you want to log in on the computer from home. To avoid long distance charges, use **ct** to have the computer call your terminal:

   ct –s1200 9=9323497<**CR**>

Because you did not specify the **–w** option, if no device is available, **ct** sends you the following message:

```
1 busy dialer at 1200 baud Wait for dialer?
```

If you type **n** (no), the **ct** command exits. If you type **y** (yes), **ct** prompts you to specify how long **ct** should wait:

```
Time, in minutes?
```

If a dialer is available, **ct** responds with

```
Allocated dialer at 1200 baud
```

This means that a dialer has been found. In any case, **ct** asks if you want the line connecting your remote terminal to the computer to be dropped:

```
Confirm hangup?
```

If you type **y** (yes), you are logged off, and **ct** calls your remote terminal back when a dialer is available. If you type **n** (no), the **ct** command exits, leaving you logged in on the computer.

Figure 9-10 summarizes the syntax and capabilities of the **ct** command.

Command Recap		
ct – connects a computer to a remote terminal		
command	*options*	*arguments*
ct	**–h, –w, –s** and others*	*telno*
Description:	**ct** connects the computer to a remote terminal and allows a user to log in from that terminal.	
Remarks:	The remote terminal must have a modem capable of answering phone calls automatically.	

*   See the *ct*(1) manual page in the *User's/System Administrator's Reference Manual* for all available options and an explanation of their capabilities.

Figure 9-10: Summary of the **ct** Command

Calling Another UNIX System: the cu Command

The **cu** command connects a remote computer to your computer and allows you to be logged in on both computers simultaneously. This means that you can move back and forth between the two computers, transferring files and executing commands on both, without dropping the connection.

The method used by the **cu** command depends on the information you specify on the command line. You must specify the telephone number or system name of the remote computer. If you specify a phone number, it is passed on to the automatic dial modem. If you specify a system name, **cu** obtains the phone number from the **Systems** file. If an automatic dial modem is not used to establish the connection, the line (port) associated with the direct link to the remote computer can be specified on the command line.

Once the connection is made, the remote computer prompts you to log in on it. When you have finished working on the remote terminal, log off and terminate the connection by typing <˜.>. You will still be logged in on the local computer.

 The **cu** command is not capable of detecting or correcting errors; data may be lost or corrupted during file transfers. After a transfer, you can check for loss of data by running the **sum** command or the **ls –l** command on the file that was sent and the file that was received. Both of these commands will report the total number of bytes in each file; if the totals match, your transfer was successful. The **sum** command checks more quickly and gives output that is easier to interpret. (See the *sum*(1) and the *ls*(1) manual pages in the *User's/System Administrator's Reference Manual* for details.)

Command Line Format

To execute the **cu** command, follow this format:

> **cu** [*options*] *telno* ⫶ *systemname*<**CR**>

The components of the command line are

telno the telephone number of a remote computer

Equal signs (=) represent secondary dial tones, and dashes (–) represent four-second delays.

systemname a system name that is listed in the **Systems** file

The **cu** command obtains the telephone number and baud rate from the **Systems** file and searches for a dialer. The **–s**, **–n**, and **–l** options should not be used together with *systemname*. (To see the list of computers in the **Systems** file, run the **uuname** command.)

Once your terminal is connected and you are logged in on the remote computer, all standard input (input from the keyboard) is sent to the remote computer. Figures 9-11 and 9-12 show the commands you can execute while connected to a remote computer through **cu**.

String	Interpretation
~.	Terminates the link.
~!	Escapes to the local computer without dropping the link. To return to the remote computer, type < ^**d**> (control-d).
~!*command*	Executes *command* on the local computer.
~$*command*	Runs *command* locally and sends its output to the remote system.
~%**cd** *path*	Changes the directory on the local computer where *path* is the path name or directory name.
~%**take** *from* [*to*]	Copies a file named *from* on the remote computer to a file named *to* on the local computer. If *to* is omitted, the *from* argument is used in both places.
~%**put** *from* [*to*]	Copies a file named *from* on the local computer to a file named *to* on the remote computer. If *to* is omitted, the *from* argument is used in both places.
~~...	Sends a line beginning with ~ (~~...) to the remote computer.
~%**break**	Transmits a <BREAK> to the remote computer (can also be specified as ~%**b**).

Figure 9-11: Command Strings for Use with **cu** (Sheet 1 of 2)

String	Interpretation
~%nostop	Turns off the handshaking protocol for the remainder of the session. This is useful when the remote computer does not respond properly to the protocol characters.
~%debug	Turns the **-d** debugging option on or off (can also be specified as ~%**d**).
~t	Displays the values of the terminal I/O (input/output) structure variables for your terminal (useful for debugging).
~l	Displays the values of the *termio* structure variables for the remote communication line (useful for debugging).

Figure 9-12: Command Strings for Use with **cu** (Sheet 2 of 2)

The use of ~%**put** requires **stty** and **cat** on the remote computer. It also requires that the current erase and kill characters on the remote computer be identical to the current ones on the local computer.

The use of ~%**take** requires the existence of the **echo** and **cat** commands on the remote computer. Also, **stty tabs** mode should be set on the remote computer if tabs are to be copied without expansion.

Sample Command Usage

Suppose you want to connect your computer to a remote computer called **eagle**. The phone number for eagle is 847–7867. Enter the following command line:

    cu -s1200 9=8477867<CR>

The **-s1200** option causes **cu** to use a 1200 baud dialer to call **eagle**. If the **-s** option is not specified, **cu** uses a dialer at the default speed, 300 baud.

When **eagle** answers the call, **cu** notifies you that the connection has been made and prompts you for a login ID:

```
connected
login:
```

Enter your login ID and password.

The **take** command allows you to copy files from the remote computer to the local computer. Suppose you want to make a copy of a file named **proposal** for your local computer. The following command copies **proposal** from your current directory on the remote computer and places it in your current directory on the local computer. If you do not specify a file name for the new file, it will also be called **proposal**.

    ~%**take proposal**<CR>

The **put** command allows you to do the opposite: copy files from the local computer to the remote computer. Say you want to copy a file named **minutes** from your current directory on the local computer to the remote computer. Type

    ~%**put minutes minutes.9–18**<CR>

In this case, you specified a different name for the new file (**minutes.9-18**). Therefore, the copy of the **minutes** file that is made on the remote computer will be called **minutes.9-18**.

Figure 9-13 summarizes the syntax and capabilities of the **cu** command.

Command Recap
cu – connects a computer to a remote computer

command	*options*	*arguments*
cu	**–s** and others*	*telno* (or) *systemname*

Description:	**cu** connects your computer to a remote computer and allows you to be logged in on both simultaneously. Once you are logged in, you can move between computers to execute commands and transfer files on each without dropping the link.

* See the *cu*(1) manual page in the *User's/System Administrator's Reference Manual* for all available options and an explanation of their capabilities.

Figure 9-13: Summary of the **cu** Command

Executing Commands on a Remote System: the uux **Command**

The **uux** command (short for UNIX-to-UNIX System command execution) allows you to execute UNIX System commands on remote computers. It can gather files from various computers, execute a command on a specified computer, and send the standard output to a file on a specified computer. The execution of certain commands may be restricted on the remote machine. The command notifies you by mail if the command you have requested is not allowed to execute.

Command Line Format

To execute the **uux** command, follow this format:

uux [*options*] *command–string*<**CR**>

The *command–string* is made up of one or more arguments. All special shell characters (such as " <>!̂ ") must be quoted either by quoting the entire *command–string* or quoting the character as a separate argument. Within the *command–string*, the command and file names may contain a *system name!* prefix. All arguments that do not contain a *systemname* are interpreted as command arguments. A file name may be either a full path name or the name of a file under the current directory on the local computer.

Sample Command Usage

If your computer is hard-wired to a larger host computer, you can use **uux** to get printouts of files that reside on your computer by entering

pr minutes ¦ uux –p host!lp<**CR**>

This command line queues the file **minutes** to be printed on the area printer of the computer **host**.

Figure 9-14 summarizes the syntax and capabilities of the **uux** command.

Command Recap		
uux – executes commands on a remote computer		
command	*options*	*arguments*
uux	**–1**, **–p**, and others*	*command-string*
Description:	**uux** allows you to run UNIX System commands on remote computers. It can gather files from various computers, run a command on a specified computer, and send the standard output to a file on a specified computer.	
Remarks:	By default, users of the **uux** command have permission to run only the **mail** and **mailx** commands. Check with your system administrator to find out if users on your system have been granted permission to run other commands.	

*   See the *uux*(1C) manual page in the *User's/System Administrator's Reference Manual* for all available options and an explanation of their capabilities.

Figure 9-14: Summary of the **uux** Command

A Summary of the File System

The UNIX System Files

This appendix summarizes the description of the file system given in Chapter 1 and reviews the major system directories in the **root** directory.

File System Structure

The UNIX System files are organized in a hierarchy; their structure is often described as an inverted tree. At the top of this tree is the root directory, the source of the entire file system. It is designated by a / (slash). All other directories and files descend and branch out from **root**, as shown in Figure A-1.

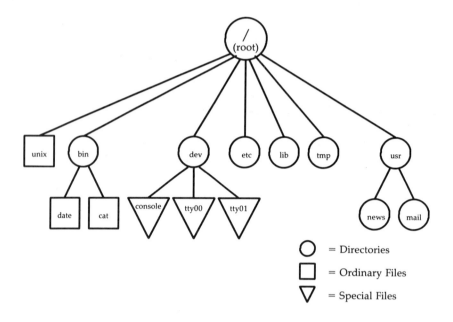

Figure A-1: Directory Tree from **root**

One path from **root** leads to your home directory. You can organize and store information in your own hierarchy of directories and files under your home directory.

Other paths lead from **root** to system directories that are available to all users. The system directories described in this book are common to all UNIX System installations and are provided and maintained by the operating system.

In addition to this standard set of directories, your UNIX System may have other system directories. To obtain a listing of the directories and files in the **root** directory on your UNIX System, type the following command line:

ls −l / <CR>

To move around in the file structure, you can use path names. For example, you can move to the directory **/bin** (which contains UNIX System executable files) by typing the following command line:

cd /bin<CR>

To list the contents of a directory, issue one of the following command lines:

ls<CR>	for a list of file and directory names
ls −l<CR>	for a detailed list of file and directory names

To list the contents of a directory in which you are not located, issue the **ls** command, as shown in the following examples:

ls /bin<CR>	for a short listing
ls −l /bin<CR>	for a detailed listing

The following section provides brief descriptions of the **root** directory and the system directories under it, as shown in Figure A-1.

UNIX System Directories

/	The source of the file system (called **root** directory)
/bin	Contains many executable programs and utilities, such as

> **cat**
> **date**
> **login**
> **grep**
> **mkdir**
> **who**

/lib	Contains available program libraries and language libraries, such as

libc.a	system calls, standard I/O
libm.a	math routines and support for languages such as C, FORTRAN, and BASIC

/dev	Contains special files that represent peripheral devices, such as

console	console
lp	line printer
tty$n$	user terminal(s)
dsk/*	disks

/etc	Contains programs and data files for system administration
/tmp	Contains temporary files, such as the buffers created for editing a file
/usr	Contains the following subdirectories, which in turn contain the data listed below:

news	important news items
mail	electronic mail
spool	files waiting to be printed on the line printer

B Summary of UNIX System Commands

Basic UNIX System Commands

Basic UNIX System Commands

at Requests that a command be run in background mode at a time you specify on the command line. If you do not specify a time, **at** displays the job numbers of all jobs you have running in **at**, **batch**, or background mode.

A sample format is

> **at 8:45am Jun 09<CR>**
> *command1*<**CR**>
> *command2*<**CR**>
> <^**d**>

If you use the **at** command without the date, the command executes within twenty-four hours of the time specified.

banner Displays a message (in words up to ten characters long) in large letters on the standard output.

batch Submits command(s) to be processed when the system load is at an acceptable level. A sample format of this command is

> **batch<CR>**
> *command1*<**CR**>
> *command2*<**CR**>
> <^**d**>

You can use a shell script for a command in **batch**. This may be useful and timesaving if you have a set of commands you frequently submit using this command.

cat Displays the contents of a specified file at your terminal. To halt the output on an ASCII terminal temporarily, use <^**s**>; type <^**q**> to restart the output. To interrupt the output and return to the shell on an ASCII terminal, press the <BREAK> or <DELETE> key.

cd Changes directory from the current one to your home directory. If you include a directory name, you can change from the current directory to the directory specified. By using a path name in place of the directory name, you can jump several levels with one command.

copy   Copies a specified directory (including its subdirectories and files) into another directory, leaving the original directory intact.

cp   Copies a specified file into a new file, leaving the original file intact.

cut   Cuts out specified fields from each line of a file. This command can be used to cut columns from a table, for example.

date   Displays the current date and time.

diff   Compares two files. The **diff** command reports which lines are different and what changes should be made to the second file to make it the same as the first file.

echo   Displays input on the standard output (the terminal), including the carriage return, and returns a prompt.

ed   Edits a specified file using the line editor. If there is no file with the name specified, the **ed** command creates one. See Chapter 5 for detailed instructions on using the **ed** editor.

grep   Searches a specified file(s) for a specified pattern and prints those lines that contain the pattern. If you name more than one file, **grep** prints the file that contains the pattern.

kill   Terminates a background process specified by its process identification number (PID). You can obtain a PID by running the **ps** command.

lc   Lists, in multiple columns, the names of all files and directories (except those that begin with a dot) in the current directory. Options are available for listing more detailed information about the contents of a directory. For more information about available options, see the *ls*(1) page in the *User's/System Administrator's Reference Manual*.

lex   Generates programs to be used in simple lexical analysis of text, perhaps as a first step in creating a compiler. See the *User's/System Administrator's Reference Manual* for details.

lp   Prints the contents of a specified file on a line printer, giving you a paper copy of the file.

lpstat   Displays the status of any requests made to the line printer. Options are available for requesting more detailed information.

ls   Lists the names of all files and directories except those whose names begin with a dot (.). Options are available for listing more detailed information about the files in the directory. (See the *ls*(1) page in the *User's/System Administrator's Reference Manual* for details.)

mail   Displays any electronic mail you may have received at your terminal, one message at a time. Each message ends with a **?** prompt; **mail** waits for you to request an option, such as saving, forwarding, or deleting a message. To obtain a list of the available options, type **?**.

When followed by a login name, **mail** sends a message to the owner of that name. You can type as many lines of text as you want. Then type <^**d**> to end the message and send it to the recipient. Press the <BREAK> key to interrupt the mail session.

mailx   **mailx** is a more sophisticated, expanded version of electronic mail.

make   Maintains and supports large programs or documents on the basis of smaller ones. See the *make*(1) page in the *Programmer's Reference Manual* for details.

mkdir   Makes a new directory. The new directory becomes a subdirectory of the directory in which you issue the **mkdir** command. To create subdirectories or files in the new directory, you must first move into the new directory with the **cd** command.

more   Displays the contents of a file, one full screen at a time. Options are available for specifying how **more** will display the file. For more information about available options, see the *more*(1) entry in the *User's/System Administrator's Reference Manual*.

mv	Moves a file to a new location in the file system. You can move a file to a new file name in the same directory or to a different directory. If you move a file to a different directory, you can use the same file name or choose a new one.
nohup	Places execution of a command in the background so that it will continue executing after you log off of the system. Error messages are placed in a file called **nohup.out**.
pg	Displays the contents of a specified file on your terminal, a page at a time. After each page, the system pauses and waits for your instructions before proceeding.
pr	Displays a partially formatted version of a specified file at your terminal. The **pr** command shows page breaks but does not implement any macros supplied for text formatter packages.
ps	Displays the status and number of every process currently running. The **ps** command does not show the status of jobs in the **at** or **batch** queues, but it includes these jobs when they are executing.
pwd	Displays the full path name of the current working directory.
rm	Removes a file from the file system. You can use metacharacters with the **rm** command, but you should use them with caution; a removed file cannot be recovered easily.
rmdir	Removes a directory. You cannot be in the directory you want to delete, and you cannot delete a directory unless it is empty. Therefore, you must remove any subdirectories and files that remain in a directory before using this command. (See **rm -r** in the *User's/System Administrator's Reference Manual* for information on removing directories that are not empty.)
sort	Sorts a file in ASCII order and displays the results on your terminal. ASCII order is as follows:

> 1. numbers before letters
> 2. uppercase letters before lowercase letters
> 3. alphabetical order

There are other options for sorting a file. For a complete list of **sort** options, see the *sort*(1) page in the *User's/System Administrator's Reference Manual*.

spell   Collects words from a specified file and checks them against a spelling list. Words not on the list or not related to words on the list (with suffixes, prefixes, and so on) are displayed.

stty   Reports the settings of certain input/output options for your terminal. When issued with the appropriate options and arguments, **stty** also sets these input/output options. (See the *stty*(1) page in the *User's/System Administrator's Reference Manual*.)

uname   Displays the name of the UNIX System on which you are currently working.

uucp   Sends a specified file to another UNIX System. (See the *uucp*(1) page in the *User's/System Administrator's Reference Manual* for details.)

uuname   Lists the names of remote UNIX Systems that can communicate with your UNIX System.

uupick   Searches the public directory for files sent to you by the **uuto** command. If a file is found, **uupick** displays its name and the system it came from, and prompts you (with a **?**) to take action.

uustat   Reports the status of the **uuto** command you issued to send files to another user.

uuto   Sends a specified file to another user. You must specify the destination in the format *system!login*. *system* must be on the list of systems generated by the **uuname** command.

vi   Edits a specified file using the **vi** screen editor. If there is no file by the name you specify, **vi** creates one. (See Chapter 6 for detailed information on using the **vi** editor.)

wc   Counts the number of lines, words, and characters in a specified file and displays the results on your terminal.

who   Displays the login names of the users currently logged in on your UNIX System and lists the terminal address for each login and the time each user logged in.

yacc   Imposes a structure on the input of a program. See the *yacc*(1) page in the *Programmer's Reference Manual* for details.

C Quick Reference to ed Commands

ed Quick Reference

The general format for **ed** commands is

[*address1,address2*]*command*[*parameter*]...<**CR**>

where *address1* and *address2* denote line addresses, and the *parameters* show the data on which the command operates. The commands appear on your terminal as you type them. You can find complete information on using **ed** commands in Chapter 5, "Line Editor Tutorial (**ed**)."

The following is a glossary of **ed** commands. The commands are grouped according to function.

Commands for Getting Started

ed *filename* Accesses the **ed** line editor to edit a specified file.

a   Appends text after the current line.

.   Ends the text input mode and returns to the command mode.

p   Displays the current line.

d   Deletes the current line.

<**CR**>   Moves down one line in the buffer.

−   Moves up one line in the buffer.

w   Writes the buffer contents to the file currently associated with the buffer.

q   Ends an editing session. If changes to the buffer were not written to a file, a warning (**?**) is issued. Typing **q** a second time ends the session without writing to a file.

Line Addressing Commands

1, 2, 3...	Denotes line addresses in the buffer.
.	Displays the current line in the buffer.
.=	Displays the current line address.
$	Denotes the last line in the buffer.
,	Addresses the first through the last line.
;	Addresses the current line through the last line.
+*x*	Adds *x* to the current line number and displays the relative address.
–*x*	Subtracts *x* from the current line number and displays the relative address.
/*abc*	Searches forward in the buffer and addresses the first line after the current line that contains the pattern *abc*.
?*abc*	Searches backward in the buffer and addresses the first line before the current line that contains the pattern *abc*.
g/*abc*	Addresses all lines in the buffer that contain the pattern *abc*.
v/*abc*	Addresses all lines in the buffer that do not contain the pattern *abc*.

Display Commands

p	Displays the specified lines in the buffer.
n	Displays the specified lines preceded by their line addresses and a tab space.

Text Input

a   Enters text after the specified line in the buffer.

i   Enters text before the specified line in the buffer.

c   Replaces text in the specified lines with new text.

.   When typed on a line by itself, ends the text input mode and returns to the command mode.

Deleting Text

d   Deletes one or more lines of text (command mode).

u   Undoes the last command given (command mode).

@   Deletes the current line (in text input mode) or a command line (in command mode).

 # or BACKSPACE
          Deletes the last character entered as text (in input mode).

Substituting Text

*address1,address2***s***/old_text/new_text/command*
          Substitutes *new_text* for *old_text* within the range of lines denoted by *address1,address2* (which may be numbers, symbols, or text). *command* may be **g**, **l**, **n**, **p**, or **gp**.

Special Characters

.	Matches any single character in search or substitution patterns.
*	Matches zero or more occurrences of the preceding character in search or substitution patterns.
[...]	Matches the first occurrence of a pattern in the brackets.
[^...]	Matches the first occurrence of a character that is not in the brackets.
.*	Matches zero or more occurrences of any characters following the period in search or substitution patterns.
^	Matches the beginning of the line in search or substitution patterns.
$	Matches the end of the line in search or substitution patterns.
\	Takes away the special meaning of the special character that follows in search and substitution patterns.
&	Repeats the last pattern to be substituted.
%	Repeats the last replacement pattern.

Text Movement Commands

m	Moves the specified lines of text after a destination line; deletes the lines at the old location.
t	Copies the specified lines of text and places the copied lines after a destination line.
j	Joins the current line with the next contiguous line.
w	Copies (writes) the buffer contents into a file.
r	Reads in text from another file and appends it to the buffer.

Other Useful Commands and Information

h   Displays a short explanation for the preceding diagnostic response (**?**).

H   Turns on the help mode, which automatically displays an explanation for each diagnostic response (**?**) during the editing session.

l   Displays nonprinting characters in the text.

f   Displays the current file name.

f *newfile*   Changes the current file name associated with the buffer to *newfile*.

!command   Allows you to temporarily escape to the shell to execute a shell command.

ed.hup   Saves the editing buffer if the terminal is hung up before a write command.

D Quick Reference to vi Commands

vi **Quick Reference**

This appendix is a glossary of commands for the screen editor **vi**. The commands are grouped according to function.

The general format of a **vi** command is

[x][command]text-object

where x denotes a number, and text-object shows the portion of text on which the command operates. The commands appear on your screen as you type them. For an introduction to the use of **vi** commands, see Chapter 6, "Screen Editor Tutorial **(vi)**."

Commands for Getting Started

Shell Commands

TERM=code   Puts a code name for your terminal into the variable **TERM**.

export TERM   Conveys the value of **TERM** (the terminal code) to any UNIX System program that is terminal-dependent.

tput init   Initializes the terminal so that it will function properly with various UNIX System programs.

> NOTE: Before you can use **vi**, you must complete the first three steps represented by the above three lines: setting the **TERM** variable, exporting the value of **TERM**, and running the **tput init** command.

vi filename   Accesses the **vi** screen editor so that you can edit a specified file.

Basic vi Commands

\<a>	Enters text input mode and appends text after the cursor.
\<ESC>	Escape; leaves text input mode and returns to command mode.
\<h>	Moves the cursor to the left one character.
\<j>	Moves the cursor down one line in the same column.
\<k>	Moves the cursor up one line in the same column.
\<l>	Moves the cursor to the right one character.
\<x>	Deletes the current character.
\<CR>	Carriage return; moves the cursor down to the beginning of the next line.
\<ZZ>	Writes changes made to the buffer to the file and quits **vi**.
:w	Writes changes made to the buffer to the file.
:q	Quits **vi** if changes made to the buffer have been written to a file.

Commands for Positioning in the Window

Positioning by Character

\<h>	Moves the cursor one character to the left.
\<BACKSPACE>	Moves the cursor one character to the left.
\<l>	Moves the cursor one character to the right.
\<space bar>	Moves the cursor one character to the right.
\<fx>	Moves the cursor right to the specified character x.

<F*x***>**	Moves the cursor left to the specified character *x*.
<t*x***>**	Moves the cursor right to the character just before the specified character *x*.
<T*x***>**	Moves the cursor left to the character just after the specified character *x*.
<;>	Continues the search for the character specified by the **<f>**, **<F>**, **<t>**, or **<T>** command. The **;** remembers the character specified and searches for the next occurrence of it on the current line.
<,>	Continues the search for the character specified by the **<f>**, **<F>**, **<t>**, or **<T>** command. The **,** remembers the character specified and searches for the previous occurrence of it on the current line.

Positioning by Line

<j>	Moves the cursor down one line in the same column.
<k>	Moves the cursor up one line in the same column.
<+>	Moves the cursor down to the beginning of the next line.
<CR>	Carriage return; moves the cursor down to the beginning of the next line.
<->	Moves the cursor up to the beginning of the next line.

Positioning by Word

<w>	Moves the cursor to the first character in the next word.
<b>	Moves the cursor to the first character of the previous word.
<e>	Moves the cursor to the end of the current word.

Positioning by Sentence

    <(>   Moves the cursor to the beginning of the sentence.

    <)>   Moves the cursor to the beginning of the next sentence.

Positioning by Paragraph

    <{>   Moves the cursor to the beginning of the paragraph.

    <}>   Moves the cursor to the beginning of the next paragraph.

Positioning in the Window

    <H>   Moves the cursor to the first line on the screen, or "home."

    <M>   Moves the cursor to the middle line on the screen.

    <L>   Moves the cursor to the last line on the screen.

Commands for Positioning in the File

Scrolling

    <^f>   Scrolls the screen forward a full window, revealing the window of text below the current window.

    <^d>   Scrolls the screen down a half window, revealing lines of text below the current window.

    <^b>   Scrolls the screen back a full window, revealing the window of text above the current window.

    <^u>   Scrolls the screen up a half window, revealing the lines of text above the current window.

Positioning on a Numbered Line

<G>	Moves the cursor to the beginning of the last line in the buffer.
<nG>	Moves the cursor to the beginning of the nth line of the file (n = line number).

Searching for a Pattern

/pattern	Searches forward in the buffer for the next occurrence of pattern. Positions the cursor under the first character of pattern.
?pattern	Searches backward in the buffer for the first occurrence of pattern. Positions the cursor under the first character of pattern.
<n>	Repeats the last search command.
<N>	Repeats the search command in the opposite direction.

Commands for Inserting Text

<a>	Enters text input mode and appends text after the cursor.
<i>	Enters text input mode and inserts text before the cursor.
<o>	Enters text input mode by opening a new line immediately below the current line.
<O>	Enters text input mode by opening a new line immediately above the current line.
<ESC>	Escape; returns to command mode from text input mode (entered with any of the above commands).

Commands for Deleting Text

In Text Input Mode

<BACKSPACE>	Deletes the current character.
<^w>	Deletes the current word delimited by blanks.
<@>	Erases the current line of text.

In Command Mode

<x>	Deletes the current character.
<dw>	Deletes a word (or part of a word) from the cursor through the next space or to the next punctuation.
<dd>	Deletes the current line.
<ndx>	Deletes n number of text objects of type x, where x may be a word, line, sentence, or paragraph.
<D>	Deletes the current line from the cursor to the end of the line.

Commands for Modifying Text

Characters, Words, Text Objects

<r>	Replaces the current character.
<s>	Deletes the current character and appends text until the <ESC> command is typed.
<S>	Replaces all the characters in the current line.
<~>	Changes uppercase to lowercase or lowercase to uppercase.

<**cw**>	Replaces the current word or the remaining characters in the current word from the cursor to the next space or punctuation with new text.
<**cc**>	Replaces all the characters in the current line.
<*n***c***x*>	Replaces *n* number of text objects of type *x*, where *x* may be a word, line, sentence, or paragraph.
<**C**>	Replaces the remaining characters in the current line, from the cursor to the end of the line, with new text.

Cutting and Pasting Text

<**p**>	Places the contents of the temporary buffer (containing the output of the last delete or yank command) into the text after the cursor or below the current line.
<**yy**>	Yanks (extracts) a specified line of text and puts it into a temporary buffer.
<*n***y***x*>	Extracts a copy of *n* number of text objects of type *x* and puts it into a temporary buffer.
<**"** *l* **y** *x*>	Places a copy of text object *x* into a register named by a letter *l*. *x* may be a word, line, sentence, or paragraph.
<**"** *x* **p**>	Places the contents of register *x* after the cursor or below the current line.

Other Commands

Special Commands

<**ĝ**>	Gives the line number of the current cursor position in the buffer and modification status of the file.
<**.**>	Repeats the action performed by the last command.

<u>	Undoes the effects of the last command.
<U>	Restores the current line to its state prior to present changes.
<J>	Joins the line immediately below the current line with the current line.
<^l>	Clears and redraws the current window.

Line Editor Commands

:	Tells **vi** that the next commands you issue will be line editor commands.
:sh	Temporarily returns to the shell to perform some shell commands without leaving **vi**.
<^d>	Escapes the temporary return to the shell and returns to **vi** so you can edit the current window.
:*n*	Goes to the *n*th line of the buffer.
:*x,z***w** *filename*	Writes lines from the number *x* through the number *z* into a new file called *filename*.
:$	Moves the cursor to the beginning of the last line in the buffer.
:.,$d	Deletes all the lines from the current line to the last line.
:r *filename*	Inserts the contents of *filename* under the current line of the buffer.
:s/*text***/***new_text***/**	
	Replaces the first instance of *text* on the current line with *new_text*.
:s/*text***/***new_text***/g**	
	Replaces every occurrence of *text* on the current line with *new_text*.
:g/*text***/s//***new_text***/g**	
	Changes every occurrence of *text* in the buffer to *new_text*.

Commands for Quitting vi

<ZZ>	Writes the buffer to the file and quits **vi**.
:wq	Writes the buffer to the file and quits **vi**.
:w *filename* **:q**	Writes the buffer to the new file *filename* and quits **vi**.
:w! *filename* **:q**	Overwrites the existing file *filename* with the contents of the buffer and quits **vi**.
:q!	Quits **vi** whether or not changes made to the buffer were written to a file. Does not incorporate changes made to the buffer since the last write (**:w**) command.
:q	Quits **vi** if changes made to the buffer were written to a file.

Special Options for vi

vi *file1 file2 file3*	Enters three files into the **vi** buffer to be edited. Those files are *file1*, *file2*, and *file3*.
:w **:n**	When more than one file has been called on a single **vi** command line, writes the buffer to the file you are editing and then calls the next file in the buffer (use **:n** only after **:w**).
vi –r *file1*	Restores the changes made to *file1* that were lost because of an interrupt in the system.
view *file1*	Displays *file1* in the read-only mode of **vi**. Any changes made to the buffer will not be allowed to be written to the file.

E Summary of Shell Command Language

Summary of Shell Command Language

This appendix is a summary of the shell command language and programming constructs discussed in Chapter 7, "Shell Tutorial." The first section reviews metacharacters, special characters, input and output redirection, variables, and processes. These are arranged by topic in the order that they were discussed in the chapter. The second section contains models of the shell programming constructs.

The Vocabulary of Shell Command Language

Special Characters in the Shell

* ? [ ] .	Metacharacters; provide a shortcut to referencing file names, by pattern matching.
&	Executes commands in the background mode.
;	Separates commands typed on one line for sequential execution.
\	Turns off the special meaning of the special character that follows.
'...'	Enclosing single quotes; turn off the special meaning of all characters.
"..."	Enclosing double quotes; turn off the special meaning of all characters except $ and

Redirecting Input and Output

<	Redirects the contents of a file into a command.
>	Redirects the output of a command into a new file or replaces the contents of an existing file with the output.
>>	Redirects the output of a command so that it is appended to the end of a file.
|	Directs the output of one command to become the input of the next command.
`command`	Substitutes the output of the enclosed command in place of `command`.

Executing and Terminating Processes

batch	Submits the following commands to be processed at a time when the system load is at an acceptable level. <^d> ends the **batch** command.
at	Submits the following commands to be executed at a specified time. <^d> ends the **at** command.
at –l	Reports which jobs are currently in the **at** or **batch** queue.
at –r	Removes the **at** or **batch** job from the queue.
ps	Reports the status of the shell processes.
kill *PID*	Terminates the shell process with the specified process ID (PID).
nohup *command list* **&**	Continues background processes after logging off.

Making a File Accessible to the Shell

chmod u+x *filename*

> Gives the user permission to execute the file (useful for shell program files).

mv *filename* **$HOME/bin/***filename*

> Moves your file to the **bin** directory in your home directory. This **bin** holds executable shell programs that you want to be accessible. Make sure the **PATH** variable in your **.profile** file specifies this **bin**. If it does, the shell will search in **$HOME/bin** for your file when you try to execute it. If your **PATH** variable does not include your **bin**, the shell will not know where to find your file and will be unable to execute your command.

filename A file that contains a shell program; becomes the command that you type to run that shell program.

Variables

positional parameter

> A numbered variable used within a shell program to reference values automatically assigned by the shell from the arguments of the command line invoking the shell program.

echo A command used to print the value of a variable on your terminal.

$# A special parameter that contains the number of arguments with which the shell program has been executed.

$* A special parameter that contains the values of all arguments with which the shell program has been executed.

named variable

> A variable to which the user can give a name and assign values.

Variables Used in the System

HOME   The default variable for the **cd** command; denotes your home directory.

PATH   Defines the path your login shell follows to find commands.

CDPATH   Defines the search path for the **cd** command.

MAIL   Gives the name of the file containing your electronic mail.

PS1 PS2   Define the primary and secondary prompt strings.

TERM   Defines the type of terminal.

LOGNAME   Defines the login name of the user.

IFS   Defines the internal field separators (normally the space, tab, and carriage return).

TERMINFO   Allows you to request that the **curses** and **terminfo** subroutines search a specified directory tree before searching the default directory for your terminal type.

TZ   Sets and maintains the local time zone.

Shell Programming Constructs

Here Document

```
command <<!
input lines
!
```

For Loop

```
for variable<CR>
        in this list of values<CR>
do the following commands<CR>
        command 1<CR>
        command 2<CR>
            .<CR>
            .<CR>
        last command<CR>
done<CR>
```

While Loop

```
while command list<CR>
do<CR>
    command1<CR>
    command2<CR>
        .<CR>
        .<CR>
    last command<CR>
done<CR>
```

If...Then

```
if this command is successful<CR>
then command1<CR>
    command2<CR>
        .<CR>
        .<CR>
    last command<CR>
fi<CR>
```

If...Then...Else

```
if command list<CR>
    then command list<CR>
    else command list<CR>
fi<CR>
```

Case Construction

```
case word<CR>
in<CR>
    pattern1)<CR>
        command line 1<CR>
            .<CR>
            .<CR>
        last command line<CR>
    ;;<CR>
    pattern2)<CR>
        command line 1<CR>
            .<CR>
            .<CR>
        last command line<CR>
    ;;<CR>
    pattern3)<CR>
        command line 1<CR>
            .<CR>
            .<CR>
        last command line<CR>
    ;;<CR>
esac<CR>
```

break and continue Statements

A break or continue statement forces the program to leave any loop and execute the command following the end of the loop.

F Setting upon the Terminal

Setting the TERM Variable

AT&T supports many types of terminals for use with the UNIX System. Because some commands are terminal-dependent, the system must know what type of terminal you are using whenever you log in. The system determines the characteristics of your terminal by checking the value of a variable called **TERM**, which holds the name of a terminal. If you have put the name of your terminal into this variable, the system will be able to execute all programs in a way that is suitable for your terminal.

This method of telling the UNIX System what type of terminal you are using is called setting the terminal configuration. To set your terminal configuration, type the command lines shown on the following screen, substituting the name of your terminal for *terminal_name*:

```
$ TERM=terminal_name<CR>
$ export TERM<CR>
$ tput init<CR>
```

These lines must be executed in the order shown; otherwise, they will not work. Also, this procedure must be repeated every time you log in. Therefore, most users put these lines into a file called **.profile** that is automatically executed every time they log in. For details about the **.profile** file, see Chapter 7.

The first two lines in the screen tell the UNIX System shell what type of terminal you are using. The **tput init** command line instructs your terminal to behave in ways that the UNIX System expects a terminal of that type to behave. For example, it sets the terminal's left margin and tabs if those capabilities exist for the terminal.

The **tput** command uses the entry in this database for your terminal to make terminal-dependent capabilities and information available to the shell. Because the values of these capabilities differ for each type of terminal, you must execute the **tput init** command line every time you change the **TERM** variable.

For each terminal type, a set of capabilities is defined in a database. This database is usually found in either the **/usr/lib/terminfo** or **/usr/lib.COREterm** directory, depending on the system.

 NOTE | Every system has at least one of these directories; some may have both. Your system administrator can tell you whether your system has the **terminfo** and/or the **.COREterm** directory.

The following sections describe how you can determine what *terminal_names* are acceptable. Further information about the capabilities in the **terminfo** database can be found on the *terminfo*(4) manual page in the *Programmer's Reference Manual*.

Acceptable Terminal Names

The UNIX System recognizes a wide range of terminal types. Before you put a terminal name into the **TERM** variable, you must make sure that your terminal is within that range.

You must also verify that the name you put into the **TERM** variable is a recognized terminal name. There are usually at least two recognized names: the name of the manufacturer and the model number. However, there are several ways to represent these names: by varying the use of uppercase and lowercase, by using abbreviations, and so on. Do not put a terminal name in the **TERM** variable until you have verified that the system recognizes it.

The **tput** command provides a quick way to make sure your terminal is supported by your system. Type

    tput –T*terminal_name* **longname**<CR>

If your system supports your terminal, it will respond with the complete name of your terminal. Otherwise, you will get an error message.

To find an acceptable name that you can put in the **TERM** variable, find a listing for your terminal in either of two directories: **/usr/lib/terminfo** or **/usr/lib/.COREterm**. Each of these directories is a collection of files with single-character names. Each file, in turn, holds a list of terminal names that all begin with the name of the file. (This name can be either a letter, such as the initial A in AT&T, or a number, such as the initial 5 in 5425.) Find the file whose name matches the first character of your terminal's name. Then list the file's contents and look for your terminal.

You can also check with your system administrator for a list of terminals supported by your system and the acceptable names you can put in the **TERM** variable.

Example

Suppose your terminal is an AT&T Teletype Model 5425. Your login is **jim** and you are currently in your home directory. First, you verify that your system supports your terminal by running the **tput** command. Next, you find an acceptable name for it in the **/usr/lib/.COREterm/A** directory. The following screen shows which commands you need to do this:

```
$ tput -T5425 longname<CR>
AT&T 4425/5425
$ cd /usr/lib/.COREterm/A<CR>
$ ls
ATT4410
ATT4415
ATT4418
ATT4424
ATT4424-2
ATT4425
ATT4426
ATT513
ATT5410
ATT5418
ATT5420
ATT5420-2
ATT5425
ATT5620
ATT610BCT
ATTPT505
$
```

Now you are ready to put the name you found, ATT5425, in the **TERM** variable. Whenever you do this, you must also export **TERM** and execute **tput init**:

```
$ TERM=ATT5425<CR>
$ export TERM<CR>
$ tput init<CR>
$
```

The UNIX System now knows what type of terminal you are using and will execute commands appropriately.

Windowing

The area of the terminal screen in which you work and display files is similar to the window of a house: both are devices that frame a part of a whole (whether the world or a file) for viewing. For this reason, the working area of a terminal screen is called a window. Until now we have assumed that your terminal screen has only one window (the whole screen). However, some terminals allow you to create more than one window on your screen. Each window on a windowing terminal has its own shell and functions almost exactly like a separate terminal. To help you take advantage of this feature, the UNIX System provides a set of software tools called the Basic Windowing Utilities.

We have already discussed how you can perform several tasks simultaneously with one screen by using tools such as background mode and the **at** command. With multiple windows, you have the additional capability of working interactively with more than one process at a time. You can keep track of several processes at once or look at more than one file simultaneously. If you have a windowing terminal and the Basic Windowing Utilities are installed on your UNIX System, you can use the techniques described in this section to make efficient use of your terminal.

Creating Windows

To create a window, you must draw it on your screen and set up the shell associated with it. The shell is the command interpreter; it allows you to work interactively with the UNIX System. Without a shell assigned to it, a window is simply a drawing on your screen.

The **layers** command allows you to draw a window on any windowing terminal. If you execute it without any arguments, you must use the mouse to draw a window. If you give specifications for windows as arguments to the **layers** command, you can program the drawing of windows and avoid using the mouse; your windows will be drawn automatically by the **layers** command.

Drawing Windows With a Mouse

The easiest way to draw windows is with the mouse. First, enter the **layers** command:

> **layers<CR>**

Next, press a button on your mouse; a pop-up menu of layer operations will appear on the screen. Choose the menu option for drawing windows (such as New), and use the mouse to draw one (see the owner's manual for the terminal for instructions).

To create more than one window, reinvoke the menu, make your selection, and draw with the mouse. (You cannot issue the **layers** command again.) In response, the terminal draws your window(s) on the screen and then waits for commands from the terminal.

Drawing Windows Without a Mouse

If you prefer to program the drawing of windows, you must first create a file containing the number and dimensions of the windows you want. Then run the **layers** command with the name of that file as an argument and the **–f** option. This option tells the command to read your specifications file. The general command line format is

> **layers –f** *file*<**CR**>

The specifications file must contain a line for each window you want in the following format:

> *origin_x origin_y corner_x corner_y command_list*

The first four fields of the line define the coordinates of the window. The *origin_x* and *origin_y* entries specify the position on the screen of the top, left-hand corner of the window, the point at which the command starts drawing. The *corner_x* and *corner_y* entries specify the position of the lower, righthand corner.

origin_x origin_y

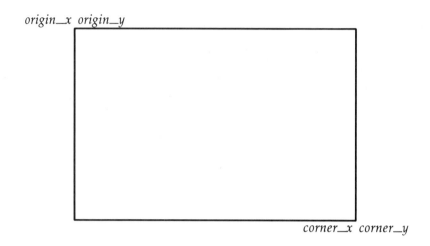

corner_x corner_y

For example, to create a large rectangular window and a small one, write a specification file with the following lines:

0	0	650	300
650	0	792	175

Windows drawn to these specifications will look like this:

The fifth field of each line in your specifications file is *command_list*. Here you must enter a command that will assign a shell to the window. You can also assign a particular terminal type or an editor to the window in this field.

The command that allows you to assign a shell to your window is **exec** (short for execute). Enter this command with an argument specifying the type of shell you want to run in the window. To run the same type of shell that normally runs in your terminal, enter the following:

exec $SHELL

To run the standard UNIX System shell, enter

exec /bin/sh

You may also want your window to provide features that are available only on a type of terminal other than the one you are using. Specify the terminal type you want and assign it to the **TERM** variable. If you include this assignment in the *commands_list* field, place it before the **exec** command. Separate all three requests (terminal type, **TERM** assignment, and **exec** command) with semicolons and leave spaces on both sides of each semicolon. For example, say you want your window to provide the features of an HP 2621 terminal running the same type of shell that you normally run on your terminal. Type the *commands_list* field in your specifications file as follows:

jim ; exec $SHELL

To summarize, the specifications file must contain a line for each window that you want to create, and each line must include five fields: four coordinates for drawing the window and one command line that assigns a shell to the window. The command line may also include the assignment of a particular editor or terminal to the window. The following example of a specifications file incorporates the previous examples of fields:

```
8       0       650     300     exec $SHELL
675     0       800     175     exec /bin/sh
0       200     800     900     jim ; exec $SHELL
0       800     792     1024    hp2621 ; TERM=hp2621 ; exec $SHELL
```

When your specifications file is ready, run the **layers** command as follows:

layers –f *specifications_file*<**CR**>

The windows you have requested will be drawn on the screen, and the shells you assigned to them will be activated and ready for your commands.

Working with Layers

Once you have windows on your screens, you need to learn how to work with them: how to navigate among them, use each one as a terminal, and delete them. You can perform all these tasks by pressing different buttons on the mouse (see the owner's manual for your terminal for specific instructions).

Programmers who want to write their own programs for creating or using windows can do so with the library of functions called **libwindows**. (See the *libwindows*(3X) page in the *Programmer's Reference Manual*.)

Glossary

acoustic coupler
A device that permits transmission of data over an ordinary telephone line. When you place a telephone handset in the coupler, you link a computer at one end of the phone line to a peripheral device, such as a user terminal, at the other end.

address
Generally, a number that indicates the location of information in the computer's memory. In the UNIX System, the address is part of an editor command that specifies a line number or range.

append mode
A text editing mode in which the characters you type are entered as text into the text editor's buffer. In this mode you enter (append) text after the current position in the buffer. See **text input mode**; compare with **command mode** and **insert mode**.

argument
The element of a command line that specifies data on which a command is to operate. Arguments follow the command name and can include numbers, letters, or text strings. For instance, in the command **lp −m myfile**, **lp** is the command and **myfile** is the argument. See **option**.

ASCII
(pronounced **as'-kee**) American Standard Code for Information Interchange, a standard for data transmission that is used in the UNIX System. ASCII assigns sets of 0s and 1s to represent 128 characters, including alphabetical characters, numerals, and standard special characters, such as #, $, %, and &.

AT&T 3B Computers
Computers manufactured by AT&T Technologies, Inc.

background
A type of program execution where you request the shell to run a command away from the interaction between you and the computer ("in the background"). While this command runs, the shell prompts you to enter other commands through the terminal.

baud rate

A measure of the speed of data transfer from a computer to a peripheral device (such as a terminal) or from one device to another. Common baud rates are 300, 1200, 4800, and 9600. As a general guide, divide a baud rate by 10 to get the approximate number of English characters transmitted each second.

buffer

A temporary storage area of the computer used by text editors to make changes to a copy of an existing file. When you edit a file, its contents are read into a buffer where you make changes to the text. For the changes to become part of the permanent file, you must write the buffer contents back into the file. See **permanent file**.

child directory

See **subdirectory**.

command

The name of a file that contains a program that can be executed by the computer on request. Compiled programs and shell programs are forms of commands.

command file

See **executable file**.

command language interpreter

A program that acts as a direct interface between you and the computer. In the UNIX System, a program called the **shell** takes commands and translates them into a language understood by the computer.

command line

A line containing one or more commands, ended by typing a carriage return (<**CR**>). The line may also contain options and arguments for the commands. You type a command line to the shell to instruct the computer to perform one or more tasks.

command mode

A text editing mode in which the characters you type are interpreted as editing commands. This mode permits actions such as moving around in the buffer, deleting text, or moving lines of text. See **text input mode**, compare with **append mode** and **insert mode**.

context search

A technique for locating a specified pattern of characters (called a string) when in a text editor. Editing commands that cause a context search scan the buffer, looking for a match with the string specified in the command. See **string**.

control character

A nonprinting character that is entered by holding down the <CTRL> key and typing a character. Control characters are often used for special purposes. For instance, when viewing a long file on your screen with the **cat** command, typing CTRL-s (ˆs) stops the display so you can read it, and typing CTRL-q (ˆq) continues the display.

current directory

The directory in which you are presently working. You have direct access to all files and subdirectories contained in your current directory. The shorthand notation for the current directory is a dot (.).

cursor

A cue printed on the terminal screen that indicates the position at which you enter or delete a character. It is usually a rectangle or a blinking underscore character.

default

An automatically assigned value or condition that exists unless you explicitly change it. For example, the shell prompt string has a default value of **$** unless you change it.

delimiter

A character that logically separates words or arguments on a command line. Two frequently used delimiters in the UNIX System are the space and the tab.

diagnostic

A message printed at your terminal to indicate an error encountered while trying to execute some command or program. Generally, you need not respond directly to a diagnostic message.

directory

A type of file used to group and organize other files or directories. You cannot directly enter text or other data into a directory.

disk

A magnetic data storage device consisting of several round plates similar to phonograph records. Disks store large amounts of data and allow quick access to any piece of data.

electronic mail

The feature of an operating system that allows computer users to exchange written messages via the computer. The UNIX System **mail** command provides electronic mail in which the addresses are the login names of users.

environment

The conditions under which you work while using the UNIX System. Your environment includes those things that personalize your login and allow you to interact in specific ways with the UNIX System and the computer. For example, your shell environment includes such things as your shell prompt string, specifics for backspace and erase characters, and commands for sending output from your terminal to the computer.

erase character

The character you type to delete the previous character you typed. The UNIX System default erase character is **#** ; some users set the erase character to the BACKSPACE key.

escape

The process of getting into the shell from within a text editor or other program.

execute

The computer's action of running a program or command and performing the indicated operations.

executable file

A file that can be processed or executed by the computer without any further translation. When you type in the file name, the commands in the file are executed. See **shell procedure**.

file
> A collection of information in the form of a stream of characters. Files may contain data, programs, or other text. You access UNIX System files by name. See **ordinary file**, **permanent file**, and **executable file**.

file name
> A sequence of characters that denotes a file. (In the UNIX System, a slash character (/) cannot be used as part of a file name.)

file system
> A collection of files and the structure that links them together. The UNIX file system is a hierarchical structure. (For more detail, see Appendix A, Summary of the File System.)

filter
> A command that reads the standard input, acts on it in some way, and then prints the result as standard output.

final copy
> The completed, printed version of a file of text.

foreground
> The normal type of command execution. When executing a command in foreground, the shell waits for one command to end before prompting you for another command. In other words, you enter something into the computer and the computer "replies" before you enter something else.

full-duplex
> A type of data communication in which a computer system can transmit and receive data simultaneously. Terminals and modems usually have settings for half-duplex (one-way) and full-duplex communication; the UNIX System uses the full-duplex setting.

full path name
> A path name that originates at the root directory of the UNIX System and leads to a specific file or directory. Each file and directory in the UNIX System has a unique full path name, sometimes called an absolute path name. See **path name**.

global
A term that indicates the complete or entire file. While normal editor commands commonly act on only the first instance of a pattern in the file, global commands can perform the action on all instances in the file.

hardware
The physical machinery of a computer and any associated devices.

hidden character
One of a group of characters within the standard ASCII character set that are not printable. Characters such as backspace, escape, and $<\hat{\ }d>$ are examples.

home directory
The directory in which you are located when you log in to the UNIX System, also known as your login directory.

input/output
The path by which information enters a computer system (input) and leaves the system (output). A terminal keyboard is an input device, and a terminal display is an output device.

insert mode
A text editing mode in which the characters you type are entered as text into the text editor's buffer. In this mode you enter (insert) text before the current position in the buffer. See **text input mode**; compare with **append mode** and **command mode**.

interactive
Describes an operating system (such as the UNIX System) that can handle immediate-response communication between you and the computer. In other words, you interact with the computer from moment to moment.

line editor
An editing program in which text is operated upon on a line-by-line basis within a file. Commands for creating, changing, and removing text use line addresses to determine where in the file the changes are made. Changes can be viewed after they are made by displaying the lines changed. See **text editor**; compare with **screen editor**.

login
> The procedure used to gain access to the UNIX Operating System.

login directory
> See **home directory**.

login name
> A string of characters used to identify a user. Your login name is different from other login names.

log off
> The procedure used to exit the UNIX Operating System.

metacharacter
> A subset of the set of special characters that have special meaning to the shell. The metacharacters are *****, **?**, and the pair **[ ]**. Metacharacters are used in patterns to match file names.

mode
> In general, a particular type of operation (for example, an editor's append mode). In relation to the file system, a mode is an octal number used to determine who can have access to your files and what kind of access they can have. See **permissions**.

modem
> A device that connects a terminal and a computer by way of a telephone line. A modem converts digital signals to tones and converts tones back to digital signals, allowing a terminal and a computer to exchange data over standard telephone lines.

multi-tasking
> The ability of an operating system to execute more than one program at a time.

multi-user
> The ability of an operating system to support several users on the system at the same time.

nroff
> A text formatter available as an add-on to the UNIX System. You can use the **nroff** program to produce a formatted on-line copy or a printed copy of a file. See **text formatter**.

operating system

The software system on a computer under which all other software runs. The UNIX System is an operating system.

option

Special instructions that modify how a command runs. Options are a type of argument that follow a command and usually precede other arguments on the command line. By convention, an option is preceded by a minus sign (−); this distinguishes it from other arguments. You can specify more than one option for some commands given in the UNIX System. For example, in the command ls −l −a directory, −l and −a are options that modify the ls command. See **argument**.

ordinary file

A file, containing text or data, that is not executable. See **executable file**.

output

Information processed in some fashion by a computer and delivered to you by way of a printer, a terminal, or a similar device.

parameter

A special type of variable used within shell programs to access values related to the arguments on the command line or the environment in which the program is executed. See **positional parameter**.

parent directory

The directory immediately above a subdirectory or file in the file system organization. The shorthand notation for the parent directory is two dots (..).

parity

A method used by a computer for checking that the data received matches the data sent.

password

A code word known only to you that is called for in the login process. The computer uses the password to verify that you may indeed use the system.

path name

A sequence of directory names separated by the slash character (/) and ending with the name of a file or directory. The path name defines the connection path between some directory and the named file.

peripheral device

An auxiliary device, under the control of the main computer, that is used mostly for input, output, and storage functions. Some examples include terminals, printers, and disk drives.

permanent file

The data stored permanently in the file system structure. To change a permanent file, you can make use of a text editor, which maintains a temporary work space, or buffer, apart from the permanent files. Once changes have been made to the buffer, they must be written to the permanent file to make the changes permanent. See **buffer**.

permissions

Access modes for directories and files that permit or deny system users the ability to read, write, and/or execute the directories and files. You determine the permissions for your directories and files by changing the mode for each one with the **chmod** command.

pipe

A method of redirecting the output of one command to be the input of another command. It is named for the | character, which redirects the output. For example, the shell command **who | wc -l** pipes output from the **who** command to the **wc** command, telling you the total number of people logged into your UNIX System.

pipeline

A series of filters separated by the | character. The output of each filter becomes the input of the next filter in the line. The last filter in the pipeline writes to its standard output or may be redirected to a file. See **filter**.

positional parameter
A numbered variable used within a shell procedure to access the strings specified as arguments on the command line invoking the shell procedure. The name of the shell procedure is positional parameter **$0**.
See **variable** and **shell procedure**.

prompt
A cue displayed at your terminal by the shell, telling you that the shell is ready to accept your next request. The prompt can be a character or a series of characters. The UNIX System default prompt is the dollar sign character (**$**).

printer
An output device that prints the data it receives from the computer on paper.

process
Generally a program that is at some stage of execution. In the UNIX System, it also refers to the execution of a computer environment, including contents of memory, register values, name of the current directory, status of files, information recorded at login time, and various other items.

program
The instructions given to a computer on how to do a specific task. Programs are user-executable software.

read-ahead capability
The ability of the UNIX System to read and interpret your input while sending output information to your terminal in response to previous input. The UNIX System separates input from output and processes each correctly.

relative path name
The path name to a file or directory that varies in relation to the directory in which you are currently working.

remote system
A system other than the one on which you are working.

root
The source directory of all files and directories in the file system. The root is designated by the slash character (/).

screen editor

An editing program in which text is operated on relative to the position of the cursor on a visual display. Commands for entering, changing, and removing text involve moving the cursor to the area to be altered and performing the necessary operation. Changes are viewed on the terminal display as they are made. See **text editor**; compare with **line editor**.

search pattern

See **string**.

search string

See **string**.

secondary prompt

A cue displayed at your terminal by the shell to tell you that the command typed in response to the primary prompt is incomplete. The UNIX System default secondary prompt is the greater-than character (>).

shell

A UNIX System program that handles the communication between you and the computer. The shell is also known as a command language interpreter because it translates your commands into a language understandable by the computer. The shell accepts commands and causes the appropriate program to be executed.

shell procedure

An executable file that is not a compiled program. A shell procedure calls the shell to read and execute commands contained in a file. This lets you store a sequence of commands in a file for repeated use. It is also called a shell program or command file. See **executable file**.

silent character

See **hidden character**.

software

Instructions and programs that tell the computer what to do. Contrast with **hardware**.

source code

The uncompiled version of a program written in a language such as C or Pascal. The source code must be translated to machine language by a program known as a compiler before the computer can execute the program.

special character

A character having special meaning to the shell program and used for common shell functions such as file redirection, piping, background execution, and file name expansion. The special characters include <, >, !, ;, &, *, ?, [, and].

special file

A file, called a device driver, used as an interface to an input/output device, such as a user terminal, a disk drive, or a line printer.

standard input

An open file that is normally connected directly to the keyboard. Standard input to a command normally goes from the keyboard to this file and then into the shell. You can redirect the standard input to come from another file instead of from the keyboard; use an argument in the form < **file**. Input to the command will then come from the specified file.

standard output

An open file that is normally connected directly to a primary output device, such as a terminal printer or screen. Standard output from the computer normally goes to this file and then to the output device. You can redirect the standard output into another file instead of to the printer or screen; use an argument in the form > **file**. Output will then go to the specified file.

string

Designation for a particular group or pattern of characters, such as a word or phrase, that may contain special characters. In a text editor, a context search interprets the special characters and attempts to match the specified pattern with a string in the editor buffer.

string variable

A sequence of characters that can be the value of a shell variable. See **variable**.

subdirectory
> A directory pointed to by a directory one level above it in the file system organization; also called a child directory.

system administrator
> The person who monitors and controls the computer on which your UNIX System runs, sometimes referred to as a super-user.

terminal
> An input/output device connected to a computer system, usually consisting of a keyboard with a video display or a printer. A terminal allows you to give the computer instructions and to receive information in response.

text editor
> Software for creating, changing, or removing text with the aid of a computer. Most text editors have two modes: an input mode for typing in text and a command mode for moving or modifying text. Two examples are the UNIX System editors, **ed** and **vi**. See **line editor** and **screen editor**.

text formatter
> A program that prepares a file of text for printed output. To make use of a text formatter, your file must also contain some special commands for structuring the final copy. These special commands tell the formatter to justify margins, start new paragraphs, set up lists and tables, place figures, and so on. Two text formatters available as add-ons to your UNIX System are **nroff** and **troff**.

text input mode
> A text editing mode in which the characters you type are entered as text into the text editor's buffer. To execute a command, you must leave text input mode. See **command mode**; compare with **append mode** and **insert mode**.

timesharing
> A method of operation in which several users share a common computer system seemingly simultaneously. The computer interacts with each user in sequence, but the high-speed operation makes it seem that the computer is giving each user its complete attention.

tool
> A package of software programs.

troff

A text formatter available as an add-on to the UNIX System. The **troff** program drives a phototypesetter to produce high-quality printed text from a file. See **text formatter**.

tty

Historically, the abbreviation for a teletype terminal. Today, it is generally used to denote a user terminal.

user

Anyone who uses a computer or an operating system.

user-defined

Something determined by the user.

user-defined variable

A named variable given a value by the user. See **variable**.

UNIX System

A general-purpose, multi-user, interactive, time-sharing operating system developed by AT&T Bell Laboratories. The UNIX System allows limited computer resources to be shared by several users and efficiently organizes the user's interface to a computer system.

utility

Software used to carry out routine functions or to assist a programmer or system user in establishing routine tasks.

variable

A symbol whose value may change. In the shell, a variable is a symbol representing some string of characters (a **string value**). Variables may be used in an interactive shell as well as within a shell procedure. Within a shell procedure, positional parameters and keyword parameters are two forms of variables. (Keyword parameters are discussed fully in "Shell Commands and Programming.")

video display terminal

A terminal that uses a television-like screen (a monitor) to display information. A video display terminal can display information much faster than printing terminals.

visual editor
See **screen editor**.

working directory
See **current directory**.

Index